Basic

Oxford
Practice Grammar

Basic

Oxford
Practice
Grammar

Norman Coe
Mark Harrison
Ken Paterson

Great Clarendon Street, Oxford, OX2 6DP, United Kingdom

Oxford University Press is a department of the University of Oxford. It furthers the University's objective of excellence in research, scholarship, and education by publishing worldwide. Oxford is a registered trade mark of Oxford University Press in the UK and in certain other countries

© Oxford University Press 2019

The moral rights of the authors have been asserted

This updated edition first published in 2019

2023 2022 2021 2020 2019

10 9 8 7 6 5 4 3 2 1

No unauthorized photocopying

All rights reserved. No part of this publication may be reproduced, stored in a retrieval system, or transmitted, in any form or by any means, without the prior permission in writing of Oxford University Press, or as expressly permitted by law, by licence or under terms agreed with the appropriate reprographics rights organization. Enquiries concerning reproduction outside the scope of the above should be sent to the ELT Rights Department, Oxford University Press, at the address above

You must not circulate this work in any other form and you must impose this same condition on any acquirer

Links to third party websites are provided by Oxford in good faith and for information only. Oxford disclaims any responsibility for the materials contained in any third party website referenced in this work

ISBN: 978 0 19 421473 5

Printed in China

This book is printed on paper from certified and well-managed sources

ACKNOWLEDGEMENTS

Ken Paterson would like to thank Jean Hope for her patience.

Front cover photograph: ShutterStock (Sheldonian Theatre/Jeffery Hamstock)

Back cover photograph: Oxford University Press building/David Fisher

Illustrations by: Working in the style of Jerome Brasseur/Beehive Illustration: John Batten/Beehive Illustration pp.53, 104, 121 (5, 6, 7), 125, 189, 198, 203; Daniela Geremia/Beehive Illustration pp.27, 30, 36, 74, 126, 155 (4); Aleksandar Sotirovski/Beehive Illustration pp.3, 8, 10, 17, 24, 25, 28, 40, 51, 80, 88, 90, 97, 121 (0, 1, 2, 3, 4), 138, 148, 149, 154, 155 (0, 1, 2, 3, 5, 6, 7), 170, 171, 206, 218.

The publisher would like to thank the following for permission to reproduce photographs: 123rf.com: pp.68 (on bus/lightpoet), 91 (suit and tie/belchonock), 98 (students with computers/goodluz), 112 (occupations/rawpixel), 165 (lamp/karlowac); Alamy Stock Photo: pp.4 (cold/XiXinXing), 98 (broken down car/CandyBox Photography), 112 (boxes/RTimages, feet/Ingram), 164 (cold man/XiXinXing), 165 (bin/Katharine Andriotis), 214 (broken down car/CandyBox Photography); Corbis p: 91 (homework/Ocean); Getty Images: pp.121 (Photodisc), 165 (keys/JackRussell/iStock); Oxford University Press: pp.4 (children running/Chris King), 47 (outside cinema/Mike Stone), 112 (children/Gareth Boden), 130 (restaurant/Gareth Boden), 133 (apples); Shutterstock.com: pp.4 (hungry/3445128471, thirsty/Evgeny Atamanenko, sad/Monkey Business Images, tired/Roman Samborskyi, scary shadow/g215, bored/wavebreakmedia, 10 (sleeping/Hung Chung Chih, learn Japanese/maicasaa, beach/Marco Antonio, tennis/Orange Line Media, couple in garden/Photodisc), 11 (De Visu), 12 (Olesia Bilkei), 29 (Africa Studio), 35 (Songquan Deng), 37 (cooking/Atamanenko, decorating tree/CroMary, writing cards/Soloviova Liudmyla, food shopping/MinDof, roof/mooremedia, wrapping/petrunjela), 47 (tennis court/isaravut, clouds/Lifestyle Graphic, phone/Kostenko Maxim, pizza/Oksana Mizina, race/Sergey Novikov, piano/Popova Valeriya, beach/Tatyana Vyc), 48 (Antonio Guillem), 61 (shutterupeire), 62 (Prostock-studio), 66 (Monkey Business Images), 68 (couple in kitchen/Foxy burrow), 75 (pathdoc), 82 (Roman Samborskyi), 86 (Maxal Tamor), 91 (asleep/Africa Studio, watch TV/Brian A Jackson, jogging/Maridav, working late/marvent, snapped cigarette/Nuttaphong Sriset, girl and grandmother/SpeedKingz), 100 (Prasit Rodphan), 112 (black and white mice/Janson George, sheep/Eric Isselee, banana/Tom K Photo, chairs/photka, knives/Planner, watches/Polryaz, cars/Rawpixel.com, walking mouse/Emilia Staslak, buses/James Steidl, standing mouse/Rudmer Zwerver), 114 (balloons/fokke baarssen, painting/Pressmaster), 115 (Monkey Business Images), 116 (cars/gallimaufry, umbrella/Romolo Tavani), 118 (pens/K303, empty bowl/Aleksei Potov, pasta/stockphoto-graf), 128 (Olena Yakobchuk), 130 (coins/Mati Nitibhon), 132 (luggage trolley/plprod, carry bags/Tero Vesalainen), 133 (cheese/Andrjuss, two slices bread/anyamuse, pens/artproem, glass milk/Tarasyuk Igor, coins/Mati Nitibhon, cars/Rawpixel.com, books/studiovin), 144 (g215), 150 (cases/Africa Studio, heavy case/Vadim Georgiev), 152 (Philip Pilosian), 164 (chilly woman/nrqemi), 165 (frame/Sandra Cunningham, cup of coffee/Fotofermer, door/Imagine Photographer, coat hanger/LightField Studios, bowl/Pointless Ltd, road sign/Shah Rohani, lightbulb/Sarunyu_foto, coffee pot/SmudgeChris, tennis court/Suti Stock Photo), 206 (mart), 214 (girl and dog/Zurijeta), 216 (Tom Wang), 219 (Ekaterina Pokrovsky), 238 (London/Aerial-motion, Marilyn Monroe/brandonht, Elvis/Dan Kosmayer).

Contents

Introduction viii
Key to symbols ix

Tenses: present

1. **Be:** Present Simple (1) 2
2. **Be:** Present Simple (2) 4
3. Present Simple (1) 6
4. Present Simple (2) 8
5. Present Continuous (1) 10
6. Present Continuous (2) 12
7. Present Simple or Present Continuous 14
8. Imperative 16

Test A 18

Tenses: past

9. **Be:** Past Simple 20
10. Past Simple 22
11. Past Continuous 24
12. Past Simple or Past Continuous 26
13. Present Perfect (1) 28
14. Present Perfect (2) 30
15. Present Perfect (3) 32
16. Past Simple or Present Perfect 34
17. Present Perfect Continuous 36
18. Present Perfect Simple or Continuous 38
19. Past Perfect 40
20. Used to 42

Test B 44

Tenses: future

21. Be going to 46
22. **Will** and **shall** 48
23. **Will** or **be going to** 50
24. Present Continuous for the future 52
25. Present tense: **when, before, after, until,** etc. ... 54
26. Future 56

Test C 58

Sentences and questions

27. Nouns, verbs, adjectives, etc. 60
28. Word order: subject, verb, object 62
29. 'Yes/no' questions 64
30. **Where, when, why, how** 66
31. **Who, what, which** 68
32. How long/far/often …? 70
33. **What … like?** 72
34. **Who** and **what**: subject and object 74
35. **Whose is this?** ~ **It's John's.** 76
36. Question tags 78
37. Short answers 80
38. **So am I, I am too, Neither am I,** etc. 82

Test D 84

v

Modal verbs

39 Ability: **can, can't, could, couldn't** ... 86
40 **Can/Could I? May I? Can/Could you?** ... 88
41 **Must, mustn't** ... 90
42 **Have to** ... 92
43 **Must/have to, mustn't/don't have to** ... 94
44 **Must, can't, may, might, could** ... 96
45 **Should, shouldn't** ... 98
46 **Should, ought to, had better** ... 100
47 **Need, needn't, needn't have** ... 102
48 **Had to do/go, should have done/gone** ... 104

Test E ... 106

Articles, nouns, pronouns, etc.

49 Articles (1): **a, an** or **the** ... 108
50 Articles (2): **a/an, the** or no article ... 110
51 Plural nouns; **one** and **ones** ... 112
52 **This, that, these, those** ... 114
53 Countable and uncountable nouns ... 116
54 **A, some, any, no** ... 118
55 **I** and **me** (subject and object pronouns) ... 120
56 **There** or **it/they** ... 122
57 **My, your; mine, yours** ... 124
58 **Myself, yourself,** etc.; **each other** ... 126
59 Direct and indirect objects ... 128
60 **Much, many; how much/many; more** ... 130
61 **A lot of, lots of, a little, a few** ... 132
62 **Something, anybody, nothing,** etc. ... 134
63 **Every/each; one/another/other/others** ... 136
64 **All, most, some, none** ... 138

Test F ... 140

Adjectives and adverbs

65 Adjectives (order) ... 142
66 Adjectives: **-ed** or **-ing** ... 144
67 Cardinal and ordinal numbers ... 146
68 Comparison: (**not**) **as … as** ... 148
69 **Too** and **enough** ... 150
70 **So** and **such** ... 152
71 Comparative adjectives ... 154
72 Superlative adjectives ... 156
73 Adverbs (1): adjectives and adverbs ... 158
74 Adverbs (2): adverbs of frequency ... 160
75 Adverbs (3): place, direction, sequence ... 162
76 Adverb + adjective; noun + noun; etc. ... 164
77 Position of adverbs in a sentence ... 166

Test G ... 168

Prepositions

78 Prepositions of place and movement ... 170
79 Prepositions of time ... 172
80 **As/like; as if/as though** ... 174
81 **In; with;** preposition + **-ing** ... 176
82 Other uses of prepositions ... 178
83 Verb + preposition ... 180
84 Adjective + preposition ... 182

Test H ... 184

Verbs

85	**Have** and **have got**	186
86	**Make, do, have, get**	188
87	Phrasal verbs (1): meanings and types	190
88	Phrasal verbs (2): separability	192
89	Passive sentences (1)	194
90	Passive sentences (2)	196
91	**Have** (something) **done**	198
92	Infinitive with/without **to**	200
93	Verb + **-ing**; **like** and **would like**	202
94	Verb + **to** or verb + **-ing**	204
95	Purpose: **for ...ing**	206
96	Verb + object (+ **to**) + infinitive	208
	Test I	210

Conditionals and reported speech

97	Zero Conditional and First Conditional	212
98	Second Conditional	214
99	Third Conditional	216
100	Reported speech (1)	218
101	Reported speech (2)	220
102	Reported questions	222
	Test J	224

Building sentences

103	**And, but, so, both ... and, either,** etc.	226
104	**Because, in case, so, so that**	228
105	**Since, as, for**	230
106	**Although, while, however, despite,** etc.	232
107	Relative clauses (1)	234
108	Relative clauses (2)	236
109	Relative clauses (3)	238
	Test K	240

Appendices

1	Nouns	242
2	Regular verbs	243
3	Irregular verbs	244
4	Adjectives and adverbs	245

Exit test 246

Index 252

Introduction

Oxford Practice Grammar is a series of three books, each written at the right level for you at each stage in your study of English. The series is intended for your use either in a classroom or when working independently in your own time.

The books are divided into units, each of which covers an important grammar topic. Each unit starts with an explanation of the grammar and this is followed by a set of practice exercises. Answers to the exercises are given at the back of the book.

You may want to choose the order in which you study the grammar topics, perhaps going first to those giving you problems. (Topics are listed in the Contents page at the front of each book and in the Index at the back.) Alternatively, you may choose to start at the beginning of each book and work through to the end.

Exam practice

The first level in the series is *Oxford Practice Grammar – **Basic***. This is suitable for elementary to pre-intermediate learners, and those working for the Oxford Test of English and Cambridge A2 Key and B1 Preliminary exams. The second is *Oxford Practice Grammar – **Intermediate*** for students who are no longer beginners but are not yet advanced in their use of English. It is suitable for those studying for the Oxford Test of English and Cambridge B2 First exam. *Oxford Practice Grammar – **Advanced*** is for those who have progressed beyond the intermediate level and who wish to increase their knowledge of English grammar and become more confident when using it. It helps students prepare for the C1 Advanced, C2 Proficiency, TOEFL, IELTS, and other advanced-level exams.

*Oxford Practice Grammar – **Basic*** is written for elementary to pre-intermediate students of English.

Grammar topics are explained simply and clearly and you are given lots of opportunity to practise.

Each new topic is presented on a left-hand page and the practice section follows on the same page or the facing page. You can therefore look across to the explanation while you are working through the exercises.

Appendices at the back of the book summarize how to form plurals of nouns, verb endings, comparative forms of adjectives, and adverbs. They also include a table of irregular verbs.

An exit test provides an opportunity for more practice, and prepares you for *Oxford Practice Grammar – **Intermediate***.

There is an interactive *Oxford Practice Grammar* website at
www.oup.com/elt/practicegrammar.

Key to symbols

The symbol **/** (oblique stroke) between two words means that either word is possible. *We put **does** before **he/she/it*** means that *We put **does** before **he***, *We put **does** before **she*** and *We put **does** before **it*** are all possible. In exercise questions this symbol is also used to separate words or phrases which are possible answers.

Brackets **( )** around a word or phrase in the middle of a sentence mean that it can be left out. *She said (that) she lived in a small flat* means that there are two possible sentences: *She said that she lived in a small flat* and *She said she lived in a small flat*.

The symbol **~** means that there is a change of speaker. In the example *When did Jasmine go to India? ~ In June.* the question and answer are spoken by different people.

The symbol ♦ in an exercise indicates that a sample answer is given.

1 Be: Present Simple (1)

1 Here are some examples of **be** in the Present Simple:

*This **is** my brother. He**'s** ten years old.*
*I**'m** a student. These **are** my books.*
*They **aren't** at home. They**'re** at the theatre.*

2 We form the Present Simple of **be** like this:

POSITIVE	FULL FORM	SHORT FORM
Singular	I am you are he/she/it is	I'm you're he's/she's/it's
Plural	we are you are they are	we're you're they're

NEGATIVE	FULL FORM	SHORT FORM
Singular	I am not you are not he/she/it is not	I'm not you aren't he/she/it isn't
Plural	we are not you are not they are not	we aren't you aren't they aren't

3 In speech, we usually use the short forms:

*She**'s** my sister.*   *He**'s** my brother.*
*I**'m** from Italy.*   *They**'re** German.*

4 We use **be**:

▶ to say who we are:
  *I**'m** Steve and this **is** my friend William. We**'re** from Scotland.*
  *I**'m** Jessica and these **are** my sisters. This **is** Amber and this **is** Penelope. Amber and Penelope **are** doctors.*

▶ to talk about the weather:
  *It**'s** cold today.*
  *It**'s** a beautiful day.*
  *It**'s** usually hot here*
  *It **isn't** very warm today.*

▶ to talk about the time:
  *It**'s** ten o'clock.*
  *It**'s** half past four.*
  *You**'re** late!*

▶ to talk about places:
  *Milan **is** in the north of Italy.*
  *John and Mary **are** in Yorkshire.*

▶ to talk about people's ages:
  *My sister **is** six years old.*

A Maria is from Brazil. She is writing about herself and her family. Put full forms of *be* in the gaps.

- ♦ I _am_ a student from Brazil.
- ♦ My parents _are not_ (not) rich.
- 1 My father _____ a teacher.
- 2 My mother _____ (not) Brazilian.
- 3 She _____ from America.
- 4 I _____ 20 years old.
- 5 My little brother _____ two.
- 6 My older brothers _____ (not) students.
- 7 They _____ in the army.
- 8 It _____ often very hot in Brazil.

B Now fill these gaps. This time, use short forms of *be*.

- ♦ I_'m_ a doctor.
- ♦ I_'m not_ (not) a bank manager.
- 1 She _____ (not) a teacher.
- 2 He _____ a student.
- 3 They _____ at home.
- 4 They _____ (not) in the park.
- 5 It _____ (not) cold today.
- 6 It _____ eight o'clock.
- 7 We _____ from Paris.
- 8 We _____ (not) from Bordeaux.
- 9 You _____ (not) 21 years old.
- 10 I _____ 24 years old.

Tenses: present

C Choose words from the box to put in the gaps.

> He's   She's   ~~They're~~   It's (x2)   are   is   We   isn't

♦ My parents live in Scotland. _They're_ teachers.
1 New York _____ in England. _____ in America.
2 Paul _____ from Germany. _____ German.
3 My sister is a doctor. _____ 30 years old.
4 _____ six o'clock! _____ are late.
5 Look at the time! Chris and Mary _____ late.

D Look at these pictures. These people are saying who they are. Write sentences using the jobs from the box.

> a pop star   a farmer   a bank manager   ~~a footballer~~   a dentist   a doctor
> ~~a police officer~~   an artist   a teacher   a film star   a scientist   a photographer

Italy — Paolo   Federico
names: I'm Paolo and this is Federico.
nationality: We're from Italy.
jobs: I'm a police officer and Federico is a footballer.

1 Sweden — Bjorn   Liv
names:
nationality:
jobs:

2 Mexico — Maria   Pedro
names:
nationality:
jobs:

3 Australia — Jim   Mary
names:
nationality:
jobs:

4 Japan — Tomoko   Akira
names:
nationality:
jobs:

5 India — Rajiv   Ikram
names:
nationality:
jobs:

2 Be: Present Simple (2)

1 We use **be**:

- to talk about how we feel:
  - I**'m** happy.   They**'re** sad.
  - They**'re** bored.   She**'s** tired.
  - We**'re** hungry.   I**'m** thirsty.
  - He **isn't** afraid.   They**'re** cold.

- to greet people:
  - William: Hello. How **are** you?
  - Jasmine: I**'m** fine thanks. How **are** you?

- to apologize:
  - I**'m** sorry I**'m** late.

- to describe things:
  - It **isn't** expensive. It**'s** cheap.
  - It**'s** an old film. It **isn't** very good.
  - These photos **are** bad!

For other uses of **be**, see **Unit 1**.

2 We use **there** + **be** to talk **about** the existence of something. **There** + **be** can be used to talk about where things are:

Singular	**There's** a supermarket in this street. **There is** a washing machine in the flat.
Plural	**There are** some good cafes in the centre of the town.

We also use **there** + **be** to talk about when things happen:

- **There is** a bus to London at six o'clock.
- **There are** taxis, but **there aren't** any buses on Sunday.
- **There isn't** another train to Manchester today.

3 We form questions with **be** in the Present Simple like this:

	QUESTIONS	
Singular	**Am** I **Are** you **Is** he/she/it	late?
Plural	**Are** we **Are** you **Are** they	late?

Here are some examples of questions using all the forms of **be**:

- **Am I** late for the film?
- **Are you** 20 years old?
- **Is he** at home now?
- **Is she** French or Italian?
- **Is it** time to go home?
- **Are we** ready to leave?
- **Are you** both at university?
- **Are they** in London today?

A Make sentences about the pictures using the words from the box. Use *He/She/They* and the Present Simple of *be*.

tired   sad   ~~thirsty~~   happy   hungry   bored   afraid   cold

♦ She's thirsty

1 He _____   2 They _____

3 _____

4 _____

5 _____

6 _____

7 _____

Tenses: present

B Use *there* + the correct form of *be* to say what we can and cannot find in the town of Smallwood.

- (a cinema: ✓) <u>There's</u> a cinema.
- (a river: ✗) <u>There isn't</u> a river.
- (restaurants: 10) <u>There are</u> ten restaurants.
1. (a castle: ✓) .... a castle.
2. (baker's shops: 2) .... two baker's shops.
3. (a zoo: ✓) .... a zoo.
4. (banks: 6) .... six banks.
5. (a luxury hotel: ✓) .... a luxury hotel.
6. (a theatre: ✗) .... a theatre.
7. (newsagents: 6) .... six newsagents.
8. (many tourists: ✗) .... many tourists.

C Write questions by putting the words in brackets ( ) in the correct order.

- (thirsty – you – are) <u>Are you thirsty?</u>
1. (a teacher – you – are) ....
2. (they – bored – are) ....
3. (is – afraid – he) ....
4. (she – tired – is) ....
5. (are – you – how) ....
6. (cold today – it – is) ....
7. (she – Spanish – is) ....
8. (they – from London – are) ....

D Complete the dialogues with the correct forms of *be*.

Steve: This ♦ <u>is</u> Jasmine, my sister.
Tom: Hello, Jasmine. ¹............... you a student?
Jasmine: No, I ²............... a dentist. I work in Brighton.

Mike: How are you, Ellie?
Ellie: I ³............... fine, thanks.
Mike: ⁴............... you hungry?
Ellie: Yes. ⁵............... there a good restaurant near here?
Mike: Yes. There ⁶............... a good, and cheap, restaurant in Wellington Street.

E Write questions using the words in brackets ( ) and a form of *be*.

QUESTIONS		ANSWERS
♦ (you/Spanish)?	<u>Are you Spanish</u>?	~ No, I'm French.
1 (you/hungry)?	...............?	~ No, I'm thirsty.
2 (she/your sister)?	...............?	~ No, she's my mother.
3 (I/late)?	...............?	~ No, you're on time.
4 (they/from America)?	...............?	~ No, they're from Canada.
5 (he/a tennis player)?	...............?	~ No, he's a footballer.
6 (you/happy)?	...............?	~ No, I'm sad.
7 (she/at home)?	...............?	~ No, she's at work.
8 (he/20)?	...............?	~ No, he's 18 years old.

3 Present Simple (1)

1 We form the Present Simple like this:

POSITIVE	
Singular	I know you know he/she/it knows
Plural	we know you know they know

I **know** the answer.
She **starts** work at nine o'clock.

We add **-s** after **he/she/it**:

| I start → he starts | I live → she lives |

If a verb ends in **-ch**, **-o**, **-sh**, **-ss** or **-x**, we add **-es** after **he/she/it**:

| I watch → he watches | you do → he does |
| they go → it goes | we wash → she washes |

If a verb ends in a consonant (**b**, **c**, etc.) + **y** (e.g. **study**), we use **-ies** after **he/she/it**:

| I study → he studies | I fly → it flies |

(For more examples, see **Appendix 2**, page 243.)

2 Now look at these examples of the negative:
I **don't like** that music.
He **doesn't listen** to his teacher.

NEGATIVE	
FULL FORM	SHORT FORM
I do not know.	I don't know.
You do not know.	You don't know.
He/She/It does not know.	He doesn't know.
We do not know.	We don't know.
You do not know.	You don't know.
They do not know.	They don't know.

Note that we say:
He does not know. (NOT He does not knows.)

3 We use the Present Simple:

▶ to talk about things that happen regularly:
He **plays** golf every day.

▶ to talk about facts:
She **comes** from France. (= She is French.)
Greengrocers **sell** vegetables.
I **don't speak** Chinese.

A Add **-s** or **-es** to the verbs in the sentences if it is necessary. If it is not necessary, put a tick (✓) in the gap.

- ♦ He work **s** in a bank.
- ♦ They live **✓** in France.
- 1 I watch _____ TV every day.
- 2 She go _____ to work by car.
- 3 The film finish _____ at ten o'clock.
- 4 We play _____ tennis every weekend.
- 5 They go _____ on holiday in August.
- 6 He speak _____ Italian and French.
- 7 She do _____ her homework every night.
- 8 We start _____ work at half past eight.

B Now finish these sentences using a verb from the box. Use each verb once. Remember to add **-s** or **-es** if necessary.

| fly | study | finish | ~~eat~~ | sell | write | drink | live |

- ♦ He **eats** toast for breakfast.
- 1 I _____ coffee three times a day.
- 2 My father _____ a new language every year.
- 3 She _____ to New York once a month.
- 4 He _____ a blog post every week.
- 5 They _____ in Ireland.
- 6 He _____ work at six o'clock.
- 7 I _____ fruit in a shop.

Tenses: present

C Write sentences using the words in brackets ( ) and the negative form of the Present Simple.

♦ (He/not/live/in Mexico) He doesn't live in Mexico.
1 (She/not/work/in a bank)
2 (I/not/play/golf)
3 (Paul/not/listen/to music)
4 (We/not/speak/French)
5 (You/not/listen/to me!)
6 (My car/not/work)
7 (I/not/drink/tea)
8 (Michelle/not/eat/meat)
9 (I/not/understand/you)

D Complete the interview using the verbs from the box. Use each verb once.

leave   start   arrive   ~~get~~   watch   work   brush   eat   have   like   drink   go   stop

Interviewer: How do you start the day, James?
James: Well, I ♦ get up at six o'clock. I get washed and dressed, and I ¹_____ breakfast at seven o'clock. After breakfast, I ²_____ my teeth. I ³_____ to work at eight o'clock.
Interviewer: When do you get to work?
James: I usually ⁴_____ at my office at about half past eight. First, I ⁵_____ a cup of coffee, and then I ⁶_____ work at just before nine o'clock.
Interviewer: Where do you work?
James: I ⁷_____ in a bank. I am a computer programmer. I ⁸_____ my job. It's very interesting.
Interviewer: When do you eat lunch?
James: I ⁹_____ work and I have lunch at one o'clock. I ¹⁰_____ a cup of tea at half past three.
Interviewer: When do you finish work?
James: I ¹¹_____ the office at six o'clock. I eat dinner when I get home. Then I ¹²_____ TV for an hour or two.

E Write facts about Jasmine using the table and the verbs in brackets ( ). A tick (✓) means that something is true. A cross (✗) means that something is not true.

♦	1	2	3	4
~~from Scotland~~ ✓	in a bank ✗	in a flat ✓	French ✓	new films ✗
~~from England~~ ✗	in a shop ✓	in a house ✗	Italian ✗	old films ✓

♦ (come)   She comes from Scotland.   She doesn't come from England.
1 (work)   She _____ in a bank.   She _____ in a shop.
2 (live)   She _____   She _____
3 (speak) _____   _____
4 (like)   _____   _____

4 Present Simple (2)

1 We use the Present Simple:

▶ to talk about feelings and opinions:

I **like** pop music. I **don't like** classical music.
She **loves** football!
Raphael **wants** a new car.
I **don't want** a cup of tea, thanks.
He **feels** sick.

▶ to talk about thoughts:

I think he's angry.

I **don't think** she likes her new job.
I **don't know** the answer.
He **doesn't understand** me.

2 We form Present Simple questions like this:

QUESTIONS			
Singular	Do	I/you	know?
	Does	he/she/it	
Plural	Do	we	know?
	Do	you	
	Do	they	

Note that we put **do** before **I/you/we/they**:
   Do you **speak** Spanish?
   Do you **work** in the town centre?
   Do they **know** the answer?

We put **does** before **he/she/it**:
   Does he **walk** to work?
   Does Steve **enjoy** his job?
   Does she **play** the piano?

Note that we say:
   Does he walk? (NOT ~~Does he walks?~~)

For other uses of the Present Simple, see **Unit 3**.

A Complete the sentences using the Present Simple form of the verbs from the box. Use each verb once.

> like   not have   ~~love~~   feel   think   not like   want   not understand

♦ She thinks that films are fantastic! She _loves_ films.
1 I .... sick. Can I have a glass of water, please?
2 I don't know the answer because I .... the question.
3 I .... he's tired. He works too hard.
4 We .... that new painting. We think it's terrible!
5 I want to call Jasmine, but I .... her phone number.
6 They're thirsty. They .... something to drink.
7 I .... your new car. It's very nice. Was it expensive?

B Write sentences about Peter using the information in brackets ( ). (✓ = like, ✓✓ = love, ✗ = not like, ✗✗ = hate)

♦ (tennis: ✗)   He doesn't like tennis.
♦ (music: ✓✓)   He loves music.
1 (coffee: ✓)   He ....
2 (films: ✗)   He ....
3 (his job: ✓✓)   ....
4 (fishing: ✗✗)   ....
5 (holidays: ✓✓)   ....
6 (golf: ✗)   ....

Tenses: present

C This is an interview with Mary Woods about herself and her husband, John. Write the questions using the ideas from the box.

like films	read books	listen to music	~~play golf~~
watch TV	play a musical instrument	go to the gym	go to the theatre
drive a car	like pop music	drink coffee	~~live in London~~
like dogs	speak any foreign languages		

QUESTIONS

♦ Do you live in London ?
♦ Does John play golf ?
1. _____ ?
2. _____ ?
3. _____ ?
4. _____ ?
5. _____ ?
6. _____ ?
7. _____ ?
8. _____ ?
9. _____ ?
10. _____ ?
11. _____ ?
12. _____ ?

ANSWERS

~ Yes, I live in north London.
~ No, but he plays tennis.
~ Yes, I speak French.
~ Yes, I like some programmes on TV.
~ Yes, he listens to music in the morning.
~ No, but he loves cats.
~ No, I don't like films.
~ Yes, he has two cups in the morning.
~ No, but I have a motorbike.
~ Yes, he plays the piano.
~ No, I prefer classical music.
~ Yes, I love musicals.
~ Yes, I read one book every week.
~ No, but he likes running.

D You are on holiday, and you are in a Tourist Information Centre. Ask questions using the table below.

A	B	C
Do	~~you~~	stop at the railway station?
Does	~~the sports centre~~	finish before 11 o'clock?
	all the banks	start here?
	the number 38 bus	~~sell maps of the city?~~
	the restaurants	change tourists' money into pounds?
	the concert	sell souvenirs?
	the sightseeing tour	have a swimming pool?
	the museum	serve typical English food?

♦ Do you sell maps of the city?
1. _____ the sports centre _____
2. _____
3. _____
4. _____
5. _____
6. _____
7. _____

5 Present Continuous (1)

1 We form the Present Continuous like this:

be + *-ing* form
I am eating.

Here are the forms of the Present Continuous:

POSITIVE	
FULL FORM	SHORT FORM
I **am** eating.	I**'m** eating.
You **are** eating.	You**'re** eating.
He/She/It **is** eating.	He**'s** eating.
We **are** eating.	We**'re** eating.
You **are** eating.	You**'re** eating.
They **are** eating.	They**'re** eating.

NEGATIVE	
FULL FORM	SHORT FORM
I **am not** eating.	I**'m not** eating.
You **are not** eating.	You **aren't** eating.
He/She/It **is not** eating.	He **isn't** eating.
We **are not** eating.	We **aren't** eating.
You **are not** eating.	You **aren't** eating.
They **are not** eating.	They **aren't** eating.

2 To make the **-ing** form, we add **-ing** to the verb:

listen → listening   play → playing
work → working   read → reading

3 But notice these irregular spellings:

win → wi**nn**ing   get → ge**tt**ing
shop → sho**pp**ing   sit → si**tt**ing
swim → swi**mm**ing   travel → trave**ll**ing
dance → danc**ing**   write → writ**ing**
shine → shin**ing**

(For more details on the spelling of the **-ing** form, see **Appendix 2**, page 243.)

4 We use the Present Continuous:

▶ to talk about actions and situations in progress now:

The bus **is coming**.

▶ to talk about actions and situations in progress around now, but not exactly at the moment we speak:

What **are** you **doing** these days?

I**'m learning** Spanish.

A Look at the pictures and the words in brackets ( ). Decide what is happening (✓) and what isn't happening (✗). Then write positive or negative sentences.

♦ (George/eat/breakfast)   ✗ George isn't eating breakfast.
  (George/sleep)   ✓ George is sleeping.
1 (They/work)
  (They/sit/in the garden)
2 (I/study/music)
  (I/learn/Japanese)

Tenses: present

3 (He/play/tennis)
  (He/win)

4 (We/spend/a day at the seaside)
  (The sun/shine)

B Complete the postcard using the words in brackets ( ) in the Present Continuous. Use full forms (e.g. *is sitting*).

Dear Peter,

Jenny and I ♦ are staying (stay) here for a week. The sun ¹_____ (shine) and it's very hot. We ²_____ (sit) on the beach and I ³_____ (drink) an orange juice.

We ⁴_____ (not/swim) because we're both tired. We ⁵_____ (watch) the boats on the sea at the moment. They ⁶_____ (travel) fast, but I can see 15 or 16. Jenny ⁷_____ (read) her book, and I ⁸_____ (write) all the postcards!

James and Jenny

C Match the two halves of the sentences. Then put in the correct form of the verb in brackets ( ).

♦ My aunt is staying (stay) with us this week
1 I _____ (go) to work by bike this week
2 My father _____ (take) some medicine
3 Anna is not in the office this week
4 Olivia needs some exercise
5 We _____ (eat) in a restaurant this week
6 Charlotte doesn't feel well
7 Tom _____ (study) more now

a so he is feeling quite drowsy.
b because she _____ (work) at home.
c so she _____ (stay) at home today.
d̶ so I am sleeping in the living room.
e because our oven is broken.
f because he wants to get a good mark.
g because I haven't got money for petrol.
h so she _____ (walk) to school this week.

♦ d   1 ___   2 ___   3 ___   4 ___   5 ___   6 ___   7 ___

6 Present Continuous (2)

1 Look at these questions:
- *Are* you *enjoying* that drink, Anna?
- *Is* he *watching* TV at the moment?
- *Are* they *working* hard?

2 We form Present Continuous questions like this:

	QUESTIONS	
Singular	Am I Are you Is she/he/it	winning?
Plural	Are we Are you Are they	winning?

3 Here are three common Present Continuous questions. They all mean 'How are you?':
- How*'s* it *going*?
- How *are* you *getting on*?
- How *are* you *doing*?

Hello. How are you doing?

Very well, thanks. And you?

4 We do not usually use the Present Continuous to talk about opinions or thoughts:
- I *like* tennis. I *know* your sister. (NOT ~~I'm liking tennis. I'm knowing your sister.~~)

We do not usually use these verbs in the Present Continuous:

like	believe	hate
love	understand	know
mean	remember	want

5 **think** and **have**:

▶ we cannot use **think** in the Present Continuous to express opinions:
- I *think* he's nice. (NOT ~~I'm thinking he's nice.~~)

▶ we can use **think** in the Present Continuous to talk about an action:
- She*'s thinking* about the film.

▶ we cannot use **have** in the Present Continuous to talk about possessions:
- I *have* a ticket. (NOT ~~I am having a ticket.~~)

▶ we can use **have** to talk about actions:
- I*'m having* breakfast. He*'s having* fun.

A Make questions by putting the words in brackets ( ) in the correct order.

◆ (enjoying – your work – you – are – ?)   Are you enjoying your work?
1. (she – having lunch – is – ?)
2. (playing football – are – they – ?)
3. (the cat – sleeping – is – ?)
4. (the sun – is – shining – ?)
5. (you – are – coming – to the cinema – ?)
6. (listening – are – they – ?)
7. (eating – at the moment – she – is – ?)
8. (it – raining hard – is – ?)
9. (I – getting better – at tennis – am – ?)
10. (are – winning the match – we – ?)

Tenses: present

B Make questions and answers using the words in brackets ( ) and the Present Continuous.

QUESTIONS

♦ (she/work/in Peru this year?)
Is she working in Peru this year?
1 (you/study/English at the moment?)
2 (they/listen/to the radio?)
3 (Peter/wash/now?)
4 (they/live/in Madrid at the moment?)
5 (David/sing/in a band this year?)

ANSWERS

(No, she/study/in Mexico)
~ No, she's studying in Mexico.
(Yes, I/work/hard)
~
(No, they/play/music)
~
(Yes, he/have/a bath)
~
(Yes, they/learn/Spanish)
~
(No, he/work/in a restaurant)
~

C Put a tick (✓) next to the correct sentences, and a cross (✗) next to the incorrect sentences.

♦ She's liking pop music. ✗
1 They're enjoying the film.
2 We're loving ice cream.
3 She's believing he's right.
4 John's thinking about my idea.
5 He's having lunch at the moment.

♦ He's learning French. ✓
6 She's eating a banana.
7 He thinks it's a good idea.
8 'Huge' is meaning 'very big'.
9 Mick is knowing Jasmine.
10 She's hating classical music.

D Complete this conversation. Use the verbs in brackets ( ) in the Present Continuous.

Paul: Hi Steve! What are you doing?
Steve: ♦ I'm going (I/go) to the bank. What are you doing?
Paul: 1 _____ (I/shop). 2 _____ (I/look) for a new tennis racket. 3 _____ (I/play) a lot of tennis at the moment, and I need a new racket.
Steve: Where is Lily? Do you know?
Paul: Yes. She isn't in England at the moment. 4 _____ (She/work) in France for a month.
Steve: What 5 _____ (she/do) in France?
Paul: 6 _____ (She/sing) in a show.
Steve: Really? What about Jacob and Lucy? What 7 _____ (they/do)?
Paul: 8 _____ (They/study) for an exam. They're always in the library at the moment.
Steve: How is your sister? Is she all right?
Paul: Yes, she's fine, but she's tired. 9 _____ (We/paint) the living room. It's hard work.
Steve: Can I help you?
Paul: No, it's OK. My father 10 _____ (help).
Steve: Well, I hope you find a good racket.

7 Present Simple or Present Continuous

Compare the Present Simple and the Present Continuous:

1 We use the Present Simple to talk about facts (things which are true at any time):
  Anna **speaks** good Spanish.
  Journalists **write** newspaper articles.
  I **come** from Norway. (= I am Norwegian.)

We use the Present Continuous to talk about actions in progress at the time of speaking:
  Anna's busy. She**'s speaking** on the phone.
  What **are you writing**? ~ An essay for college.
  Look! The bus **is coming**.

2 We use the Present Simple for situations that exist over a long time, and for actions that are repeated (e.g. people's habits, or events on a timetable):
  Mike **works** for an advertising company.
  He **lives** in Paris. (= His home is in Paris.)

We use the Present Continuous for things that continue for a limited period of time around now (e.g. holidays, visits, temporary jobs, school or university courses):
  John **is working** in the USA for six months.
  He**'s living** in New York.

Jasmine **travels** a lot in her job.
I **do** a lot of sport.

We can use words like **usually, often, every**:
  We **usually go** out to dinner at weekends.
  I **often go** to football matches on Sundays.
  The buses **leave every** hour.

Jasmine**'s travelling** around Europe for a month.
I**'m doing** a one-year course in tourism.
We**'re painting** the flat.

3 We use the Present Simple with thinking and feeling verbs (e.g. **know, forget, notice, understand, recognise, remember, like, love, hate, want, prefer, need**):
  I **don't know** which train to catch.

We do not usually use the Present Continuous with thinking and feeling verbs:
  NOT ~~I'm knowing someone who lives in Venice.~~

4 We use **have** in the Present Simple to talk about possession:
  I **have** a new car.

We use **think** in the Present Simple to express opinions:
  I **think** she's interesting.

We use **have** and **think** in the Present Continuous to talk about actions:
  I**'m having** fun.
  He can't come, he**'s having** dinner at the moment.
  I **am thinking** about my work.

A Complete the sentences with the verbs in brackets ( ). Use the Present Simple (*I do*) or the Present Continuous (*I am doing*).

♦ I *leave* (leave) home at seven o'clock every morning.
1 She usually .... (work) in the Sales Department in London, but at the moment she .... (do) a training course in Bristol.
2 Emilia .... (wash) her hair every day.
3 He .... (try) very hard in every game that he .... (play).

Tenses: present

4 Excuse me. I think that you _____ (sit) in my seat.
5 _____ (you/listen) to music very often?
6 Don't talk to me now. I _____ (write) an important essay.
7 Why _____ (they/drive) on the left in Britain?
8 It _____ (not/get) dark at this time of year until about ten o'clock.
9 It usually _____ (rain) here a lot, but it _____ (not/rain) now.
10 A: What are you doing?
   B: I _____ (bake) a cake. Why _____ (you/smile)? _____ (I/do) something wrong?

B This is Anna's first message in English to David. There are some mistakes in it. Cross out the incorrect forms and write in the correct form. Put a tick (✓) if the form of the verb is correct.

Hi David,
I live ♦ ✓ in a large flat in Rome. I'm having ♦ have two sisters. They are called Rosa and Maria. We are getting up ¹ _____ at seven o'clock every morning, and we have ² _____ coffee and a small breakfast. I leave ³ _____ the flat at eight and walk to the university. I am finishing ⁴ _____ classes at five every day, and I arrive ⁵ _____ home at six. This month I work ⁶ _____ very hard for my first exams. At the moment, I eat ⁷ _____ breakfast in the kitchen of our flat: my mother drinks ⁸ _____ coffee, and my sisters are messaging ⁹ _____ their friends. On Saturday afternoons I am playing ¹⁰ _____ tennis with my friends, or I go ¹¹ _____ to the cinema. Today, I'm going to see a new English film! Sometimes I am watching ¹² _____ American films on TV, but I'm not understanding ¹³ _____ the words! Are you liking ¹⁴ _____ films?
With best wishes,
Anna

C Write the sentences using the words in brackets ( ) and the Present Simple or the Present Continuous.

♦ (Usually she/work/at the office, but this week she/work/at home.)
   Usually she works at the office, but this week she's working at home.

1 (You/not/eat/very much at the moment. Are you ill?)

2 (She/know/three words in Italian!)

3 (I/take/the bus to work this week, but usually I/walk.)

4 (I/study/Japanese this year. It's very difficult.)

5 (you/watch/the television at the moment?)

6 (I/not/remember/the name of the hotel.)

7 (She/speak/three languages.)

8 (The sun/shine/. It's a beautiful day!)

8 Imperative

1 These are imperatives:
Go. Help. Come. Wait.

We use the imperative like this:
Come in! Have a cup of tea.
Turn left at the pharmacy.
Don't touch! It's hot.

Note that sometimes the imperative is one word, but often we give more information:
Help!
Help me!
Help me with my suitcase.

We can say *please* after an imperative to be more polite:
Help me with my suitcase, please.
Hurry up, please. We're late.
Come here, please.
Listen to me, please.

2 We form the negative like this:
Don't be late.
Don't forget your books!
Don't wait for me.

We normally use the short form *Don't*.

3 We use the imperative:
- to give instructions:
  Turn right at the corner.
  Don't forget your passport.
- to give warnings:
  Look out! There's a car coming.
  Be careful! That box is very heavy.
- to give advice:
  Have a rest. You look tired.
  Take a coat. It's cold today.
  Don't see that film. It's terrible!
- to ask people to do things:
  Come in please, and sit down.
  Listen to this song. It's wonderful.
  Pass the butter, please.
- to make offers:
  Have another orange juice.
  Make yourself a cup of coffee.
- to 'wish' things:
  Have a good trip!
  Have a nice holiday!

A Make complete sentences by filling the gaps with words and phrases from the box. Use each word or phrase once.

| Turn left | Come in | ~~Don't wait~~ | Don't forget | Stop the car! | Help me! | Have |
| Don't listen | Pass | Don't be late! | Open | Come | Catch | Take |

♦ *Don't wait* for me. I'm not coming tonight.
1 .... an umbrella with you. It's raining.
2 .... a rest. You look tired.
3 .... at the end of the road.
4 .... I can't swim!
5 .... to take your passport.
6 .... There's a cat in the road.
7 .... to my party, please.
8 .... your books at page 84.
9 .... the salt, please.
10 .... to that song. It's terrible.
11 .... The bus leaves at nine o'clock.
12 .... and have a glass of lemonade.
13 .... the first train in the morning.

Tenses: present

B Steve is emailing a friend. Put the verbs from the box into the gaps.

open   forget   ~~come~~   be   bring   have   turn   wait   make

Hi Paul,

♦ *Come* and see me next weekend. I'm staying in a house by the sea. Don't ¹_____ to bring your swimming costume with you! It isn't difficult to find the house. When you get to the crossroads in the town, ²_____ right and drive to the end of the road. ³_____ careful because it is a dangerous road! ⁴_____ some warm clothes with you because it is cold in the evenings here. If I am not at home when you arrive, don't ⁵_____ for me. The key to the house is under the big white stone in the garden. ⁶_____ the front door and ⁷_____ yourself a cup of tea in the kitchen! ⁸_____ a good journey!

Best wishes,
Steve

C What are these people saying? Look at the pictures and match the words from the box to make imperatives.

Come	right.
Have	out!
Pass	~~me!~~
Turn	an orange juice.
~~Help~~	your umbrella.
Don't	in.
Don't forget	to me!
Listen	the milk, please.
Look	touch it!

♦ *Help me!*
1 ....
2 ....
3 ....
4 ....
5 ....
6 ....
7 ....
8 ....

Test A: Tenses – present

A Kate and Amber are talking about their daily lives. Complete their conversation using the verbs in brackets ( ) in the Present Simple. Use short forms if you can.

Kate: ✦ *Do you get up* (you/get/up) early?

Amber: No, not really. ¹_____ (My sister/go) to the bathroom first at about eight o'clock. ²_____ (not/get up) until about eight thirty. What about you?

Kate: Well, ³_____ (Mike/try) to get me up at about seven, but ⁴_____ (he/not/usually/succeed)!

Amber: ⁵_____ (I/be/not) very hungry in the morning. What about you? ⁶_____ (you/eat) much for breakfast?

Kate: ⁷_____ (I/not/usually/like) to eat much, but ⁸_____ (Mike/study) for an hour before breakfast, so ⁹_____ (he/eat) quite a lot.

Amber: ¹⁰_____ (he/have) a big lunch as well?

Kate: ¹¹_____ (I/not/know). ¹²_____ (He/not/tell) me!

Amber: ¹³_____ (you/drive) to work?

Kate: Yes. ¹⁴_____ (there/not/be) any buses. What about you?

Amber: Well, ¹⁵_____ (my sister/want) to buy a new car, but at the moment, ¹⁶_____ (we/both/walk).

B Felix is on holiday in Portugal with his wife, Charlotte, and their children, Tom and Ellie. He's emailing their oldest child, Simon, who is at home in England. If the Present Continuous form is correct, put a tick (✓). If it's wrong, either change the spelling or change it to the Present Simple.

Hi Simon,

How are you geting ✦ *getting* on? We're thinking ✦ *We think* it's great here. Everyone is having ✦ ✓ a good time. I'm siting ¹_____ in the hotel Business Centre. Tom is swimming ²_____ in the pool. Ellie is lying ³_____ on the beach, and Charlotte is shoping ⁴_____. We're liking ⁵_____ Portugal. We're all relaxing. ⁶_____. What are you doing? Are you working hard ⁷_____ at the moment? I'm knowing ⁸_____ your exams start tomorrow. Good luck! Is it raining ⁹_____ in England? The sun is shineing ¹⁰_____ here, of course! I'm learning ¹¹_____ a bit of Portuguese, but not very much. I'm understanding ¹²_____ some of the things that people say, but only if the words are similar to English. Hope to hear from you soon!

Love,
Dad

Tenses: present

C Hazel and Isaac are on the phone. Complete their conversation using the verbs in brackets ( ) in either the Present Simple or Present Continuous. Use short forms if you can.

Isaac: ♦ _Are you working_ ? (you/work)
Hazel: Yes. ¹ _____ (I/finish) a piece of homework for tomorrow. Why? What are you doing?
Isaac: Well, ² _____ (I/think) about my homework, but I'm afraid ³ _____ (I/not/actually/do) it at the moment. I'm tired and bored. ⁴ _____ (you/want) to go out?
Hazel: No. Look at the weather. ⁵ _____ (it/rain). ⁶ _____ (I/never/go out) in the rain. By the way, ⁷ _____ (you/know) the new girl in our class, the one with glasses? ⁸ _____ (I/think) ⁹ _____ (she/come) from Venezuela. Anyway, ¹⁰ _____ (she/stay) with Peter's family this month.
Isaac: Yes, I know. ¹¹ _____ (she/do/well) at school, isn't she? Peter says ¹² _____ (she/speak) three languages: Spanish, English and French. ¹³ _____ (I/not/speak/any languages) other than English!

D This is the opening part of a book. One unnecessary word has been crossed out already as an example. Find 21 more and cross them out.

Today is the 1 June 1964. The sun ~~shines~~ is shining and the birds sing are singing. What is does everyone doing do? Well, Mrs Green is reads reading a newspaper. She is reads reading a newspaper every day before breakfast. Her husband, Mr Green, is danceing dancing in the garden. He likes is liking dancing in the morning.

Have you another cup of coffee, darling', says Mr Green.

But I'm still drink drinking my first cup, dear', replies Mrs Green, 'and anyway, where's our daughter today? She is usually bringing brings me my coffee.'

Mary,' says Mr Green (but he doesn't stop dance dancing), 'she's she works working in London this week. Don't you remember?'

Stopping Stop dancing and listening listen to me. I never forget forgetting anything. I was just giving you a little test. Anyway, it's time for work.'

'Alright, darling, but don't forget not your briefcase.'

Thank you, dear. Don't dancing dance too hard!'

E It's the beginning of a new term at university. Complete these sentences for new students, using the words from the box.

~~leave (✗)~~   show (✓)   smoke (✗)   ~~work (✓)~~   check (✓)   give (✗)   copy (✗)

♦ _Work_ hard, but take a break now and again!
♦ _Don't leave_ your bags or coats in the lecture hall.
1 _____ that you know all the examination dates.
2 _____ your computer password to another student.
3 _____ your ID card when you enter the building.
4 _____ in the lecture halls or classrooms.
5 _____ your essays from the Internet!

9 Be: Past Simple

1 We form the Past Simple of **be** like this:

	POSITIVE
Singular	I **was** you **were** he/she/it **was**
Plural	We/you/they **were**

	NEGATIVE	
	FULL FORM	SHORT FORM
Singular	I **was not** you **were not** he/she/it **was not**	I **wasn't** you **weren't** he/she/it **wasn't**
Plural	we/you/they **were not**	we/you/they **weren't**

	QUESTIONS	
Singular	**Was** I **Were** you **Was** he/she/it	right?
Plural	**Were** we/you/they	right?

Here are some examples with **was** and **were**:
- I **was** in New York last week.
- We **were** at home yesterday evening.
- They **weren't** late this morning.
- **Was** it a good film?

2 Look at these examples of how we use the Past Simple of **be**:

▶ **was**/**were** + facts about the past:
- John F. Kennedy **was** an American president.
- Our first house **was** in the centre of town.
- A: **Were** your answers correct?
- B: No, they **were** all wrong!
- Olivia **wasn't** at the party.

▶ **was**/**were** + place and time:

	+ PLACE	+ TIME
We **were**	in Spain	in June.
She **wasn't**	at home	last night.

- George and Joanna **weren't** in London at the weekend. They **were** in Brighton.
- Steve and Mary **were** here at six o'clock.

▶ **was**/**were** + adjective (e.g. **cold**, **tired**):
- It **was cold** yesterday.
- They **were tired** after the journey.
- The train **was late** again this morning.
- A: **Were** your exams easy?
- B: The first exam **was** easy, but the second one **wasn't**.

A Complete the sentences using *was* or *were*.

♦ Today I am happy but yesterday I <u>was</u> sad.
1. Now Jasmine is at home but last week she _____ on holiday.
2. Today it's raining but yesterday it _____ sunny.
3. This year there is a jazz festival here and last year there _____ a pop festival.
4. Today Mr Brown is at work but yesterday he _____ ill.
5. These days there are houses here but 100 years ago there _____ trees.
6. Today I feel fine but yesterday I _____ in bed all day.
7. My mother is a manager now but she _____ a shop assistant last year.
8. Today is Saturday and we are at home, but yesterday we _____ at school.
9. This summer we are staying at home but last summer we _____ in Greece.
10. Today Tina and Jack are tired because yesterday they _____ at the gym.

Tenses: past

B Mary spent last weekend in Madrid. Ask her some questions using the words in brackets ( ) and *was* or *were*.

- (your hotel/good?) Was your hotel good?
1. (your room/comfortable?)
2. (the weather/nice?)
3. (the streets/full of people?)
4. (the shops/expensive?)
5. (the city/exciting at night?)
6. (the museums/interesting?)
7. (the people/friendly?)
8. (your flight/OK?)

C George and Sally have been married for 50 years. They are talking about their first house. Complete their conversation using words from the box, and following the model of the two examples.

| new | Italian | ~~big~~ | green | cheap | ~~cold~~ | bad |

George: The house was warm.
Sally: No, it ♦ wasn't warm, it was cold.
George: The garden was small.
Sally: No, it ♦ wasn't small, it was big.
Sally: The neighbours were French.
George: No, they ¹
George: The living room was red.
Sally: No, it ²
Sally: Our first chairs were expensive.
George: No, they ³
George: The kitchen was old.
Sally: No, it ⁴
George: The local shops were good.
Sally: No, they ⁵

D Complete these conversations with *was*, *wasn't*, *were*, or *weren't*.

Peter: ♦ Was Paul at work today?
Julie: No, he ¹ _____ in the office. I think he's sick.

Henry: ² _____ you in South America last year?
Steve: Yes. I ³ _____ in Bolivia on business, and then my wife and I ⁴ _____ in Brazil for a holiday.

Olivia: Raphael and I ⁵ _____ at home in London last week. We ⁶ _____ at Mike's house in Cornwall. It was lovely there. Do you know Mike?
Jasmine: Yes, I ⁷ _____ at Mike's party in Oxford in the summer. ⁸ _____ you there?
Olivia: No, we weren't there. Raphael and I ⁹ _____ in Portugal in the summer.

10 Past Simple

1 We form the Past Simple of regular verbs by adding **-ed** to the verb:

walk → walk**ed**	watch → watch**ed**
open → open**ed**	ask → ask**ed**

There are some exceptions:

▸ verbs ending with **-e**:

+ **-d**:	live → liv**ed**	like → lik**ed**

▸ verbs ending with a consonant and **-y**:

-y → **-ied**:	apply → appl**ied**	try → tr**ied**

▸ most verbs ending with one vowel and one consonant:

-p → **-pped**:	stop → sto**pped**	plan → plan**ned**

(For more details on the form of the Past Simple, see **Appendix 2**, page 243.)

2 Many verbs have an irregular Past Simple form:

do → did	have → had
take → took	buy → bought
come → came	stand → stood
find → found	ring → rang
go → went	say → said

(For more details, see **Appendix 3**, page 244.)

3 We form the negative with **didn't** and the infinitive (e.g. **do**, **take**, **understand**):

I **didn't understand**. (NOT didn't understood)

We form questions with **did** and the infinitive (e.g. **watch**):

Did you **watch** the film?

4 We use the Past Simple to talk about an action or situation in the past which is finished. We often say when it happened (e.g. **yesterday**, **last night**):

Chris **phoned** me **yesterday**. He **wanted** to ask me something.
Did you **enjoy** the concert **last night**?

5 We can use the Past Simple with **for** to talk about something that continued for a period of time, and ended in the past:

I **lived** in Rome **for two years**. Then I went to work in Japan.

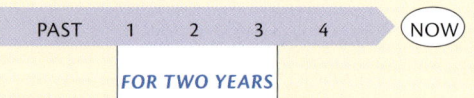

A Put a tick (✓) next to the correct forms of the Past Simple, and cross out those which are incorrect. You can look at **Appendix 3**, page 244, before you do the exercise.

walked ✓	drinked	went	played	writed	swam
~~taked~~	wrote	cooked	gived	spent	finded
drank	asked	flew	made	sended	buyed
gave	meeted	took	left	found	winned
met	passed	stoped	followed	sent	eated
won	cryed	comed	drove	bought	brought
leaved	swimmed	cried	stopped	ate	crossed

B Complete the sentences using the Past Simple form and the words in brackets ( ).

♦ We *went* (go) on holiday to Scotland last year.
1 I .... (take) a taxi from the airport to the city centre.
2 We .... (walk) to the park and then we .... (play) tennis.
3 The man in the shop .... (say) something to the woman, but she .... (not/hear) him.

Tenses: past

4 I .... (ring) the doorbell and a woman .... (open) the door.

5 I .... (download) three films at the weekend, but I only .... (watch) one.

6 A: .... (you/understand) the film?
   B: No. I .... (try) to understand it, but the actors .... (speak) very quickly.

7 A: .... (you/buy) some clothes at the market?
   B: Yes, I .... (buy) a pair of trousers and a shirt.

8 A: .... (you/enjoy) the festival?
   B: Yes. It .... (not/rain) and we .... (listen) to some good music.

C Make sentences using the Past Simple form and the words in brackets ( ).

♦ (When/you/leave/the party?) *When did you leave the party?*

1 (When/you/finish/your exams?)

2 (I/wait/for an hour, but he/not/phone.)

3 (you/watch/the news on TV last night?)

4 (Mark/stop/playing tennis, and he/start/playing golf instead.)

5 (He/ask/me a question, but I/not/know/the answer.)

6 (I/live/there for a few years, but I/not/like/the place.)

D It's the beginning of a new term at university. Two students, Nick and Elliot, are talking about the summer holidays. Complete their conversation using the Past Simple form of the words in brackets ( ).

Nick: What ♦ *did you do* (you/do) in the summer?
Elliot: I ¹............... (take) a trip around Europe by train.
Nick: ²............... (you/go) on your own, or with some friends?
Elliot: A couple of friends ³............... (come) with me.
Nick: How many countries ⁴............... (you/visit)?
Elliot: I ⁵............... (go) to six or seven countries. I ⁶............... (have) a great time, and I really ⁷............... (love) all of them.
Nick: Which one ⁸............... (you/like) most?
Elliot: Sweden, I think. I ⁹............... (enjoy) exploring the marvellous countryside and I ¹⁰............... (take) lots of photographs.
Nick: When ¹¹............... (you/arrive) back home?
Elliot: Last week. I'm still rather tired.

11 Past Continuous

1 We form the Past Continuous like this:

POSITIVE		
I/He/She/It	was	waiting.
You/We/They	were	

NEGATIVE	FULL FORM	SHORT FORM	
I/He/She/It	was not	wasn't	waiting.
You/We/They	were not	weren't	waiting.

QUESTIONS	
Was I/he/she/it	waiting?
Were you/we/they	

(For rules on the spelling of **-ing** forms (e.g. **waiting**), see **Appendix 2**, page 243.)

2 Look at these examples:

A: What **were** you **doing** at seven o'clock last night?
B: I **was driving** home from work.

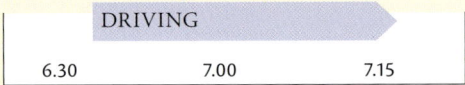

I **was living** in Japan in 2001. (I lived there from 1999 to 2003.)

We use the Past Continuous for an action or situation that was in progress at a particular time in the past (e.g. at 7 p.m., in 2001).

3 Now look at this:

When I **walked** into the room, Anna **was working** on her laptop and Joseph **was reading**.

We use the Past Simple (**walked**) for a completed action. We use the Past Continuous (**was working**) for an action in progress in the past.

Anna   Joseph

4 We can use **when** or **while** before the Past Continuous:

I met her **when/while** we **were working** for the same company. (**when** = during the time)

We can only use **when** (NOT ~~while~~) before the Past Simple:

When I **met** her, we were working for the same company. (**when** = at the time)

A Complete the sentences using the Past Continuous form of the words in brackets ( ).

♦ It _was snowing_ (snow) when I left home this morning.
1 I tried to explain my problem to her, but she .... (not/listen).
2 He .... (talk) on the phone when I arrived.
3 A lot of people .... (wait) for the seven-thirty bus last night.
4 I .... (live) in London when I met them.
5 I nearly had an accident this morning. A car .... (come) towards me, but I moved quickly out of the way.
6 At the end of the first half of the game, they .... (win).
7 It was a sunny afternoon and people .... (sit) on the grass in the park. Then it suddenly started to rain.
8 Which hotel .... (you/stay) in when you lost your passport?
9 Fortunately, I .... (not/drive) too fast when the child walked into the road in front of me.
10 I looked out of the window, and I saw that it .... (not/rain) any more.
11 What .... (you/do) at three o'clock yesterday afternoon?

Tenses: past

B Describe what the people in the picture were doing when Nick came into the room. Use the correct verb from the box in the Past Continuous.

brush   watch   ~~read~~   listen   write   eat   paint   sit   play

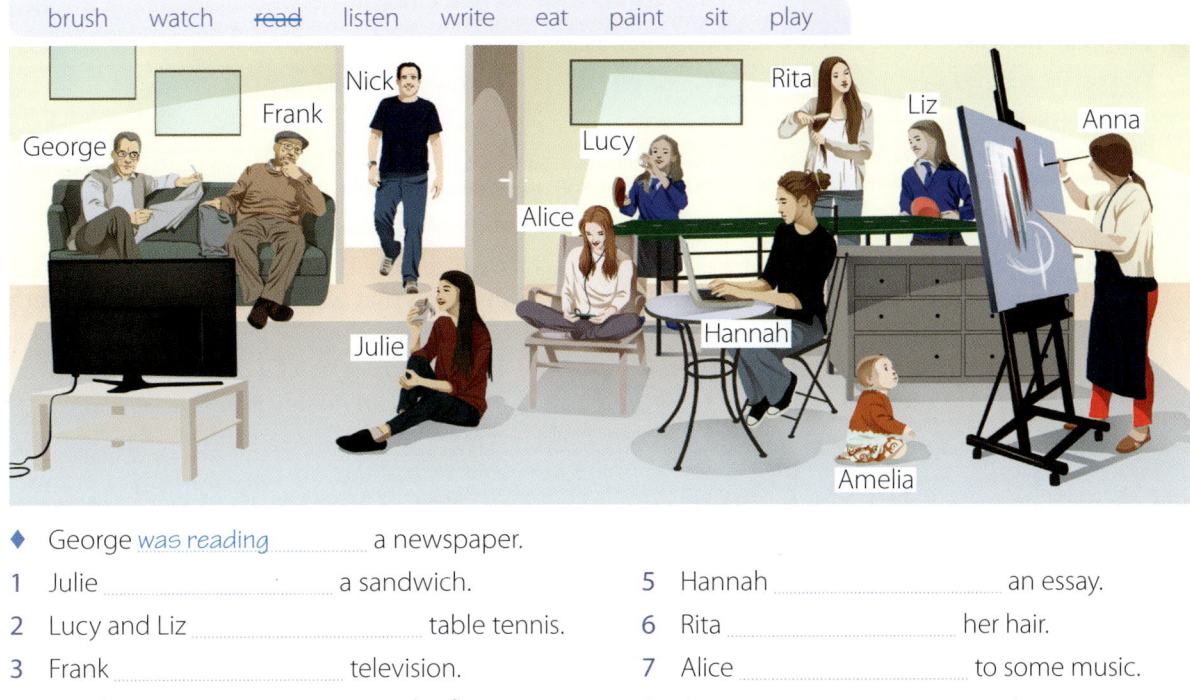

- George *was reading* a newspaper.
1. Julie _____ a sandwich.
2. Lucy and Liz _____ table tennis.
3. Frank _____ television.
4. Amelia _____ on the floor.
5. Hannah _____ an essay.
6. Rita _____ her hair.
7. Alice _____ to some music.
8. Anna _____ a picture.

C Look at the information about Sian and Nathan. Complete the sentences about them using the Past Continuous (*I was doing*) or the Past Simple (*I did*).

SIAN	
2000–06	lived in New York
2003–06	studied at university
2006	left university
2006–10	worked as a translator
2009	met Nathan
2012	married Nathan

NATHAN	
2002–10	lived in Washington
2003–05	did a course in computing
2005–10	worked as a computer programmer
2009	met Sian
2010–15	ran his own company
2012	married Sian

- In 2002, Sian *was living* in New York.
1. In 2004, Nathan _____ in Washington.
2. In 2004, Sian _____ at university.
3. In 2004, Nathan _____ a course in computing.
4. When Sian _____ university in 2006, Nathan _____ as a computer programmer.
5. When Nathan _____ Sian, she _____ as a translator.
6. While Sian _____ as a translator, she _____ Nathan.
7. In 2012, Nathan _____ his own company.
8. While he _____ his own company, Nathan _____ Sian.

12 Past Simple or Past Continuous

1 Compare the Past Simple and the Past Continuous:

PAST SIMPLE	PAST CONTINUOUS
He **talked** to her last week.	He **was talking** to her when I saw him.
I **didn't talk** to her yesterday.	I **wasn't talking** to anyone, I was watching the TV.
Did you **talk** to your sister?	**Were** you **talking** to her before I came?

2 We use the Past Simple to talk about a complete event in the past:

Last Saturday morning, Paul **played** football in the park.

PAST — PAUL **PLAYED** FOOTBALL. — NOW

We often use the Past Continuous to talk about an action that was in progress, when something else happened:

Last Saturday, Paul **was playing** football in the park when he saw Jasmine.

PAST — PAUL **WAS PLAYING** FOOTBALL. — NOW
HE SAW JASMINE.

Here are some more examples:
On Sunday I **made** a cake.
It **rained** a lot on Saturday morning.

Here are some more examples:
My phone rang while I **was making** a cake.
It **was raining** when we left home.

3 We often use the Past Simple to talk about one event that followed another event:

When Anna James **left** university, she **went** to work for a bank. She **left** the bank after five years, and **wrote** a book which …

In a story we often use the Past Continuous to say what was in progress, when something happened:

The sun **was shining**. People **were sitting** under the trees or **walking** around the park. Suddenly a car **drove** into the park …

A Use the Past Simple and the Past Continuous to make sentences from the words in brackets ( ).

♦ (The police/arrive/while/I/have/breakfast)
   The police arrived while I was having breakfast.

1 (The storm/start/while/they/drive/home)

2 (I/see/an accident/while/I/wait/for the bus)

3 (Mary/go/to several concerts/while/she/stay/in London)

♦ (I/have/breakfast/when/the police/arrive)
   I was having breakfast when the police arrived.

4 (My father/cook/the dinner/when/he/burn/his fingers)

5 (The soldiers/prepare/to leave/when/the bomb/explode)

B Complete these texts using the Past Simple or the Past Continuous of the verbs in brackets ( ).

♦ Beethoven _wrote_ (write) nine symphonies; he _was writing_ (write) another symphony when he died.

1 Last Saturday Tom wanted to make two salads. He _____ (make) the first one in five minutes. He _____ (make) the second one when his guests _____ (arrive), and they _____ (help) him to finish it.

2 The artist Gaudí _____ (design) several houses in Barcelona, Spain. Later he _____ (start) work on a church. He _____ (work) on the church when he _____ (die).

3 Last month a bank robber _____ (escape) while the police _____ (take) him to prison. Later they _____ (catch) him again, and this time they _____ (lock) him up without any problem.

4 Raphael's football team were lucky last Saturday. After 20 minutes they _____ (lose), but in the end they _____ (win) the game by four goals to two.

5 John Lennon _____ (sing) and _____ (play) on many records with the Beatles. After that he _____ (record) several songs without the Beatles. He _____ (prepare) a new record when Mark Chapman _____ (shoot) him.

6 The evening was getting darker; the street lights _____ (come) on. People _____ (hurry) home after work. I _____ (stand) in a queue at the bus stop. Suddenly, somebody _____ (grab) my bag.

C A police officer is interviewing Mary Croft about last Friday evening. Look at the pictures and complete the conversation. Use the Past Simple or the Past Continuous of the words in brackets ( ).

Police officer: What time ♦ _did you get_ (you/get) home from work?
Mary: At about six o'clock.
Police officer: And what ¹ _____ (you/do) after you got home?
Mary: I read the news.
Police officer: Did anything happen while ² _____ (read)?
Mary: Yes, my phone ³ _____ (ring).
Police officer: What ⁴ _____ (you/do) when your husband came home?
Mary: I was watching TV, and I ⁵ _____ (drink) a cup of coffee.
Police officer: Did you and your husband stay at home?
Mary: No, I ⁶ _____ (drink) my coffee. Then I put on my raincoat, and we ⁷ _____ (go) out at seven o'clock.
Police officer: Why ⁸ _____ (you/put) your raincoat on?
Mary: Because it ⁹ _____ (rain), of course.

13 Present Perfect (1)

1 We form the Present Perfect using the present tense of **have** + a past participle:

POSITIVE	
FULL FORM	SHORT FORM
I/you **have arrived**	I**'ve arrived**
he/she/it **has arrived**	he**'s arrived**
we/you/they **have arrived**	we**'ve arrived**

NEGATIVE	
FULL FORM	SHORT FORM
I/you **have not arrived**	**haven't arrived**
he/she/it **has not arrived**	**hasn't arrived**
we/you/they **have not arrived**	**haven't arrived**

QUESTIONS
Have I/you **arrived**?
Has he/she/it **arrived**?
Have we/you/they **arrived**?

2 Regular past participles end in **-ed** or **-d**:

played   travelled   arrived   washed

(For more regular past participles see **Appendix 2**, page 243.)

Many past participles are irregular:

buy → **bought**   make → **made**   go → **gone**

(For irregular past participles see **Appendix 3**, page 244.)

3 We use the Present Perfect:

▶ to talk about recent actions:

At 18.00, Anna arrived home.
At 18.01, we can say: Anna **has arrived** home.
From 18.30 to 19.00, Anna ate her dinner.
At 19.01, we can say: She**'s eaten** her dinner.

▶ to talk about our lives:

I**'ve sailed** across the Atlantic.
I**'ve seen** gorillas in Africa.
I **haven't danced** the Flamenco.

4 When we ask people about their lives, we often use **ever** (= at any time):

Have you **ever** been to Australia?
ANSWER: Yes, I have./No, I haven't.

When people talk about their lives, they sometimes use **never** (= not at any time):
I've **never** learnt French.

Note that **ever** and **never** come before the past participle.

A Use short forms (*I've seen, she's gone*) of the Present Perfect to make positive or negative sentences with the words in brackets ( ).

♦ (He/lose/his passport.)   He's lost his passport.
♦ (She/not/see/her sister.)   She hasn't seen her sister.
1 (We/finish/our work.)
2 (They/buy/a new house.)
3 (They/not/phone/the doctor.)
4 (They/go/to the cinema.)
5 (You/eat/four bananas!)
6 (You/not/take/any photographs.)

Now use the words in brackets ( ) and the Present Perfect to make questions.

- (you/see/John?) — Have you seen John?
7. (you/be/to Canada?)
8. (they/cook/our breakfast?)
9. (Jasmine/make/any mistakes?)
10. (we/visit/all the museums?)

B James is talking about his life. Put the past participle of the verbs in brackets ( ) in the gaps.

I've ♦ *seen* (see) a lot of beautiful places in my life, and I've ¹ _____ (do) a lot of interesting things. I've ² _____ (travel) in North and South America, for example. I've ³ _____ (visit) all the big American cities. I've ⁴ _____ (drive) across Mexico. I haven't ⁵ _____ (be) to Argentina, but I've ⁶ _____ (work) in Peru and Bolivia. I've ⁷ _____ (swim) in the Pacific Ocean, the Atlantic Ocean, and the Mediterranean Sea. I've ⁸ _____ (eat) in the best restaurants in Paris, and I've ⁹ _____ (sing) Italian songs in Rome. I haven't ¹⁰ _____ (make) much money in my life, but I've ¹¹ _____ (meet) a lot of interesting people and I've ¹² _____ (take) a lot of wonderful photographs!

C Read the questions. If they refer to a recent event, put a tick (✓). If they refer to someone's life, rewrite the sentence using *ever*.

- Have you had coffee? — ✓
- Have you been to Jamaica? — Have you ever been to Jamaica?
1. Have you bought your ticket?
2. Have you flown in a helicopter?
3. Have you washed your hands?
4. Have you spoken to a prince or princess?
5. Have you had anything to drink?

D Write true short answers (*Yes, I have./No, I haven't.*) to the following questions.

1. Have you ever been to New York?
2. Have you bought a newspaper this week?
3. Have you played a computer game today?
4. Have you ever made a grammatical mistake in English?
5. Have you learnt something new today?
6. Have you ever danced the tango?
7. Have you used your phone yet today?

14 Present Perfect (2)

1 We use the Present Perfect to talk about something that happened in the past, but we do not say exactly when it happened:

I've seen this film before. (= before now)

We often use the Present Perfect in this way for things that happened in the past, and that have a result now:

I've seen this film before. I don't want to see it again now.

She's left the company. She doesn't work there now.

We often use the Present Perfect with **ever** (= at any time) and **never** (= at no time):

Have you ever met a famous person?

He has never worked in a factory.

2 We can use the Present Perfect with **for** and **since** to talk about situations or actions in a period of time from the past until now.

We use **for** with a period of time (e.g. **three months**), and **since** with a point in time (e.g. **Tuesday**):

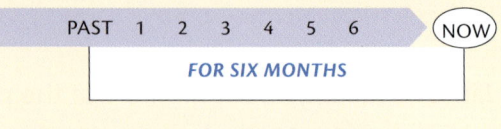

*We've lived here **for** six months.*

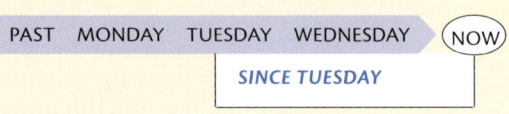

*I haven't seen Tom **since** Tuesday.*

3 **Gone** and **been**
Look at the difference between these two sentences:

*He's **been** to Paris.* (= He is now at home again.)

*He's **gone** to Paris.* (= He is in Paris now.)

He's been means 'he has finished his trip'.
He's gone means 'he has begun his trip'.

A Look at the pictures that show what Jenny has done in her life. Complete the sentences about her, using the Present Perfect form of the verbs in brackets ( ).

♦ She _has worked_ (work) as a secretary and as a schoolteacher.
1 She _____ (live) in Paris since 2015.
2 She _____ (visit) Canada and the USA.
3 She _____ (be) married for four years.
4 She _____ (write) four books.
5 She _____ (climb) Mont Blanc twice.

Tenses: past

B Complete the sentences using the Present Perfect form of the verbs in brackets ( ).

♦ Don't take my plate away. I _haven't finished_ (not/finish) my meal.

1. A: What's that book about?
   B: I don't know. I _____ (not/read) it.
2. I _____ (lose) my pen. Can I borrow yours, please?
3. My father _____ (buy) an expensive new car.
4. A: I _____ (book) a room here for tonight.
   B: Yes madam, what's your name, please?
5. I _____ (make) some sandwiches. Would you like one?
6. I'm not sure what the problem with the car is. It _____ (not/happen) before.
7. A: _____ (you/reply) to that letter from the bank?
   B: No I haven't, but I'll do it soon.

C Write this conversation using the Present Perfect and the words in brackets ( ).

♦ Rob: (you/ever/want/to work in another country?)
   Have you ever wanted to work in another country?

1. Noah: (Yes, in fact I/work/abroad twice.)
2. (I/work/in Ireland and in Brazil.)
3. (What about you?/you/ever/have/a job abroad?)
4. Rob: (No, I/never/want/to leave my home town.)
5. (I/live/here for 20 years, and I/never/think/of working abroad.)
6. Noah: (Really? Well, I/apply/for another job abroad.)

D Make sentences using the words in brackets ( ) with the Present Perfect and *for* or *since*.

♦ (I/not/play/tennis/last summer.)
   I haven't played tennis since last summer.

1. (I/know/her/more than ten years.)
2. (I/not/eat/anything/lunchtime.)
3. (you/live/in this town/a long time?)
4. (Charlotte/be/a good friend/we were at school together.)
5. (you/see/Jack/the party last week?)

15 Present Perfect (3)

1 We use **just** with the Present Perfect to talk about things that happened a short time before now:

have + just + PAST PARTICIPLE
It has just finished.

Could I speak to Jasmine, please? ~ I'm afraid she has just left. (= She left a short time ago.)
Is that a good book? ~ I don't know. I've just started it. (= I started it a short time before now.)

2 Look at this example with **already**:

Do you want something to eat? ~ No thanks, I've already eaten. (= I ate before now.)

We use **already** with the Present Perfect to emphasize that something happened before now, or before it was expected to happen. We use **already** like this:

have + already + PAST PARTICIPLE
I've already heard that story.

Here is another example:
Nicola: *Is Sarah going to phone you later?*
Robert: *No. She's (= She has) already phoned me.* (= Sarah phoned before Nicola expected her to phone.)

3 We use **yet** with a negative verb to say that something has not happened, but we think that it will happen:

The post hasn't arrived yet. (= The post has not arrived, but it probably will arrive.)
I haven't finished this work yet. (= I haven't finished this work, but I will finish it.)
They haven't replied to my letter yet.

We use **yet** in questions to ask whether something that we expect to happen has happened:

Have you paid the bill yet? (= Perhaps you have not paid the bill, but you are going to pay it soon.)
Has it stopped raining yet? (= Perhaps it has not stopped raining, but it will stop raining soon.)
Have you found a job yet?

Notice that we usually put **yet** at the end of a negative statement or question:

They haven't replied to my message yet.
Have you found a job yet?

A Complete the dialogues using *just* and the words in brackets ( ). Use the Present Perfect.

♦ A: What's happening in this programme?
  B: I don't know. It's just started. (It/start)

1 A: _____ (I/come) back from my holiday.
  B: Did you have a good time?

2 A: Could I have a copy of *Sports World*, please?
  B: Sorry. _____ (I/sell) the last copy.

3 A: How's Lucy?
  B: She's very happy. _____ (She/finish) her exams.

4 A: _____ (I/have) a message from Mike.
  B: Oh yes? What did he say?

5 A: Have you heard from Alice and Frank recently?
  B: Yes, _____ (they/move) to another town.

6 A: Have you still got the same car?
   B: No, _____ (I/buy) a new one.

7 A: Would you like something to eat?
   B: No, thanks. _____ (I/have) breakfast.

B Make sentences using the Present Perfect with *already* or *yet* and the words in brackets ( ).
Use the Present Perfect.

♦ (I/not/read/today's news.) yet
  I haven't read today's news yet.

1 (you/decide/which one to buy?) yet

2 (I/explain/this to you three times.) already

3 (Their baby son/start/talking.) already

4 (you/phone/Jasmine?) yet

5 (The game/not/finish.) yet

6 (I/have/lunch.) already

7 (He/spend/all his money.) already

C Complete the conversation using *just*, *already* or *yet* and the words in brackets ( ).
Use the Present Perfect.

Julia: Are you having a good time here?
Anna: Yes, I haven't been here long, and ♦ I've already visited (I/visit) a lot of interesting places.
Julia: ¹ _____ (you/visit/the Art Gallery).
Anna: No, ² _____ (I/not/do/that), but I'm going to do it.
Julia: What about the theatre? ³ _____ (you/see/a play)?
Anna: No, but ⁴ _____ (I/book/a ticket) for one. It's called *The Friends*.
        I did it online five minutes ago. Would you like to come with me?
Julia: Thanks, but ⁵ _____ (I/see/that play). I saw it last month.
Anna: ⁶ _____ (I/hear) that The Adventurers are going to give a concert next
        week. Do you like them?
Julia: Yes, I do. ⁷ _____ (they/make) a really good new album. It came out a
        couple of days ago.
Anna: I really want to get a ticket.
Julia: ⁸ _____ (they/not/sell/all the tickets). But be quick! They're a very
        popular group.

16 Past Simple or Present Perfect

Compare the Past Simple and the Present Perfect:

1 We use the Past Simple to talk about something that happened at a particular time in the past:
  I **met** John **at four o'clock**.
  When **did** Jasmine go to India? ~ **In June**.
  Martin **bought** a new car **last week**.

We use the Present Perfect to talk about the past, but not about when things happened:
  I've **met** John's girlfriend. She's nice.
  Have you ever **been** to India? ~ Yes, I have.
  I **have** never **bought** a new car.

2 We use the Past Simple for situations or actions during a period of time that ENDED in the past:
  I **worked** there **for two years**. I left last year.

I WORKED THERE FOR TWO YEARS.

We **lived** in that house **for a long time**; then we moved to this one.
Our company **opened** two new shops **last summer**.

We use the Present Perfect for situations or actions during a period of time from the past to NOW:
  He **has worked** here **for two years**.
  (= He still works here.)

HE HAS WORKED HERE FOR TWO YEARS.

We've **lived** in this flat **since we got married**.
(= We still live in it.)
We opened two shops last summer. **Since then** (= since that time), we **have opened** two more.

3 Notice how we often move from the Present Perfect to the Past Simple:
  Peter: **Have** you ever **played** this game before?
  Maria: Yes, I **played** it once when I was in England.
  Peter: **Did** you win?
  Maria: No, I **lost**.

A Complete the conversation by choosing the correct form in brackets ( ).

Sarah: ♦ _Have you ever been_ (Have you ever been/Did you ever go) to the United States?
James: Yes, ¹ _____ (I've been/I went) to California last year.
Sarah: ² _____ (Have you liked/Did you like) it?
James: Yes, ³ _____ (I've enjoyed/I enjoyed) the trip a lot.
Sarah: What ⁴ _____ (have you done/did you do) there?
James: ⁵ _____ (I've visited/I visited) Hollywood, Disneyland and San Francisco.
       ⁶ _____ (Have you been/Did you go) to California, Sarah?
Sarah: No, but ⁷ _____ (I've booked/I booked) a holiday there. I've got my ticket and I'm going next week!

B Complete the dialogues using the Present Perfect (*I have seen*) or Past Simple (*I saw*) of the words in brackets ( ).

A: I ♦ _saw_ (see) Jack last night.
B: Oh really. I ¹ _____ (not/see) him for months. How is he?

34

Tenses: past

A: We ² _____ (go) to the theatre last Saturday.
B: ³ _____ (you/enjoy) the play?
A: Yes, it ⁴ _____ (be) very good.

A: I ⁵ _____ (never/hear) of this group before. Are they famous in your country?
B: Yes, they are very popular. They ⁶ _____ (be) famous in my country for years.

A: What ⁷ _____ (you/do) last weekend?
B: I ⁸ _____ (stay) at home. I ⁹ _____ (need) a rest.

A: ¹⁰ _____ (you/ever/win) a competition?
B: Yes, I ¹¹ _____ (win) a photography competition in 2015.

A: So, John is your best friend. ¹² _____ (you/meet) him when you were at university?
B: Yes. We ¹³ _____ (be) friends for more than ten years.

C Complete this paragraph about the London Underground using the Present Perfect or Past Simple forms of the verbs in brackets ( ).

The London Underground

London ♦ _has had_ (have) an underground train system since the 19th century. The London Underground ¹ _____ (start) in 1863, when Victorian engineers and workers ² _____ (build) the Metropolitan railway. This railway line ³ _____ (go) from Paddington Station to Farringdon Street Station, and steam engines ⁴ _____ (pull) the coaches. 12 more lines ⁵ _____ (open) since then. The world's first underground electric railway ⁶ _____ (open) in 1890. This line ⁷ _____ (go) from the City of London to Stockwell in South London. Since the London Underground ⁸ _____ (begin), many other cities, such as New York and Moscow, ⁹ _____ (build) their own systems.

17 Present Perfect Continuous

1 We form the Present Perfect Continuous like this:

POSITIVE		
	FULL FORM	SHORT FORM
I/You/We/They	have been cooking.	've been cooking.
He/She/It	has been cooking.	's been cooking.

NEGATIVE		
I/You/We/They	have not been cooking.	haven't been cooking.
He/She/It	has not been cooking.	hasn't been cooking.

QUESTIONS		
Have	I/you/we/they	been cooking?
Has	he/she/it	been cooking?

(For details about **-ing** forms see **Appendix 2**, on page 243.)

2 We use the Present Perfect Continuous for an action or situation that began in the past and continues until now:

You're late! I've been waiting for you.

We often use **for** and **since** with the Present Perfect Continuous. We use **for** with a period of time, and **since** with a point in time:

I've been waiting for you for two hours.
I've been waiting for you since six o'clock.

3 Here are some more examples:

PAST   NOW

Julia has been talking on the phone for an hour. (= She started talking on the phone an hour ago and she is still talking.)
You've been sitting there since one o'clock. (= You started sitting there at one o'clock and you are still sitting there.)

4 We use the Present Perfect Continuous for actions that are done many times in a period of time from the past until now:

She's been having driving lessons for a couple of months. (= She started a couple of months ago; she is still having lessons.)
I've been playing tennis since I was a small child.

5 We can use **How long ...?** with the Present Perfect Continuous:

How long have you been living here? I have been living here for three years.

A Complete the sentences by putting the verbs in brackets ( ) into the Present Perfect Continuous.

♦ She _has been learning_ (she/learn) Spanish for six months.
1 The roads are very wet; _____ (it/rain) for hours.
2 _____ (we/play) this game for hours. Let's stop now!
3 _____ (Emilia/learn) French at school for three years.
4 _____ (I/read) this book for months, but I haven't finished it yet.
5 _____ (we/watch) this programme for hours.
6 _____ (the neighbours/make) a lot of noise again today?
7 _____ (I/save) my money for a holiday.
8 _____ (you/listen) to me carefully?

Tenses: past

B Put *for* or *since* into the gaps.

♦ I've been working in this office *since* last summer.
1 Have you been doing this course _____ a long time?
2 I've been driving this car _____ more than ten years.
3 She has been planning the party _____ the beginning of the month.
4 George has been telling the same stories _____ several years.
5 We've been waiting for a reply _____ we contacted them last week.
6 What have you been doing _____ the last time that I saw you?
7 You've been writing that application _____ more than two hours.
8 He's been feeling ill _____ a few days.

C Write sentences to describe what each member of the Wyatt family has been doing to prepare for Christmas. Use words from the box and the Present Perfect Continuous to describe the pictures.

wrap	make
decorate	shop
write	~~put up~~
a cake	cards
~~decorations~~	presents
the tree	for food

♦ *John has been putting up decorations.*
1 Mary and Steve _____
2 Martha _____
3 Mia _____
4 Tom _____
5 Joseph _____

D Write a sentence for each of the following situations, using the Present Perfect Continuous and *for* or *since*.

♦ She started her course a month ago and she is still doing it.
  She has been doing her course for a month.
♦ I started reading this novel last weekend and I'm still reading it.
  I have been reading this novel since last weekend.
1 It started raining at three o'clock and it is still raining.

2 He started playing chess when he was ten years old and he still plays it.

3 I started work at eight o'clock and I'm still working.

4 Helen started looking for another job two months ago and she's still looking.

5 We arrived here two hours ago and we're still waiting.

18 Present Perfect Simple or Continuous

1 Compare the Present Perfect Simple and Present Perfect Continuous:

We use the Present Perfect Simple (**have painted**) to talk about a past activity that is now completed:

> We'**ve painted** the rooms. (= The rooms are now painted.)
> Anna'**s mended** her bike. (= She can ride it now.)

We use the Present Perfect Continuous (**have been painting**) to emphasize the activity itself, which may or may not be completed:

> We'**ve been painting** the flat. That's why it smells. We still have three rooms to paint.
> Anna's hands are dirty because she'**s been mending** her bike.

2 We use the Present Perfect Simple to ask and answer **How many?** and **How much?**:

> A: How many rooms **have** you **painted**?
> B: We'**ve painted** three of them.

We usually use the Present Perfect Continuous to ask **How long?**, and with **since** and **for**:

> I **have been travelling** for six months.
> A: How long **have** you **been waiting**? **Have** you **been queuing** for a long time?
> B: Yes, I'**ve been waiting** since two o'clock.

For more details about **How long?**, **How many?** and **How much?** see **Unit 32**.

3 Note that we usually use the Present Perfect Simple (not the Continuous):

▶ to talk about short actions with **have**, **stop**, **break**, etc.
> Anthony **has had** an accident on his bike.

▶ with verbs of thinking (e.g. **know**, **decide**, **forget**, **notice**):
> I'm sorry. I'**ve forgotten** your name.

▶ to talk about the last time that something happened:
> I **haven't eaten** meat for two years. (= I last ate meat two years ago.)

Note that we can use the Present Perfect Simple or the Continuous with **work**, **teach**, and **live**, with no difference in meaning:

> I **have taught** here for two years.
> OR I **have been teaching** here for two years.

A Write out the sentences in brackets ( ). Use the Present Perfect Simple (*I have done*).

♦ He's late again. (How many times/he/arrive/late this month?)
   How many times has he arrived late this month?

1 What a good week! (We/sell/much more than we expected.)

2 (How much money/you/spend/this week?)

3 (How many people/Jasmine/invite/to her party?)

Tenses: past

Now use the Present Perfect Continuous (*I have been doing*).

4 It's still raining. (It/rain/for hours.)

5 That noise is awful. (They/drill/holes in the wall all morning.)

6 Are you still here? (How long/you/sit/here?)

B Five friends have just finished some jobs. Look at the table and complete the dialogues. Use the Present Perfect Simple or the Present Perfect Continuous.

	ACTIVITY	NOW
Lucas	~~sweep the floors~~	he is sweating
Rachel	~~cut the grass~~	she is tired
Paul	do the washing-up	he has soft hands
Laura	peel the onions	she has red eyes
Tim	defrost the freezer	he has cold hands

♦ Lucas, why are you sweating?   ~ Because I *have been sweeping the floors.*
♦ Is the lawn finished?   ~ Yes, Rachel *has cut the grass.*
1 Paul, why are your hands so soft?   ~ Because I
2 Are the onions ready for the pan?   ~ Yes, Laura .... them.
3 Rachel, you look tired.   ~ Yes, I
4 Tim, your hands are very cold.   ~ Yes, I
5 Are the floors clean?   ~ Yes, Lucas .... them.
6 Why are your eyes red, Laura?   ~ Because I
7 Are the plates clean?   ~ Yes, Paul
8 Is the freezer all right now?   ~ Yes, Tim

C Complete the conversations using the verbs in brackets ( ). Use the Present Perfect Simple or the Present Perfect Continuous.

Ellen: Where are you and your family going to live?
Owen: Well, we've ♦ *been talking* (talk) about that for weeks, but we haven't
        ♦ *decided* (decide) anything yet.

Tina: Excuse me. Have you ¹ .... (stand) in this queue for a long time?
Jacob: Yes, I've ² .... (queue) for almost an hour.

Sara: Why are you crying?
Joe: Because my brother has ³ .... (have) an accident. He's
        ⁴ .... (break) both his legs.

Lucy: Excuse me. Has someone ⁵ .... (leave) this bag here?
Ben: I don't know. I've ⁶ .... (sit) here all afternoon, but I haven't
        ⁷ .... (notice) it until now.

19 Past Perfect

1 We form the Past Perfect with **had** and the past participle of a verb (e.g. **started**, **taken**):

	FULL FORM	SHORT FORM
I/You/He/She/It/We/They	had started.	'd started.

I **had taken** it. OR I'**d taken** it.
They **had not started**.
OR They **hadn't started**.

2 Look at this:

> A year ago:
> Jenny is flying to Rome. She thinks, 'I have never been on a plane before now.'
>
> Now:
> Jenny flew to Rome last year. She **had** never **been** on a plane before that.

When we talk about an event or situation in past time we use the Past Simple (e.g. **flew**); if we talk about an event before that time, we use the Past Perfect (e.g. **had been**). Here is another example:

> Last Saturday at the cinema:
> Mary: We don't need to queue because I've already bought the tickets.
>
> Now, talking about last Saturday:
> Mary: We didn't need to queue because I **had** already **bought** the tickets.

Note that we can use **never** and **already** before the past participle (e.g. **been**, **bought**).

3 If we talk about a series of past events in order, we use the Past Simple:

> A: I saw a beautiful bird in my garden.
> B: I went to get my phone to take a photo.
> C: The bird **flew** away.
> D: I returned with my phone.

PAST   A   B   C   D   NOW

We need the Past Perfect to make it clear that one of the events is not in order:

> D: I returned with my phone.
> C: The bird **had** already **flown** away.
>   (= The bird had gone before I returned.)

Also, compare these sentences using **when**:

Past Simple: **When** I returned with my phone, the bird **flew** away. (= It went after I returned.)

Past Perfect: **When** I returned with my phone, the bird **had flown** away. (= It went before I returned.)

4 The Past Perfect is used in reported speech:

> 'I have suffered from asthma for many years.'
> She told the doctor that she **had suffered** from asthma for many years.

(For more on reported speech, see **Units 100–102**.)

A Write sentences about what these people had already done or had never done before. Use the Past Perfect, and *already* or *never*.

♦ Last summer Mary won a gold medal for the third time.
   She had already won two gold medals before that.

♦ Last year Nathan visited Scotland for the first time.
   He had never visited Scotland before that.

1 Last weekend Tom rode a horse for the first time.
   He .... before that.

2 Last summer Julian ran in a marathon for the sixth time.
   He .... before that.

3 Last week Lucy wrote a poem for the first time.
   She .... before that.

Tenses: past

4 Last week Anna appeared on TV for the first time.
   She _____ before that.

5 Last summer Anthony played tennis at Wimbledon for the fifth time.
   He _____ before that.

6 Last year Abigail wrote her third novel.
   She _____ before that.

B In each case you have two events in the order in which they took place. Write the information in one sentence using the words in brackets ( ).

♦ **A:** The driver started the car. **B:** Lady James appeared.
   (When Lady James/appear/, the driver/already/start/the car)
   When Lady James appeared, the driver had already started the car.

1 **A:** We put the fire out. **B:** The firefighters arrived.
   (When the firefighters/arrive/, we/already/put/the fire out.)

2 **A:** James finished the work. **B:** The manager came back.
   (When the manager/come/back, James/already/finish/the work.)

3 **A:** I went to bed. **B:** Raphael called.
   (When Raphael/call/, I/already/go/to bed.)

4 **A:** Alice and Jack had lunch. **B:** Their children came home.
   (When their children/come/home, Alice and Jack/already/have/lunch.)

5 **A:** Owen prepared the supper. **B:** His wife got home from work.
   (When his wife/get/home from work, Owen/already/prepare/the supper.)

6 **A:** The thieves spent the money. **B:** The police caught them.
   (The thieves/already/spend/the money/when the police/catch/them.)

C Use the Past Perfect to complete the sentences.

♦ Last summer Grace said, 'I've always wanted to fly in a helicopter.'
   Grace said that she had always wanted to fly in a helicopter.

1 Jacob said, 'Jack has just gone out.'
   Jacob told us that Jack _____

2 Robert said to Charlotte, 'Have you been to Cambridge?'
   Robert asked Charlotte if she _____

3 When the boys came home, Mrs Brock said, 'I've made some sandwiches.'
   Mrs Brock told the boys that she _____

4 'I know your cousin,' said Tom. 'I met her in Amsterdam.'
   Tom said he knew my cousin because he _____

5 Rob was talking to Abigail, and he said, 'Have you ever been to Japan?'
   Rob asked Abigail if she _____

20 Used to

1 We can use the Present Simple to talk about present situations or habits:

- situations:
  My sister **works** as a translator.
  Andrew **lives** in London.

- habits:
  Peter usually **wears** jeans.
  I often **eat** a sandwich for lunch.
  Mike **doesn't smoke** anymore.
  Does John **drive** to work every day?

2 Look at these sentences with the Past Simple:

- situation:
  Henry **lived** in France for many years.

- habit:
  When I was young, I **ran** three miles every day.

The verbs are in the Past Simple and the sentences are about past situations or habits.

3 Look at these sentences with **used to**:

Charlotte **used to live** in Ireland.
Many people **used to make** their own bread.
My husband **used to work** at home.

We use **used to** to talk about a past situation or habit that continued for months or years, and to emphasize that the situation today is different:

Charlotte doesn't live in Ireland **now**.
Nowadays people usually buy bread from a shop.
My husband doesn't work at home **now**.

Compare the Past Simple and **used to**:

- Past Simple:
  When he was young, he **ran** three miles every day. (He may or may not run three miles every day now.)

- **used to**:
  When I was young, I **used to run** three miles every day. I don't do that now. (I don't run three miles every day now.)

We make negative sentences and questions with **did** + **use to**:

Lucy **didn't use to like** black coffee.
Paul **didn't use to smoke**.
Did Oliver **use to cycle** to school?
Did your parents **use to read** to you?

4 We do not use **use to** for present situations or habits; we use the Present Simple:

Anna **sings** in a band. (NOT ~~Anna uses to sing in a band.~~)
Joe **doesn't cycle** to school. (NOT ~~Joe doesn't use to cycle to school~~)

A Look at the table of people who have changed what they eat or drink and complete the sentences.

name		in the past		now	
Anna	Grace	meat	tap water	fish	bottled water
Tom	Mary	coffee	tinned fruit	tea	fresh fruit
Robert	Lucy	white bread	margarine	brown bread	butter

♦ Anna _used to eat_ meat, but now she _eats fish_.
♦ Tom _drinks tea_ now, but _he used to drink_ coffee.
1 Robert _____ white bread, but now _____ brown bread.
2 Grace _____ tap water, but now _____ bottled water.
3 Mary _____ fresh fruit now, but _____ tinned fruit.
4 Lucy _____ butter now, but _____ margarine.

Tenses: past

Now complete these questions.

♦ *Did Anna use to eat meat?* ~ Yes she did, but now she eats fish.
5 _____ white bread? ~ Yes he did, but now he eats brown bread.
6 _____ tinned fruit? ~ Yes she did, but now she eats fresh fruit.
7 _____ tap water? ~ Yes she did, but now she drinks bottled water.

Now complete these sentences.

♦ Anna *didn't use to eat* _____ fish, but she does now.
♦ Tom drinks tea now, but he *didn't use to drink* _____ it.
8 Lucy _____ butter, but she does now.
9 Mary eats fresh fruit now, but she _____ it.
10 Grace drinks bottled water now, but she _____ it.

B Tick (✓) the sentences which are correct and cross out the sentences which are incorrect.

♦ When he was at primary school, Anthony used to work very hard. ✓
♦ ~~Last year Peter used to get a new bicycle for Christmas.~~
1 I didn't use to watch TV much, but I do now.
2 When he was a teenager, my grandfather used to buy all the Beatles' records.
3 Paul used to go the cinema almost every weekend.
4 Did Grace used to go to the concert last night?
5 Paul used to be really fit when he played a lot of volleyball.
6 John use to spend a lot of money on that new jacket he bought last week.
7 Kate didn't use to come to school yesterday because she was sick.
8 Jasmine used to play tennis a lot, but she doesn't have time now.
9 Did you use to go to the seaside for holidays when you were a child?
10 We used to live in Canada before we came here.

C Complete the sentences with the words in brackets ( ) to say what these people used to do and what they do now.

♦ (Andrew/get up/seven o'clock/now/half past seven)
Andrew used to get up at seven o'clock, but now he gets up at half past seven.

♦ (I/swim/before work/now/after work)
I used to swim before work, but now I swim after work.

1 (Dan/play/violin/now/guitar)

2 (Anna/be/best friends/Annie/now/Cathy)

3 (Lucy/have/dancing lessons/now/riding lessons)

4 (I/buy CDs/now/download all my music)

5 (John and Abigail/live/London/now/Cardiff)

6 (David/drive/Fiesta/now/Jaguar)

Test B — Tenses – past

A Anna is emailing her new Spanish friend, Pilar. If the verb tenses are wrong, correct them. If they are right, put a tick (✓).

I'll try to answer some of your questions. ◆ I have moved _I moved_ to London from Bristol in 2009. That means ◆ I've been here ✓ for almost ten years now. (Wow! Time flies, doesn't it?) ¹ I was living .... in the south of the city when ² I was starting .... going out with my husband, Mel. (We were both studying French at the time ³ we have met .... at University College.) In fact, ⁴ I've stayed .... in flats all over London! My favourite flat ⁵ had .... a balcony and you could see a small park in the square. ⁶ I had never forgotten .... that flat, or my flatmates. Anyway, that's enough about me. How long ⁷ have you lived .... in Madrid? ⁸ Have you been .... born there? London and Madrid are so big, aren't they? ⁹ I didn't see .... all the different parts of London yet! I saw an old friend by chance about a week ago when ¹⁰ I walked .... to work, and she lives on a boat in north London. ¹¹ I have visited .... her last week. ¹² I've never seen .... such a small kitchen! My friend cooked a meal for us.

B Sara is talking to her husband. They've been married for 40 years. Six Past Simple verb forms should be Past Perfect. One has been corrected for you as an example. Find the other five, cross them out and rewrite them.

Sara: We first met in 1977, didn't we, at the cinema?

Brian: Yes. When we arrived, ◆ ~~the film already began~~. _the film had already begun._

Sara: I saw it before anyway.

Brian: Really? You didn't tell me that.

Sara: No. I wanted you to take me to the cinema the following week!

Brian: So you already decided you liked me!

Sara: And then you took me to your favourite restaurant, but it closed a week before!

Brian: Oh dear. What did we do next?

Sara: We went to a pub to meet your friends, but it was empty. Everyone went home, because England was playing Germany at Wembley.

Brian: What an evening!

Sara: That's not all! When I got home I couldn't open the front door because I left my keys at the pub.

Tenses: past

C Anna is talking to her mother on the phone. Underline the verbs that should be in the Present Perfect Continuous or Past Continuous form, and then correct them. One has been done as an example. Find five more.

'I'm so tired, Mum, I've studied [*I've been studying*] all day from five o'clock this morning. In fact, I did some maths when you rang just now. I still haven't finished and now I've got a headache because I've worked harder than I've ever done before! Sorry, what did you say? You've never had a problem with maths? But you're a teacher! You've read books and things all your life! Dad says you learnt French verbs on Saturday morning in the park when he first met you! Anyway, I haven't finished yet. My friend Stevie will be OK, though. Every time I've visited her in the last month, she has worked hard.'

D Paul, Caroline, Jo and Rob are talking about some of the holidays they've had. Put the verbs in brackets ( ) in the Past Simple, Past Continuous or Present Perfect form.

Paul: Do you remember when ♦ *we went* (we go) to Morocco, Caroline?
Caroline: Unfortunately, yes. ¹ _____ (You/lose) your passport, just after we arrived.
Paul: That's right. ² _____ (We/sail) near the coast, and I was looking at the fish, and ³ _____ (it/just drop) into the sea! ⁴ _____ (you/two/visit) North Africa?
Jo: No. ⁵ _____ (We/be) to Ghana, though. ⁶ _____ (We/fly) there in 2001, didn't we, Rob?
Rob: Sorry, Jo. ⁷ _____ (I/not/listen). ⁸ _____ (I/have) such a busy day today! Actually, ⁹ _____ (I/fall) asleep on the sofa when ¹⁰ _____ (Paul/ring) and invited us around.
Jo: So you need a holiday, don't you?
Caroline: ¹¹ _____ (Paul and I/go) to this really great country hotel, The Woodland Spa, about a month ago. ¹² _____ (We/read) the Sunday newspapers, and ¹³ _____ (we/see) this advertisement. ¹⁴ _____ (Paul/not/stop) talking about it since we got back!
Paul: It was fantastic!
Rob: ¹⁵ _____ (it/have) a jacuzzi in the bathroom?
Jo: ¹⁶ _____ (be/there) a bowl of fruit in your bedroom?
Caroline: All of that. And ¹⁷ _____ (you/never/see) such a beautiful swimming pool in your life!
Jo: It sounds lovely. Better than that hotel ¹⁸ _____ (Rob and I/stay) in last year in Devon.
Rob: Oh dear. ¹⁹ _____ (It/be) terrible. One night ²⁰ _____ (we/talk) in our room, and the owner knocked on the door at ten o'clock in the evening and told us to go to sleep!
Jo: ²¹ _____ (I/not/enjoy) a holiday in the UK for years, I'm afraid.

21 Be going to

1 We form sentences with **be going to** like this:

BE GOING +	TO	+ INFINITIVE
It is going	to	snow.

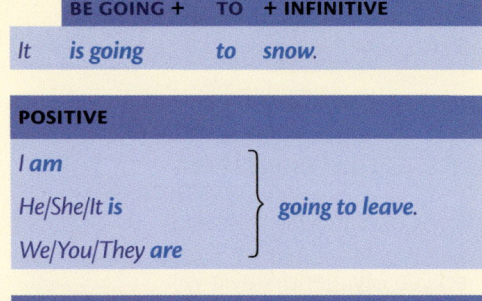

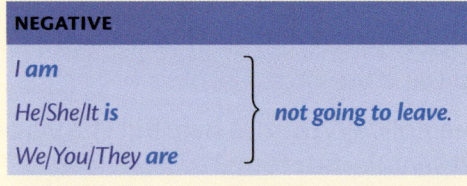

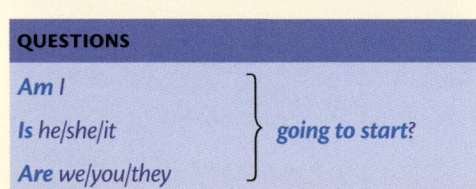

2 Note that we usually use the short form of **be** (**I'm**, **he/she/it's**, **we/you/they're**):

They**'re** going to leave.
He**'s** going to spend a week by the sea.

3 The negative short form is **I'm not going to**:
I'm not going to play tennis today.

With **he**, **she** and **it**, there are two negative short forms:
He/she/it **isn't** going to come.
He/she/it**'s not** going to come.

With **you**, **we** and **they**, there are also two negative short forms:
You/we/they **aren't** going to come.
You/we/they**'re not** going to come.

4 We use **be going to** for the future. We use it:

▶ to talk about things we have decided to do in the future:
A: What **are** you **going to do** tomorrow?
B: **I'm going to visit** Paul in Brighton.
A: **Are** you **going to drive**?
B: No, **I'm going to take** the train.

▶ to predict the future, using information we know now:
Look at that blue sky! It**'s going to be** hot.
I've eaten too much. I**'m going to be** ill.
Look at the time. It's two o'clock. They **aren't going to come** now.

A Paul has decided what he's going to do in his life. Complete the sentences, using short forms of *be going to* and the verbs in brackets ( ).

♦ I 'm going to study (study) music at university.
1 I _____ (travel) all over the world.
2 I _____ (not/work) in an office.
3 I _____ (marry) a very rich woman.
4 We _____ (have) 11 boys.
5 They _____ (become) a football team.
6 They _____ (win) the World Cup.
7 I _____ (play) the piano every night in a cafe.
8 My wife _____ (not/cook) or clean.
9 We _____ (eat) in restaurants every day.

B Write positive sentences with short forms of *be going to* and the words in brackets ( ).

♦ (I/see/a film tonight.)   I'm going to see a film tonight.
1 (She/buy/a new car tomorrow.)
2 (They/work/hard this year.)
3 (It/rain/this afternoon.)

Tenses: future

Write negative sentences with short forms of *be going to* and the words in brackets ( ).

- ♦ (They/not/catch/that train!)   They're not going to catch that train!
- 4 (Paul/not/drive/to Scotland.)
- 5 (We/not/finish/it today.)
- 6 (She/not/buy/a new house.)

Write questions with *be going to* and the words in brackets ( ).

- ♦ (you/have/a holiday this year?)   Are you going to have a holiday this year?
- 7 (they/win/the match?)
- 8 (Mary/leave/her job?)
- 9 (you/take/the exam in June?)

C Keiko is Japanese. She's going to spend a week by the sea in England. Ask her some questions. Use *be going to*, the verbs in brackets ( ), and the words from the box.

| an umbrella | in a luxury hotel | to a club | fish and chips |
| in the sea | ~~a lot of English~~ | golf every day | |

- ♦ (speak)   Are you going to speak a lot of English?
- 1 (play)
- 2 (take)
- 3 (swim)
- 4 (eat)
- 5 (stay)
- 6 (go)

D Make sentences about the pictures using short forms of *be going* to and the words from the box.

> It/rain
> They/eat/a pizza
> They/not/play/tennis
> He/not/win/the race
> She/have/a swim
> They/watch/a film
> ~~He/make/a phone call~~
> He/play/the piano

- ♦ He's going to make a phone call.
- 1
- 2
- 3
- 4
- 5
- 6
- 7

22 Will and shall

1 We use **will** to talk about the future. Look at this example:

It's now five o'clock. I'll stop work at six.

2 We make sentences with **will** like this:

WILL + INFINITIVE
I **will stop**.

We use **I will** or **I'll**, and **I will not** or **I won't**. We usually use the short forms (**I'll**, **he'll**, **I won't**, **he won't**) when we speak.

POSITIVE	FULL FORM	SHORT FORM
I/He/She/It/We/You/They	will go.	'll go.

NEGATIVE	FULL FORM	SHORT FORM
I/He/She/It/We/You/They	will not go.	won't go.

QUESTIONS	FULL FORM	SHORT FORM
will go.	I/he/she/it/we/you/they	go?

3 We use **will** to talk about future facts, and things that we think will happen in the future:

*My father **will be** 50 years old tomorrow.*
*Jasmine **will love** your new dress.*
*He's a good manager. He **won't make** any mistakes.*

We also use will to ask about the future:
***Will** they **win** this game?*

4 We use **I'll** when we make a quick decision to do something. For example, when the doorbell rings, we say:
***I'll** answer it.*

Here is another example:
A: *Does anyone want to come with me tonight?*
B: *Yes, **I'll** come.*

We use **Shall I ...?** or **I'll ...** when we want to do things for other people:

OFFER:	**Shall I make** you a cup of coffee?
OFFER:	**I'll make** you a cup of coffee.

We use **Shall we ...?** to suggest things that we can do:

SUGGESTION:	**Shall we** see a film tonight?

A Complete the dialogues with *will* or *won't* and the verbs from the box. Use short forms of *will* where you can.

> have   take   ~~phone~~   finish   be (x2)   win   make

♦ A: Are you coming to the cinema on Sunday?
　B: I'm not sure. I 'll phone _____ you on Saturday.

1 A: Don't change your clothes now. We _____ late.
　B: No, we won't. We _____ a taxi.

2 A: George is going to have a party at the weekend.
　B: Why?
　A: It's his birthday. He _____ 30 on Saturday.

3 A: She _____ the tennis match tomorrow.
　B: Why not?
　A: She _____ mistakes. She always makes mistakes in important matches.

4 A: _____ Steve _____ the work tonight?
　B: No, he won't finish. He _____ time.

48

Tenses: future

B Put the best phrase from the box in each gap. Start your sentences with *I'll*.

> phone for a taxi   help you to look for it   ~~carry some of them~~
> go with you   give you some money   make you a sandwich
> open a window   ask her to phone you tonight   give you the name of a language school

♦ A: I want to take these books home, but they're very heavy.
B: I'll carry some of them.

1 A: I feel sick. It's so hot in this room.
B: _____

2 A: I want a cup of coffee, but I don't have any money.
B: _____

3 A: I'm hungry. I didn't have any lunch.
B: _____

4 A: I want to learn Japanese.
B: _____

5 A: I've lost my passport.
B: _____

6 A: It's ten o'clock. I'll be late if I walk.
B: _____

7 A: I want to speak to Jasmine. It's very important.
B: _____

8 A: I want to go to the museum, but I don't know the way.
B: _____

C Put *Shall I* or *Shall we* in the gaps to complete the dialogues.

♦ A: I'm hungry. Are you going to the shops?
B: Yes. Shall I _____ get you something to eat?

♦ A: We need a holiday.
B: What a good idea! Shall we _____ go to Florida?

1 A: I'm going to get some tickets for the concert next week. _____ buy you one?
B: Yes please. I'd love to come.

2 A: _____ go to a restaurant tonight?
B: OK, but I don't have any money. Will you pay for me?

3 A: I want to go to Italian classes, but I've never learnt a foreign language before.
B: _____ come with you?
A: That's very kind of you.

4 A: Where is our meeting?
B: At John's office on Baker Street.
A: _____ walk or take a taxi?

5 A: You look thirsty. _____ get you a drink?
B: Yes, please. Can I have an orange juice or some water?

6 A: It's a beautiful day! _____ have a picnic?
B: Wonderful idea! Who shall we invite?

23 Will or be going to

1 Compare **will** and **be going to**:

We use **will** with an infinitive (**do**, **go**, **be**, **arrive**, etc.):

INFINITIVE
John **will arrive** tomorrow.

We use **be going** with **to** + infinitive (**to do**, **to be**, **to rain**, etc.):

TO + INFINITIVE
It's **going to rain** soon.
My friends **are going to come** tonight.
It **isn't going to rain** today.
What **are you going to do** on Sunday?

2 We use **will** for actions that we decide to do now, at the moment of speaking:

PAST → NOW SPEAKING / DECISION

I like this coat. I think I**'ll buy** it.
A: What would you like to eat?
B: **I'll have** a pizza, please.

We can use **will** for offers and promises:
I'll carry your case for you. (OFFER)
I **won't forget** your birthday again. (PROMISE)

We use **be going to** for actions that we have decided to do before we speak:

PAST DECISION → NOW SPEAKING

I'm going to clean my room this afternoon.
(I decided to clean it this morning.)

We can ask questions about people's plans:
Are you going to take the three o'clock train?
(= Have you decided to take the three o'clock train?)

3 We use **will** to talk about things that we think or believe will happen in the future:

I'm sure you**'ll enjoy** the film.
I'm sure it **won't rain** tomorrow. It**'ll be** another beautiful, sunny day.

We use **be going to** for something that we expect to happen, because the situation now indicates that it is going to happen:

He's running towards the goal, and he**'s going to score**.

A Complete the sentences using the words in brackets ( ) and *'ll* or a form of *be going to*.

♦ A: Are you going to watch TV tonight?
 B: Yes, *I'm going to watch* (I/watch) my favourite programme at nine o'clock.

1 A: What _____ (you/eat) tonight? What food have you bought?
 B: I haven't bought any food.
 A: Well, why don't you come to my house? _____ (I/cook) us something nice to eat.

2 A: I'm going into the centre of town tomorrow. _____ (I/buy) some new clothes.
 B: Oh, what _____ (you/get)?
 A: _____ (I/look) for a T-shirt and some jeans.
 B: I'd like to go into the centre too. _____ (I/come) with you.

3 A: _____ (I/leave) work late tomorrow. There is a meeting at six o'clock.
 B: Oh, I didn't know that. Well, _____ (I/see) you after the meeting.

4 _____ (I/phone) Tom at six o'clock. I promised to phone him this evening.

5 A: Are you going to have a holiday in the summer?
 B: Yes, _____ (I/travel) around Europe with a friend.

Tenses: future

B Look at the office scenes in the pictures and match them to the sentences. Cross out the incorrect sentences.

♦ Relax, I'll answer it. / ~~Relax, I'm going to answer it~~.
a You look hot, I'll open a window. / You look hot, I'm going to open a window.
b Next year, we're going to enter the Japanese market. / Next year, we'll enter the Japanese market.
c Thanks, I'm going to have an orange juice. / Thanks, I'll have an orange juice.
d Have a rest, I'm going to do the photocopying. / Have a rest, I'll do the photocopying.
e Thursday is no good for me, I'm afraid. I'll meet the new manager of our Tokyo office. / Thursday is no good for me, I'm afraid. I'm going to meet the new manager of our Tokyo office.

C You are at a party. Here are some of the questions you are asked. Reply using the words in brackets ( ) and *will* or *be going to*.

♦ A: Hi, nice to see you. Would you like a drink?
B: (I/have/a coke, please) I'll have a coke, please.

1 A: What are you doing these days?
B: (Nothing much, but I/start/a new job soon)

2 A: Would you like something to eat?
B: (Thanks, I/have/a sandwich)

3 A: What are your plans for the weekend?
B: (I/do/some shopping tomorrow and I/go/for a swim on Sunday)

4 A: Why is Maria standing by the piano?
B: (She/sing/, I'm afraid)

5 A: This cake looks delicious. Are you going to have some?
B: (No, but I'm sure you/enjoy/it)

6 A: How are you getting home?
B: (David/give/me a lift)

24 Present Continuous for the future

1 Look at these examples:
I**'m flying** home tomorrow.
He**'s starting** a new job on Monday.
Anthony and Anna **are coming** at the weekend.

In each example, we are using the Present Continuous (see **Units 5** and **6**), but we are talking about the future, not the present.

2 Look at this example:

You bought a plane ticket **last week**.
You can now say:
I**'m flying** home **next week**.

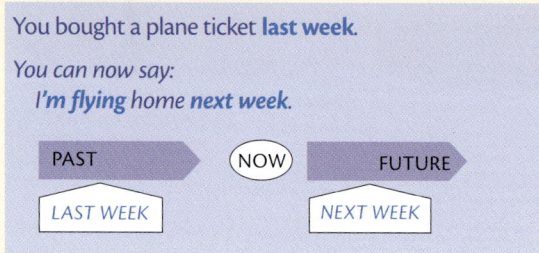

We use the Present Continuous to talk about things we have arranged in the past to do in the future.

Here are some more examples:

A bank wrote to Steve and asked him to start work **next week**.
We can now say:
He**'s starting** a new job **next week**.

John said to Anthony and Anna:
Would you like to come for dinner on Sunday?
Anthony and Anna said:
Yes.
John now says:
Anthony and Anna **are coming** on Sunday.

3 The important part of a Present Continuous for the future sentence is often a time or day (e.g. **next week**, **in July**, **tomorrow**, **on Sunday**):

PRESENT: I'm leaving **now**.
FUTURE: I'm leaving **tomorrow**.
PRESENT: We're having a party **at the moment**. Can I phone you tomorrow?
FUTURE: We're having a party **in July**.

4 We do not use the Present Continuous for future events that we cannot arrange or have not arranged:

The sun will shine tomorrow.
(NOT ~~The sun is shining tomorrow.~~)
The Irish team will win next week.
(NOT ~~The Irish team are winning next week.~~)

A Write sentences about the past events in brackets ( ) using the words from the box. Use short forms of the Present Continuous for the future.

I/eat/in a new restaurant tonight	I/go/to the doctor tomorrow
I/fly/to Florida in August	~~I/study/English in London in May~~
I/go/to a concert next Tuesday	I/see/Mary this weekend

♦ (You paid for an English course in London yesterday.)
   I'm studying English in London in May.

1 (You booked a table at a new restaurant last week.)

2 (You bought a ticket for a concert last month.)

3 (You called your doctor this morning.)

4 (You paid for a holiday at a travel agent's last week.)

5 (You talked to Mary on the phone this morning.)

Tenses: future

B Mark is an explorer. Look at the things he has arranged to do. Match the pictures with the words from the box. Write sentences about what he is doing next year using the Present Continuous. Say when he is doing each thing.

he/drive/across the Sahara
he/walk/across the Antarctic
~~he/run/across/Africa~~
he/fly/over the Amazon
he/climb/Mount Everest
he/sail/across the Pacific

♦ January   1 March   2 May

3 July   4 September   5 November

♦ He is running across Africa in January.
1
2
3
4
5

C Complete these dialogues using the Present Continuous for the future and the words in brackets ( ). Use short forms where possible.

♦ Steve: *Are you doing* (you/do) anything this weekend?
♦ Megan: *I'm seeing* (I/see) a film on Sunday. Do you want to come?

1 Pete: Jasmine, Joe and Ellie _____ (come) to my house on Friday night.
  Mark: _____ (you/have) a party?
  Pete: No, we aren't. _____ (We/play) cards. Would you like to come?

2 David: _____ (I/fly) to New York on Sunday.
  Chris: _____ (you/see) John there?
  David: Yes, _____ (we/meet) at the airport.

3 Raphael: Mary and I _____ (drive) to Scotland next Wednesday.
  Mike: _____ (you/stay) in Edinburgh?
  Raphael: No. _____ (we/visit) my mother in Aberdeen.

4 Paul: _____ (I/start) a new job on Monday.
  Arthur: Really? What is it?
  Paul: _____ (I/sell) cars. Do you need a new car?

25 Present tense: when, before, after, until, etc.

1 Look at this sentence:

When the programme ends, I'll do the washing-up.

To talk about an event in the future, we usually use the Present Simple (e.g. **ends**) after **when**, **before**, **after**, **until** and **as soon as**. We do not use **will**:

I'm going to finish this work before I go. (NOT ... *before I will go.*)
Wait here until I get back.
I'll phone you as soon as I arrive.

2 We can use **when** + Present Simple to refer to a time when something will happen:

I'll buy an ice cream when I'm in the newsagent's.

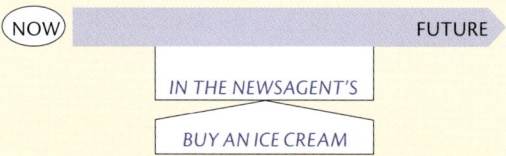

When you see her, give her my message.

We use **until** + Present Simple to mean from now to a time in the future:

We'll sit outside until it gets dark. (= We'll sit outside from now to when it gets dark.)

We use **as soon as** + Present Simple with the meaning 'immediately after':

They'll start playing as soon as it stops raining. (= They will start playing immediately after the rain stops.)

3 We use **when** + Present Perfect (e.g. **I have done**) to talk about an action that must, or will, happen before the next action can happen:

When I've found a job, I'll look for a place to live. (= First I will find a job; then I will look for a place to live.)

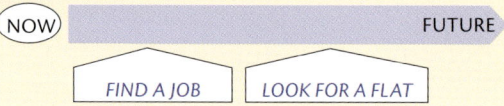

When Simon has saved enough money, he'll buy a car. (= First Simon must save the money; then he can buy a car.)

4 With **after** we can use either the Present Simple or the Present Perfect with no difference in meaning:

After she takes/has taken the course, she'll be a qualified teacher. (= When she has done her course, she'll be a qualified teacher.)

A Complete the sentences by putting *when*, *before*, *after*, *as soon as* or *until* into the gaps. Sometimes more than one answer is possible.

♦ I'll stay in this job _until_ I find a better one.
1 I'm going to keep working _____ I finish this.
2 Remember to buy some stamps _____ you're in the post office.
3 _____ I speak to him on the phone tonight, I'll ask him.
4 We can go for a meal _____ we've seen the film.
5 I'll keep looking for it _____ I find it.
6 I'll wait for them _____ it gets dark, and then I'll leave.
7 Don't forget to lock the door _____ you go out.
8 _____ I've found the information, I'll phone you.
9 We'll wait _____ it stops raining, and then we'll go out.
10 _____ you see John, give him my regards.
11 Put in your application _____ the closing date arrives.
12 You shouldn't wait. You should reply _____ you receive the invitation.
13 Book a table _____ you go to the restaurant. It's often full.

Tenses: future

B Complete the dialogues using the Present Simple or *will* forms of the verbs in brackets ( ). Sometimes you do not need to change the word in brackets.

♦ A: Could you post this letter for me today, please?
B: Yes, I 'll do _____ (do) it when I go _____ (go) to the shops.

1 A: I might be late tonight.
B: OK. I _____ (wait) until you _____ (arrive).

2 A: I'm leaving next week.
B: I _____ (see) you before you _____ (go), won't I?

3 A: Have you decided what you're going to do at the weekend yet?
B: No, but I _____ (phone) you as soon as I _____ (know) what I'm going to do.

4 A: Have you done that homework yet?
B: No, not yet. I _____ (do) it when I _____ (have) enough time.

5 A: I don't want to go to that party tonight.
B: Well, I'm sure you _____ (enjoy) it when you _____ (get) there.

6 A: Could you tell Tom to call me, please?
B: Yes, I _____ (tell) him when I _____ (see) him tomorrow.

7 A: Mr Jackson isn't in at the moment.
B: I see. Well, I _____ (wait) until he _____ (come) back.

8 A: Have you booked a hotel in London yet?
B: No, but we _____ (book) one before we _____ (go) there.

9 A: Don't forget to write to Peter.
B: OK. I _____ (do) it as soon as I _____ (get) home.

10 A: _____ (you/see) Jack when you _____ (be) in Madrid?
B: Yes, I hope I will. I _____ (phone) him when I _____ (arrive) in Spain.

C Complete the sentences using the Present Perfect or *will* forms of the verbs in brackets ( ).

♦ When you have *wrapped* (wrap) that parcel, I 'll _____ (post) it for you.
1 I _____ (pay) the bill when I have borrowed some money from somebody.
2 When I've found a car that I want to buy, I _____ (ask) my bank to lend me the money to buy it.
3 After the plane _____ (land), you may unfasten your safety belts.
4 When you _____ (check) all your answers, hand in your question paper.
5 I _____ (read) this book when I'm on holiday.
6 When I _____ (read) this magazine, I'll start work.
7 You _____ (feel) better when you have had something to eat.
8 When you _____ (finish) your work, you can go home.
9 She _____ (be) pleased when she hears the news.
10 Let's go for a walk after we _____ (have) dinner.

55

26 Future

1 We can talk about future time with different verb forms, for example:

- **will**: *I'll come with you.*
- **be going to**: *He's going to come with us.*
- Present Continuous:
  We're coming tomorrow.
- Present Simple:
  When he arrives, we'll have dinner.

2 When we talk about events in the future that we expect to happen but that are not in our control, we can use **will** or **be going to**:
  Anna will be (OR is going to be) 12 next week.
  We won't see (OR aren't going to see) those birds again until next spring.
  Will they finish (OR Are they going to finish) the building soon?

3 When we talk about events in the future that are in our control (i.e. we can decide what will happen), we use **will** differently from **be going to**. We use **will** at the time we decide what to do; we use **be going to** after we have decided what to do. Look at these examples:
  John: *Can somebody help me, please?*
  Helen: *Yes, I'll help you.*
  (Here, Helen decided after John asked.)

Now compare:
  Laura: *John needs some help.*
  Helen: *I know. I'm going to help him.*
  (Here, Helen had decided before Laura spoke.)

4 Look at these examples:
  If it rains, they'll stay (OR they're going to stay) at home.
  We'll have (OR we're going to have) lunch after the programme finishes.

When a sentence has two parts that refer to the future, we use the Present Simple after **if**, **when**, **before**, **after**, **as soon as** and **until**, and in the other part of the sentence we use **will** or **be going to**:

WHEN/AFTER ETC. +	SIMPLE PRESENT	+ WILL/BE GOING TO
After	it finishes	we'll have lunch.

5 We use the Present Continuous to talk about a future arrangement that we have made with someone else:
  A: *Can you come and see us this evening?*
  B: *I can't. I'm playing squash with Sam.*
  Peter can't come to the cinema with us tonight because he's meeting Jasmine for dinner.

A Liz has come back to London from Amsterdam. Her brother Tom has just met her at Liverpool Street Station. In the sentences below, think about when the person decides to do something. Put a tick (✓) if you think the underlined phrase is correct. Otherwise write the correct form of *will* or *be going to* in the gaps.

Tom: Hi Liz. Do you want some tea or coffee after your journey?

Liz: Thanks. ♦ <u>I'll</u> ✓ _____ have a tea.

Tom: ♦ <u>I'm going to</u> I'll _____ carry your bag – you look tired. ¹ <u>We'll</u> _____ go to that cafe, over there. Here we are. So, welcome back to England. How was Holland?

Liz: Well, it was great to have some time to think, and I've made some decisions. ² <u>I'll</u> _____ talk to the boss tomorrow, and ³ <u>I'll</u> _____ ask him if I can move to another department.

Tom: Good. I'm sure ⁴ <u>he'll</u> _____ give you what you want. Now, would you like something to eat?

Tenses: future

Liz: Um, yes. [5] I'm going to _____ have a sandwich. Thanks. What about you?

Tom: No, thanks, I don't want to spoil my appetite. I've reserved a table for this evening at the Mexican restaurant in Leicester Square. [6] I'll _____ take Charlotte. What are you going to do this evening?

Liz: I haven't thought about it. [7] I'll _____ probably cook something. Oh, and I must ring Dad. Did you remember that it's his birthday tomorrow?

Tom: Yes, I remembered. [8] He'll _____ be 50. Promise me you'll relax a bit?

Liz: Sure.

Tom: OK. [9] I'll _____ get you a taxi. Call me tomorrow. [10] You won't _____ forget, will you?

B Write sentences using the words in brackets ( ), *will* and the Present Simple.

♦ (Tom/help/us/when/he/come/home)   Tom will help us when he comes home.
1 (I/buy/the tickets/before/I/go/to work)
2 (As soon as/Henry/arrive, we/have/something to eat)
3 (The play/start/after/the music/stop)
4 (He/not/stop/until/he/finish/the job)
5 (When John/get/here, we/go/to the beach)

C Look at Anna's diary for next week and complete the sentences. If Anna has an arrangement with someone else, use the Present Continuous, but if she does not, use *be going to*.

	MORNING	AFTERNOON/EVENING
Monday	10.00 take Tim to the airport	wash the car
Tuesday	do some shopping	
Wednesday	11.00 take the dog to the vet	tidy my flat
Thursday	12.30 cook lunch for mother	buy a new squash racket
Friday	9.00 play squash with Mary	paint her bedroom
Saturday	wash my hair	6.00 meet Tim at the airport

♦ Anna *is taking* _____ Tim to the airport on Monday morning.
♦ On Monday evening Anna *is going to wash* _____ the car.
1 On Tuesday she _____ some shopping because on Thursday she _____ lunch for her mother.
2 She can't see anyone on Wednesday morning because she _____ the dog to the vet.
3 On Wednesday evening she _____ her flat.
4 On Thursday afternoon she _____ a new squash racket because _____ squash with Mary on Friday morning.
5 On Friday afternoon she _____ her bedroom.
6 She _____ her hair on Saturday morning because she _____ Tim at the airport at six o'clock.

Test C: Tenses – future

A Alex is talking on the phone to his girlfriend, Rosemary. Use *shall* or short forms of *will* or *be going to* to complete the conversation.

Alex: Hi! It's Alex here.
Rosemary: Hi! I'm drying my hair at the moment.
Alex: ♦ *Shall I ring* (I/ring) you back?
Rosemary: No, it's OK. ¹_____ (I/finish) drying it later. How are things going?
Alex: Not bad, thanks. What ² _____ (you/do) on Saturday after you've seen your mum?
Rosemary: I'm not really sure. ³ _____ (we/meet up) around six in the evening?
Alex: OK. But I may be a little late. ⁴ _____ (I/watch) the final at tennis club in the afternoon. ⁵ _____ (I/get) you a ticket, if you like.
Rosemary: No thanks. It sounds a bit boring. I'm sure ⁶ _____ (you/enjoy) it more on your own. Anyway, ⁷ _____ (I/buy) some new books in town, I think, if I've got enough money.
Alex: ⁸ _____ (I/lend) you some. I've just been paid.
Rosemary: Don't worry. I'll have my credit card.

B Steve is writing an email to Joanna, a work colleague. Complete his message using the words in brackets and the Present Continuous, *shall* or a short form of *will*.

Hi Joanna,

I've just arrived in Mexico City. I didn't get much sleep on the plane so I think ♦ *I'll go* (I/go) to bed for an hour or two this morning. As you know from my schedule, ¹ _____ (I/meet) Carl this afternoon, and then ² _____ (I/fly) to Monterrey tomorrow morning. ³ _____ (I/send) you the documents after Carl has signed them? By the way, Carl says ⁴ _____ (you/come) to Mexico at the weekend. If ⁵ _____ (you/stay) near the Hotel Victoria, ⁶ _____ (you/bring) me the green folder on my desk? I forgot it, I'm afraid. Also, I'm sorry but ⁷ _____ (not/be able) to meet you at the airport. I'm sure you've heard already that ⁸ _____ (I/visit) the new headquarters building of Carl's company in Acapulco.

Best wishes,
Steve.

C Mike is talking to his teenage daughter about the visit of her uncle and his children. Complete their conversation with the words from the box.

> I'm / taking / you're / ~~is~~ / I'll / am / won't / will / Shall / arrive

Ellie: I just want to go out, Dad.
Mike: I know, but your Uncle Paul ♦ *is* _____ coming tomorrow with Steve and Sara.
Ellie: So? What's it got to do with me?
Mike: You know ¹ _____ moving out of your room tomorrow morning, don't you?

Ellie: I ² .... move! I don't want to! Why should I?

Mike: We've talked about this already. ³ .... I tell Uncle Paul that he can't come?

Ellie: Where ⁴ .... I going to sleep then?

Mike: Before they ⁵ ...., we'll make a bed for you in my room.

Ellie: OK. But that's all ⁶ .... going to do.

Mike: Almost. Remember you're ⁷ .... the children to the circus on Sunday.

Ellie: I won't go. Circuses are cruel to animals!

Mike: It's a circus without animals. We've talked about this before. I'll give you some money. When you get there, the kids ⁸ .... want some ice cream.

Ellie: OK. I'll sleep in your room and ⁹ .... take little Steve and Sara to the circus, but next weekend I'm going to Michelle's party, and I'll need a new pair of jeans, but I don't have any money. Can you help?

D Jasmine is telling her classmates what will happen when they arrive at the school's mountain centre in Scotland. Cross out the word *will* or the form *'ll*, if they are wrong.

'You'll meet Tim, one of the team of guides, as soon as you ~~will~~ arrive at the centre. He'll show you where to eat and sleep. Tim will check your bags when you will get up, to make sure you're ready for the day. It's important to have food and drink and an extra pullover. Before you'll start walking, Tim will make sure you have your own map, in case you get lost. It's a fantastic place to go walking. You'll be able to see the sea after you will get to the top of the mountain! But it can become cold very quickly. You'll have to listen to Tim until you'll know the right thing to do if the weather changes suddenly. Don't worry, though. You'll have a good time. You'll enjoy the views as soon as you will get there!'

E Four friends are in a restaurant on holiday. Complete their conversation by crossing out the incorrect future forms.

Laura: *Are you going to/~~Shall you~~ order some food, Tom?

Tom: Yes, but I'll have a chat with the waiter first when he ¹comes/will come to the table. There are some dishes I just don't understand.

Ben: We haven't made any plans for this afternoon, have we? What are we ²doing/going to do?

Karen: It's too hot to go for a walk again.

Tom: Don't worry. ³I'm carrying/I'll carry you!

Ben: After you ⁴finish/will finish lunch, you won't be able to carry anyone!

Karen: Don't order too much food, Tom. ⁵I'm playing/I'll play in a volleyball match on the beach this evening. It's not a serious game, but there is an interesting prize.

Ben: What is it?

Karen: ⁶I'll/I'm going to tell you if you agree to play a practice match with me this afternoon.

Tom: ⁷Am I calling/Shall I call the waiter? ⁸I'm dying/I'm going to die of hunger in a moment.

Laura: Look. He's coming over. Ben, for the first time in your life, why don't you have something different from a pizza?

27 Nouns, verbs, adjectives, etc.

1 Look at this:

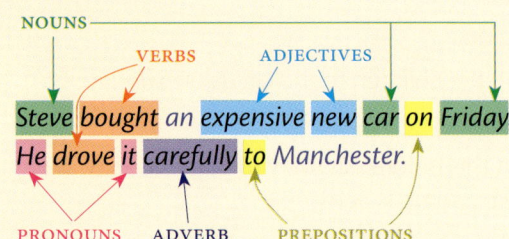

2 Nouns describe things or people or animals:

| butter | car | woman | dog | problem |

Some nouns (proper nouns) are the names of people, places and things. We begin proper nouns with capital letters (A, B, etc.):

| Jasmine | Paris | Oxford Street | June |
| a Rolls-Royce | | the Tower of London | |

3 Verbs describe actions or situations:

| work | play | live | meet | stay | see |

They **work** hard. (**work** = verb)
I **saw** Peter. (**saw** = verb)

4 We use auxiliary verbs (**be**, **have**, **do**, **will**, **can**, **may**, **must**, etc.) before another verb:
They **are** working hard. (**are** = auxiliary)
I **have** seen Peter. (**have** = auxiliary)
I **must** go now. (**must** = auxiliary)

5 We put adjectives (e.g. **wonderful**) before nouns:
We had a **wonderful** day.

We can also use adjectives after the verbs **be**, **look**, **seem**, **feel**:
He's **hungry**.   She **looks tired**.

Sometimes we put **very** before adjectives:
It's **very hot** today.
He bought a **very expensive** car.

6 We normally use adverbs to describe verbs:
She walked **quickly**.   He sings **well**.

Most adverbs end in **-ly**:

| clearly | slowly | badly |

7 We use pronouns (**I**, **you**, **he**, **she**, etc.) to replace nouns:
David has a new job. **He** is enjoying **it**.

8 We use prepositions (**in**, **on**, **at**, etc.) when we are talking about places and times:

| PLACE: | She's **at home**. It's **in the box**. |
| TIME: | I'll see you **on Monday**. They went on holiday **in June**. |

A Put the underlined words in the correct columns in the table.

NOUN	VERB	AUXILIARY	ADJECTIVE	ADVERB	PROUNOUN	PREPOSITION
			wonderful			

I had a <u>wonderful</u> holiday in <u>Spain</u> last year.
She <u>lives</u> in a <u>large</u> flat in New York.
Peter walked <u>quickly</u> <u>to</u> work.
We <u>met</u> them in Green Street <u>on</u> Friday.
You <u>must</u> come and visit me in Scotland.
My teacher spoke <u>slowly</u> but I didn't understand her.

<u>Mary</u> and Lily <u>are</u> studying Japanese at college.
I <u>have</u> lost my <u>bag</u>.
They bought a <u>big</u> old <u>house</u> in the country.
She <u>swims</u> fast and <u>she</u> can ski <u>well</u>, too.

Sentences and questions

B Complete the sentences with words from the box. Use each word once.

NOUN	VERB	AUXILIARY	ADJECTIVE	ADVERB	PRONOUN	PREPOSITION
~~job~~	find	~~has~~	beautiful	badly	I	on
match	pass	must	sick	easily	you	at
Saturday	do	carefully	in			

♦ Paul <u>has</u> just started a new <u>job</u>.
1 You'll .... the books .... the table.
2 .... bought some .... flowers and gave them to my wife.
3 She played .... and lost the tennis ....
4 .... haven't seen your grandfather for a long time – you .... visit him at the weekend.
5 Don't worry! You'll .... the exam ....
6 Listen .... ! The money is .... the box.
7 I'm playing golf on .... you want to play with me?
8 I feel .... What did we eat .... the restaurant?

C In this text, circle the letters that should be capital letters.

Josephine got a job in (n)ew (y)ork in june. She went there with her husband, mike. They are living in an apartment on madison avenue. Yesterday, they wanted to look at the sights. They saw the statue of liberty and walked through manhattan. Last monday, josephine started her new job. Josephine and mike want to live the rest of their lives in america.

D Put the word in brackets ( ) in the correct place (a–i).

♦ (on)   I'm ª flying ᵇ to ᶜ Mexico /ᵈ Sunday.   <u>d</u>

1 (interesting) Iª saw ᵇ a ᶜ very ᵈ film ᵉ last ᶠ night.   ....

2 (quickly)   Goª or ᵇ you'll ᶜ miss ᵈ the ᵉ train!   ....

3 (can)   Iª see ᵇ the ᶜ mountains ᵈ from ᵉ my ᶠ window. ....

4 (it)   Sheª sent ᵇ me ᶜ a ᵈ ticket ᵉ but ᶠ I ᵍ left ʰ at ⁱ home. ....

5 (go)   Youª look ᵇ sick. You ᶜ must ᵈ and ᵉ see ᶠ a ᵍ doctor. ....

6 (in)   Iª stayed ᵇ there ᶜ for ᵈ a ᵉ week ᶠ June.   ....

7 (very)   Maryª gave ᵇ Christopher ᶜ a ᵈ expensive ᵉ present. ....

8 (road)   There'sª snow ᵇ on ᶜ the ᵈ so ᵉ drive ᶠ carefully. ....

28 Word order: subject, verb, object

1 In English, the order of words in a statement is subject + verb + object:

SUBJECT +	VERB +	OBJECT
I	enjoy	good food.
Peter	is watching	TV.
She	drank	a cup of coffee.

2 Some verbs (e.g. **go**) do not have an object:
   Steve **has gone**.
   The train **didn't arrive**.
   Anna and Tom **are swimming**.

Some verbs (e.g. **like**) always need an object:

SUBJECT +	VERB +	OBJECT
I	like	music.
She	wants	a drink.

3 After the verb **be**, we can use an object or an adjective:

	OBJECT
She is	a doctor.

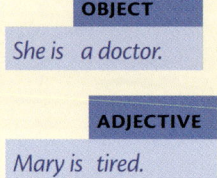

	ADJECTIVE
Mary is	tired.

We can also put adjectives after the verbs **look**, **seem** and **feel** (see **Unit 65**):
   Mary **looks** tired.

4 Now look at this example:

John gave **Mary** an apple.
John gave **her** an apple.

After some verbs (e.g. **give**, **send**, **bring**), we can talk about a person (**Mary**, **her**) and an object:

	VERB +	PERSON +	OBJECT
He	sent	Jasmine	a book.
Anna	made	Tom	a cup of tea.
Anna	brought	him	a cup of tea.
He	left	them	some money.
She	wrote	him	an email.

5 We usually put information about times or places at the end of the sentence:

		PLACE
I had a holiday		in Spain.

	TIME
They gave their son a watch	yesterday.

A There are ten sentences in the box. Circle each sentence.

(She didn't come) he is rich they like sport we are studying she is a teacher the bus hasn't arrived they've gone I didn't like the programme they sent me a postcard Paul and Joe have left

B Put the words in brackets ( ) in the correct order.

♦ (bought – she – a TV)   She bought a TV.
1 (the match – won – they)
2 (is eating – he – a pizza)
3 (Anna – films – loves)
4 (saw – three cats – I)
5 (tennis – we – played)
6 (wants – a new house – Steve)
7 (forgot – my passport – I)

Sentences and questions

8 (a photo – she – is taking)
9 (drank – an orange juice – he)
10 (golf – they – like)
11 (Joe – Mexico – visited)
12 (lost – we – our money)

C If the words are in the correct order, put a tick (✓). If not, write the correct sentence.

- Mary has phoned. ✓
- Brilliant was the film. — The film was brilliant.
1 The boys are playing football.
2 Michael not has come.
3 The children are looking tired.
4 Anna eggs does not eat.
5 Mary ate a large piece of cake.

D Write sentences with the word in brackets ( ) in the correct place.

- She wrote a letter. (me) — She wrote me a letter.
1 They sent an invitation. (us)
2 Michelle gave a present. (Mike)
3 I made a sandwich. (her)
4 Tom bought a new phone. (Ellie)
5 My uncle gave a job. (me)
6 She left a message. (you)
7 Mary is sending some flowers. (them)
8 She brings a coffee every day. (him)

E Put the word in brackets ( ) in the correct place in the sentence.

- (bought) We _bought_ a house _____ in Italy _____.
1 (him) They _____ gave _____ a new car _____.
2 (was) I _____ thirsty _____ this morning.
3 (last night) My friends _____ didn't arrive _____.
4 (her bag) She _____ lost _____.
5 (an actor) David _____ is _____.
6 (a photograph) I _____ sent _____ her _____.
7 (stayed) We _____ in Turkey _____ for a week.
8 (his wife) Paul _____ met _____ in Scotland _____.
9 (yesterday) We _____ didn't win _____ the match _____.
10 (her) I _____ wrote _____ an email _____.
11 (wonderful) The film _____ was _____.
12 (today) They _____ left _____.
13 (me) She _____ brought _____ a cake _____.
14 (ate) They _____ their dinner _____ at seven o'clock _____.

29 'Yes/no' questions

1 Here are some 'yes/no' questions:
- Are you hungry?
- Shall I get the door?
- Did you enjoy the film?

We call them 'yes/no' questions because the answer is either 'yes' or 'no':
- Are you hungry?   Yes, I am./No, I'm not.

2 We form 'yes/no' questions like this:

▶ We put the verb **be** before the subject:

BE +	SUBJECT +	
Are	they	busy?
Is	he	ready?
Was	she	here?

▶ Or, we put an auxiliary verb (**be**, **have**, **will**, **shall**, **can**, **may**, etc.) before the subject:

AUXILIARY +	SUBJECT +	VERB
Is	Mark	leaving?
Have	they	gone?
Will	they	win?
Can	you	sing?

(For auxiliary verbs, see **Unit 27**.)

▶ With Present Simple verbs, we put **do** or **does** before the subject:

DO +	SUBJECT +	VERB	
Does	she	work	in Paris?
Do	they	live	in New York?
Do	you	play	tennis?
Does	he	like	ice cream?

Note that we say:
- Does she play tennis? (NOT ~~Does she plays tennis?~~)

▶ With Past Simple verbs, we put **did** before the subject:

DID +	SUBJECT +	VERB	
Did	she	visit	Paris?
Did	he	go	to Spain?

3 Here are all the forms of **do** questions:

PRESENT SIMPLE		
Do	I/you/we they	work?
Does	he/she/it	
PAST SIMPLE		
Did	I/he/she/it/you/we/they	work?

A Make 'yes/no' questions from these statements.

♦ You are learning a language.   *Are you learning a language?*
1 She is thirsty.
2 He can swim well.
3 They were tired after the match.
4 She will return to Mexico.
5 I may leave now.
6 They have all left.
7 We shall wait a little longer.

B Make 'yes/no' questions from these statements. Start your questions with *Do, Does* or *Did*.

♦ You listen to music.   *Do you listen to music?*
1 They work in London.
2 She visits her uncle.

Sentences and questions

3 We began the course in March.
4 Her car goes very fast.
5 You bought a new table.

C You have met an English girl, Jasmine, in Paris. Use the words in brackets ( ) to ask her some questions. Her answers are on the right. They will help you choose the right tense for your questions.

- (like/it here) You: Do you like it here? ~ Jasmine: Yes, I do.
- (studying/French) You: Are you studying French? ~ Jasmine: Yes, I am.
1 (like/French music) You: ? ~ Jasmine: Yes, I do.
2 (staying/in the centre) You: ? ~ Jasmine: No, I'm not.
3 (come/by plane) You: ? ~ Jasmine: Yes, I did.
4 (have got/a flat) You: ? ~ Jasmine: Yes, I have.
5 (working/in Paris) You: ? ~ Jasmine: No, I'm not.
6 (visited/the museums) You: ? ~ Jasmine: Yes, I have.
7 (find/your flat easily) You: ? ~ Jasmine: No, I didn't.
8 (like/French food) You: ? ~ Jasmine: Yes, I do.

D You want to study English in London. You call a language school to ask some questions. Put the words in brackets ( ) in the right order to make questions.

- (of London? – Is – near the centre – the school) Is the school near the centre of London?
1 (homework? – give – Do – the teachers)
2 (the classes – small? – Are)
3 (organize – trips? – Does – the school)
4 (a certificate – I get – Will – at the end of the course?)
5 (a place now? – I – reserve – Shall)
6 (pay – I – Can – by credit card?)

E David has just spent a week on holiday in Greece with his wife Mary. Ask him some questions about his holiday using words and phrases from the box. Use his answers to help you.

~~Did~~	Was	the sea	~~Mary~~	~~enjoy~~	comfortable?
Did	Was	the airport	Mary	busy?	the beaches?
Did	Was	the restaurants	learn	expensive?	any Greek?
Were	the hotel	you	like	warm?	~~the holiday?~~

- You: Did Mary enjoy the holiday? ~ David: Yes, she had a good time.
1 You: ~ David: Yes, there were thousands of people at the airport.
2 You: ~ David: Yes, the water was very warm.
3 You: ~ David: No, they were quite cheap.
4 You: ~ David: No, it's a difficult language for me.
5 You: ~ David: Yes, she swam and sunbathed every day.
6 You: ~ David: Yes, it was a lovely hotel.

30 Where, when, why, how

1 **Where**, **when**, **why**, and **how** are question words. We use them like this:

▶ **Where**
We use **where** to ask about places:
Where is Mike? ~ He's at home.

▶ **When**
We use **when** to ask about times and dates:
When will you phone? ~ At six o'clock.

▶ **Why**
We use **why** to ask about the reason for something:
Why is Mary taking a taxi? ~ Because her car isn't working.

▶ **How**
We use **how** to ask 'in what way?':

How did he get to Brighton? ~ He went by train.

We also use **how** to ask about people's health or happiness:
Hello. How are you? ~ I'm fine, thanks.

2 We form questions with **where**, **when**, **why** and **how** like this:

▶ In questions with **be**, we put the subject after **be**:

	BE	+	SUBJECT	
Why	is		Paul	angry?
Where	are		they?	
Why	is		he	here?

▶ In questions with an auxiliary verb (**will**, **is**, **are**, **can**, **must**, etc.), we put the subject after the auxiliary verb:

	AUXILIARY	SUBJECT	+	VERB	
Why	are	they		leaving?	
How	will	she		get	there?
When	will	you		phone?	

(For auxiliary verbs, see **Unit 27**.)

▶ In questions with a Present Simple or Past Simple verb, we put a form of **do** before the subject:

	DO	+	SUBJECT	+	VERB	
Where	does		she		live?	
Why	did		you		phone	the police?
Where	did		he		live?	

A Put the words in brackets ( ) in the correct order to make questions.

♦ (you – where – live – do – ?) *Where do you live?*

1 (do – get up – you – when – ?) ....
2 (she – does – where – come – from – ?) ....
3 (leaving – they – are – when – ?) ....
4 (he – is – why – waiting – ?) ....
5 (are – you – how – ?) ....
6 (did – to Scotland – how – get – you – ?) ....
7 (is – where – the town centre?) ....
8 (Paul – drive – so fast – does – why – ?) ....
9 (when – the film – does – start – ?) ....
10 (will – how – you – travel – ?) ....
11 (is – running – she – why – ?) ....
12 (did – where – buy – you – that picture – ?) ....

Sentences and questions

B Put *Where*, *When*, *Why* or *How* in the gaps to complete the questions.

- *Where* are you going? ~ To the shops.
1. .... are you leaving? ~ At six o'clock.
2. .... does she take a taxi to work? ~ Because she doesn't have a car.
3. .... did they get to France? ~ By boat.
4. .... is he studying Spanish? ~ Because he wants to work in Spain.
5. .... do you have breakfast? ~ At seven-thirty.
6. .... is the restaurant? ~ In Carlton Street.
7. .... are you feeling today? ~ I've got a headache.
8. .... did she buy that dictionary? ~ In the bookshop near the station.
9. .... did Grace go to the police? ~ Because she lost her passport.

C Use the 'full' answers to write questions with *where*, *when*, *why* or *how*. (We usually use the short, underlined answers when we reply to a question.)

- Question: *When did you lose your bag?*
  Answer: (I lost my bag) On Saturday morning.
1. Question: ....
   Answer: (I met Joanna) At a club in the centre of town.
2. Question: ....
   Answer: (got home) By bus.
3. Question: ....
   Answer: (I'm looking for a new job) Because I want more money.
4. Question: ....
   Answer: (The nearest hospital is) In Park Street.
5. Question: ....
   Answer: (You get to Park Street) On the number 38 bus.
6. Question: ....
   Answer: (They're going to see the film) On Friday evening.
7. Question: ....
   Answer: (She left the party at ten o'clock) Because she was tired.
8. Question: ....
   Answer: (He's studying English) At a language school in Edinburgh.

D If the underlined words are wrong, change them. Put a tick (✓) if they are right.

- How is *does* she get to work in the mornings?
- Where do ✓ you normally go for your holidays?
1. How is .... your father?
2. Why do .... you working so hard at the moment?
3. When does .... she finish work yesterday afternoon?
4. Why do .... you go to the bank every day?
5. Where does .... Peter yesterday?
6. Where do .... Mike live?
7. How do .... you get from the art gallery to the swimming pool?

31 Who, what, which

1 We use **who** to ask about people:
 A: **Who** are you going to visit?
 B: I'm going to visit my sister.
 Who did Jasmine invite to her party?

2 We use **what** and **which** to ask about things:
 What film did you see at the cinema?
 Which newspaper do you want, The Times or the Daily Telegraph?

We normally use **what** when there are many possible answers:

We normally use **which** when there is a small number of possible answers:

3 When we form questions, we normally put a form of be or an auxiliary verb (e.g. **can**, **will**, **do**) after **who**, **what** and **which**:
 Who is the President of Peru?
 Who can speak Chinese?
 Who did you meet at the party?
 What's the capital of India? ~ New Delhi.
 What's she doing?
 What was the name of your teacher?
 What does your father do?
 Which car **will** you buy, the Fiat or the Ford?
 Which shirt **do** you prefer, the red or the blue?

A Put *who*, *what* or *which* in the gaps.

QUESTIONS		ANSWERS
♦	**What** did you eat last night?	~ Fish, peas and potatoes.
1	_____ are you messaging?	~ Steve.
2	_____ restaurant do you prefer, the Pizza Palace or the Spaghetti King?	~ The Pizza Palace.
3	_____ 's the answer to question 13?	~ I don't know.
4	_____ bus do we take to the museum, the number 24 or the number 38?	~ The number 38.
5	_____ did you invite to the party?	~ Anthony, Steve and Kathryn.
6	_____ are you doing at the weekend?	~ I'm driving to Bristol.
7	_____ pen is yours, the green one or the blue one?	~ The green one.
8	_____ has been to Africa?	~ I have.
9	_____ 's the capital of Scotland?	~ Edinburgh.
10	_____ 's the boy in the photo?	~ My cousin.

B Complete the dialogues using the words from the box.

| is | ~~What~~ | do | Who | is | are | What | did | Who | is | are | Which | were |

♦ A: **What** did you do this morning? B: We bought a new car.
1 A: Where _____ you buy that painting? B: We bought it in Mexico.
2 A: Where _____ the nearest bank? B: In the High Street.

Sentences and questions

3 A: Why _____ you tired yesterday evening? B: I worked very hard all day.
4 A: When _____ you get up in the morning? B: I get up at seven o'clock.
5 A: _____ car do you prefer, the family car or the sports car? B: The sports car.
6 A: What _____ they doing? B: They're playing tennis.
7 A: _____ did you meet at the station? B: I met Jasmine.
8 A: Who _____ they? B: They're my sisters.
9 A: _____ is the name of the hotel? B: It's called the Bridge Hotel.
10 A: _____ does she like best? B: Tom.
11 A: Who _____ the richest person in the world? B: I don't know!
12 A: Which film _____ better? B: The French one.

C Complete the questions. (We usually use the short, underlined answers when we reply to a question.)

♦ A: Which <u>song do you prefer?</u>
   B: (I prefer) <u>The Spanish song</u>.

1 A: What _____?
  B: (She bought) <u>Bread and milk</u>.

2 A: Which _____?
  B: (They use) <u>The blue book</u>.

3 A: What _____?
  B: (I saw) <u>The Arc de Triomphe and the Eiffel Tower</u> (in Paris).

4 A: Who _____?
  B: (I met) <u>My aunt and uncle</u> (at the airport).

5 A: Which _____?
  B: (I am catching) <u>The 13.30</u> (train).

6 A: Who _____?
  B: (I will visit) <u>My sister and her family</u> (in Paris).

D Write questions to match the answers. Begin your questions with *who*, *what* or *which*.

♦ <u>Who is he?</u>
  He's my brother.

1 _____?
  Jack drinks coffee in the morning.

2 _____?
  I'm going to see a film tomorrow.

3 _____?
  They are playing cricket.

4 _____?
  I prefer the blue book.

5 _____?
  She likes Peter.

6 _____?
  He bought the small car.

69

32 How long/far/often ...?

1 We use **How long ...?** to ask about a period of time:
   How long have you been waiting? ~ About 20 minutes.
   How long will the journey take? ~ Three hours.

We use **from ... to** or **from ... until** to talk about a period of time:
   She was a student **from** 2007 **to** 2012.
   Tomorrow I'm working **from** nine o'clock **until** six o'clock.

2 We use **How far ...?** to ask about the distance from one place to another. We can use **from** and **to** with the places we are asking about:
   How far is it **from** Amsterdam **to** Paris? ~ 475 kilometres.
   How far are the shops **from** here? ~ Not far.

3 We use **How often ...?** to ask about the number of times something happens. We can use phrases like **every day**, **once a week**, etc. in the answer:
   How often do the buses run? ~ **Every hour**.
   How often do you play squash? ~ **Twice a week**.

4 We can use **How much ...?** to ask about the price of something:
   How much is a return ticket to Florence?
   How much did you pay for this car?

5 We use **How much ...?** with an uncountable noun to ask about the amount of something. An uncountable noun cannot be plural because it describes something that cannot be counted (e.g. **bread**, **work**, **weather**, **money**, **music**, **meat**, **milk**, **cheese**).
   How much bread is there in the cupboard?
   How much work have you done today?

6 We use **How many ...?** with a plural noun to ask about numbers:
   How many students are in your class? ~ 15.
   How many people went to the party? ~ Ten.

7 We use **How old ...?** to ask about someone's age:
   How old are you? ~ I'm 19.

Note that we say:
   I am 19. OR: 19. (NOT I have 19.)

We can also say:
   I'm 19 years old. (NOT I'm 19 years.)

A Complete the questions using the words in brackets and *How long, How old, How often*, etc. Put the verbs into the correct tense.

QUESTIONS	ANSWERS
♦ (How/you/stay/in New Zealand?) How long did you stay in New Zealand?	~ I stayed there for six months.
1 (How/he/go/to the gym?)	~ He goes every day.
2 (How/a single room/cost?)	~ It costs £50 a night.
3 (How/be/you when you went to live in Australia?)	~ I was 15 when I went there.
4 (How/exams/you/going to take?)	~ I'm going to take three exams.
5 (How/the course/last?)	~ It will last for two years.
6 (How/be/it from here to the nearest bus stop?)	~ It's about 200 metres.

Sentences and questions

B Write questions using the words in brackets ( ) and *How old, How much, How many,* etc. Put the verbs into the correct tense.

♦ A: How old is your husband? (your husband/be)
B: He is 34. He'll be 35 next month.

1 A: _____ (languages/you/speak)
B: I speak three – English, French and Chinese.

2 A: _____ (it/be/from here to the airport)
B: It's about 25 kilometres.

3 A: _____ (the meal/cost)
B: I can't remember, but it wasn't very expensive.

4 A: _____ (you/stay there)
B: I stayed there from June until October.

5 A: _____ (you/brush your teeth)
B: I brush them twice a day.

6 A: _____ (cheese/you/buy)
B: I bought half a kilo.

C Complete each of these sentences by putting one word into each gap.

♦ It was my birthday last week. I am 21 years old.
1 The programme lasts _____ eight-thirty _____ ten o'clock.
2 There is a train to the centre _____ 30 minutes in the morning.
3 How _____ money have you got?
4 How far is it _____ here _____ the city centre?
5 My grandfather is 70 _____ _____.
6 How _____ countries have you visited?

D Write Rob's questions to complete the dialogue. Start with *How* each time.

Anna: I'm doing a course in computer programming.
Rob: Oh really. ♦ How long have you been doing it?
Anna: I've been doing it for about a month. It's at the local college.
Rob: 1 _____ ?
Anna: I go there twice a week.
Rob: 2 _____ ?
Anna: The lessons last for three hours, from two o'clock until five o'clock.
Rob: 3 _____ ?
Anna: I study at home every evening.
Rob: 4 _____ ?
Anna: There are about 25 people in my class.
Rob: 5 _____ ?
Anna: They're all about the same age as me.
Rob: 6 _____ ?
Anna: It's not far from my home.
Rob: 7 _____ ?
Anna: It doesn't cost anything. My company is paying.

33 What ... like?

1 Look at this question and answer:
- A: **What's** Julie **like**?
- B: She's kind and very clever.

We use **What ... like?** to ask about a person's physical appearance (tall, short, pretty, etc.) or character (interesting, boring, friendly, unfriendly, etc).

We can also use **What ... like?** to ask about places, books, films and events (e.g. a party, a football match):
- A: **What's** Rio de Janeiro **like**?
- B: Well, the beaches are wonderful but the traffic is awful.
- A: **What's** Spielberg's latest film **like**?
- B: It's excellent.

2 We use **look like** to talk about someone's appearance:
- A: **What** does Julie **look like**?
- B: She's tall with brown hair.

We can also use **like** with **taste**, **feel**, **sound**, and **smell**:
- A: **What** does that **taste like**?
- B: It **tastes like** cheese.
- A: What is this material?
- B: I don't know. It **looks like** wool but it **feels like** cotton.

3 We can also use **like** with the question word **Who** and in statements to mean 'similar to':
- A: **Who's** Julie **like** – her father or her mother?
- B: She's **like** her mother. (= She is similar to her mother.)
- Rio de Janeiro is **like** Buenos Aires. (= Rio is similar to Buenos Aires.)

4 The word **like** in **What's she like?** is a preposition; it is not the verb **like**. Here is an example of **like** used as a verb:
- A: What music does Julie **like**?
- B: She **likes** rock music.

5 We usually use **How ...?**, not **What ... like?**, when we ask about someone's health or temporary state:
- A: **How's** your brother today?
- B: He's feeling much better.
- A: **How** was your boss today?
- B: He was very friendly today!

A Write questions using the words in brackets and *is, are*, or *look*. Sometimes more than one question is possible.

♦ (What/Ellie/like)
A: What is Ellie like ? B: She's clever, but she's a bit boring.

♦ (What/Jasmine/like)
A: What does Jasmine look like ? B: She's quite short and has dark hair.

1 (What/Peter/like)
A: ? B: He's not a very interesting person.

2 (What/Anna's parents/like)
A: ? B: They're very friendly.

3 (What/Tom/like)
A: ? B: He's very tall, and he has blond hair.

4 (What/Eva/like)
A: ? B: She's tall and strong.

5 (What/Rob and Tom/like)
A: ? B: They're very amusing.

6 (What/Lucy/like)
A: ? B: She's tall and slim, and she wears glasses.

Sentences and questions

B Read the following descriptions.

> Kiwis are a round, brown fruit with a rough skin. They have almost no smell, but they are sweet, with a flavour similar to strawberries.
> A double bass is a musical instrument. It is the largest member of the violin family. It has a deep sound.

Now for each of the answers, write a question about kiwis or a double bass, using *look/sound/taste/smell/feel* + *like*.

QUESTIONS	ANSWERS
♦ What do kiwis look like?	~ They're round and brown.
1 _____?	~ It has a deep sound.
2 _____?	~ They don't really have a smell.
3 _____?	~ They have a flavour like strawberries.
4 _____?	~ Like a very big violin.
5 _____?	~ They are rough to the touch.

C Use the words in brackets ( ) to write a question with the preposition *like* or the verb *like*. Add any other necessary words.

♦ (What music/you/like)
   A: What music do you like? B: I like rock music.
♦ (What/Julie/like)
   A: What is Julie like? B: She is very amusing.
1 (Who/your sister/like)
   A: _____? B: She likes a boy in her class.
2 (What/Paul's brothers/like)
   A: _____? B: They think they're clever, but I don't.
3 (What/Jasmine/like/for breakfast)
   A: _____? B: She likes toast and marmalade.
4 (Who/you/like)
   A: _____? B: I'm like my mother.
5 (What/Mary's husband/like)
   A: _____? B: He is rather boring. He's not like her.

D Write questions with *What … like?* (for things that are permanent) or *How …?* (for health or temporary situations). Use a form of *be* and the other words in brackets ( ).

♦ (be/Atlanta) What is Atlanta like? ~ It's a very modern city.
♦ (be/Mike/yesterday) How was Mike yesterday? ~ He felt a lot better.
1 (be/John's flat) _____? ~ It's very big, and it has a wonderful view over the city.
2 (be/your boss/yesterday) _____? ~ He was tired but friendly.
3 (be/a squash racquet) _____? ~ It's similar to a tennis racket, but lighter.
4 (be/your sister) _____? ~ She's very well, thank you.
5 (be/Portugal) _____? ~ It's very interesting. There are lots of things to see.

34 Who and what: subject and object

1 Compare these examples:

Mary   Mary

SUBJECT

Anna: Who **told** you?

Mary: James told me.

This is a subject question.

OBJECT

Anna: Who **did** you **tell**?

Mary: I told William.

This is an object question.

2 Compare subject and object questions with **who**:

In the sentence *Who told you?*, **Who** is the subject. Here is another example:

SUBJECT

Anna: Who **wrote** Hamlet?

(= **Somebody** wrote *Hamlet*. Who?)

Mary: Shakespeare wrote *Hamlet*.

When **who** is the subject, the order of the words is the same as in a statement:

SUBJECT

Who	**is going to come** with me?
Who	**lives** in that old house?
Who	**wants** some more coffee?

In the sentence *Who did you tell?*, **Who** is the object. Here is another example:

OBJECT

Anna: Who **did** you **meet** last night?

(= You met **somebody**. Who?)

Mary: I met a couple of friends.

When **who** is the object, we use an auxiliary (**be**, **do**, **have**, etc.) before the subject:

OBJECT

Who	**are** you **going to invite**?
Who	**did** Laura **ask** for help?
Who	**have** you **told** about this?

3 Compare subject and object questions with **what**:

SUBJECT

What **is** in this dish?

(= **Something** is in it. What?)

OBJECT

What **did** you **buy** at the shops?

(= You bought **something**. What?)

A Write questions beginning with *Who* or *What* from the sentences in brackets ( ).

♦ (Eric met somebody.) — Who did Eric meet?
♦ (Somebody ate the last piece of cake.) — Who ate the last piece of cake?
1 (Somebody wants some more coffee.)
2 (Something happened at the end of the story.)
3 (Somebody is going to pay the bill.)
4 (He had something for breakfast.)
5 (Their email said something.)
6 (Somebody knows the answer to my question.)
7 (They saw something.)
8 (She is phoning somebody.)

Sentences and questions

B Use the 'full' answers to write questions using *Who* or *What*. (We usually use the short, underlined answers when we reply to a question.)

QUESTIONS	ANSWERS
♦ Who were you talking to on the phone ?	~ (I was talking to) Elizabeth (on the phone).
♦ What was the result of the game ?	~ (The result of the game was) 2–0 to Italy.
1 .... ?	~ Anita and Frank (went on the trip).
2 .... ?	~ I'm not sure (what's happening in this film).
3 .... ?	~ (I'm going to call) Jasmine.
4 .... ?	~ (I watched) that new comedy programme (on TV last night).
5 .... ?	~ John (sent these flowers).
6 .... ?	~ (I bought) a book (in that shop).
7 .... ?	~ Some good news (has made Tom so happy).

C Read this story and then complete the questions.

Two days ago Robert took his driving test. He failed it. Afterwards he met his friend Raphael. He told Raphael that he had failed his test. Then he said, 'Don't tell anyone. It's a secret.' Raphael said, 'OK, I won't tell anyone.' Later that day, Raphael met Emilia for coffee and he said, 'Robert failed his driving test.' Emilia laughed. 'Poor Robert,' she said.

QUESTIONS	ANSWERS
♦ (What/Robert/do/two days ago?) What did Robert do two days ago?	~ He took his driving test.
1 (What/happen?)	~ He failed it.
2 (Who/take/his/driving test?)	~ Robert.
3 (What/Robert/fail?)	~ His driving test.
4 (What/Robert/say/to Raphael?)	~ He said, 'Don't tell anyone.'
5 (Who/meet/for coffee?)	~ Raphael and Emilia.

D Complete the questions for the answers using the words in brackets ( ).

♦ (Mark Chapman/kill)	Who did Mark Chapman kill ?	~ He killed John Lennon.
♦ (John Lennon/kill)	Who killed John Lennon ?	~ Mark Chapman killed John Lennon.
1 (the Nobel Prize/win)	Who .... for Physics in 1909?	~ Marconi and Braun.
2 (Marconi and Braun/invent)	What .... ?	~ Short wave radio.
3 (Everest/climb)	Who .... with Hillary?	~ Sherpa Tenzing.
4 (Prince Harry/marry)	Who .... ?	~ He married Meghan Markle.
5 (Hiroshima/destroy)	What .... ?	~ An atomic bomb.
6 (Churchill/smoke)	What .... ?	~ Cigars.

35 Whose is this? ~ It's John's.

1 's and '

We use the apostrophe (') to talk about possession:

This is Mike**'s** house. (= The house belongs to Mike.)

Here are the rules:

- Singular noun (e.g. **Mary**) + **'s**:
  Where is **Tom's** bike?

- Irregular plural noun (e.g. **men**) + **'s**:
  Have you got the **children's** books?

- Regular plural noun (e.g. **teachers**) + **'**:
  We have eight children. This is the **boys'** bedroom, and this is the **girls'** bedroom.

2

We use the apostrophe for people, but not normally for things. We use **of** for things:

The **boys'** room. (NOT The room of the boys.)
The end **of** the film. (NOT The film's end.)

We say:
I'm going to the **newsagent's**, the **baker's**, the **butcher's** ...

because we mean 'the newsagent's shop/the baker's shop/the butcher's shop'.

3 We use **whose** to ask about possession:

A: **Whose** car is that? (= Who does that car belong to?)
B: It's **John's**. (= It belongs to John.)

A: **Whose** shoes are those?
B: They're mine. (= They belong to me.)

The word **whose** does not change:
Whose book is that?
Whose books are those?

We often use **this**, **that**, **these** and **those** (see **Unit 52**) in our questions. We often use **mine**, **yours**, **his**, etc. (see **Unit 57**) in our answers:

Whose watch is **that**? ~ It's **Steve's**.
~ It's **his**.

(We don't need to say: It's Steve's watch.)

4 **Whose** sounds the same as **who's** but it is different in meaning:

Whose coat is this? (= Who does this coat belong to?)
Who's coming? (= Who is coming?)
Who's finished? (= Who has finished?)

A Complete these questions and answers. Use *Whose* and the words in brackets ( ) in each question. Use *It's* or *They're* in each answer.

	QUESTIONS	ANSWERS	
♦	(books/be) Whose books are those?	~ They're	Mike's.
♦	(car/be) Whose car is that?	~ It's	hers.
1	(pens/be) _____ those?	~ _____	mine.
2	(umbrella/be) _____ that?	~ _____	Paul's.
3	(house/be) _____ that?	~ _____	Steven King's.
4	(clothes/be) _____ those?	~ _____	his.
5	(rings/be) _____ those?	~ _____	Carla's.
6	(bike/be) _____ that?	~ _____	Christine's.
7	(painting/be) _____ that?	~ _____	John's.
8	(bag/be) _____ that?	~ _____	hers.
9	(apple/be) _____ that?	~ _____	Michelle's.
10	(motorbike/be) _____ that?	~ _____	my grandfather's.
11	(taxi/be) _____ that?	~ _____	ours.
12	(jackets/be) _____ those?	~ _____	the tennis players'.

Sentences and questions

76

Sentences and questions

B Rewrite each sentence using an apostrophe (') and *This is* or *These are*.

- This umbrella belongs to Lucy. — This is Lucy's umbrella.
- These books belong to the students. — These are the students' books.
1. These keys belong to Peter.
2. This football belongs to the boys.
3. This house belongs to my teacher.
4. These bikes belong to my sisters.
5. This room belongs to the children.
6. This chair belongs to the manager.
7. These suitcases belong to Mark.
8. These bags belong to the women.
9. This laptop belongs to Jasmine.

C Complete the conversation using the names of shops from the box and apostrophes (').

| fishmonger | chemist | hairdresser | travel agent |
| greengrocer | butcher | newsagent | ~~baker~~ |

Mike: Have we got everything we need for the weekend?

Anna: I hope so. I went to the ♦ baker's for some bread. Then I went to the bank. After that, I bought some apples at the ¹ ...., and some cough medicine at the ² ....

Mike: Did you get any meat?

Anna: Yes. I went to the ³ .... and bought some beef. I also got some fish at the ⁴ .... What did you get?

Mike: Well, I had a cup of coffee and a piece of cake, and then I bought a newspaper at the ⁵ .... Then I went to the ⁶ .... to pick up some tickets.

Anna: Did you get any milk or sugar or tea?

Mike: No, I'm sorry. I forgot. But I did go to the ⁷ .... for a haircut. Do you like it?

D Complete these sentences with *Who's* or *Whose*.

- Who's finished their homework?
- Whose flat are you staying in?
1. .... going to the cinema tonight?
2. .... watch is that?
3. .... got an answer to question number three?
4. .... playing football in the park on Sunday?
5. .... house is near to the railway station?
6. .... bags are these?
7. .... chair is that?
8. .... been to France this year?

36 Question tags

1 A question tag is a short question (e.g. **isn't it?**, **haven't we?**) that we can add at the end of a statement:

   Henry: *We've met before,* **haven't we?**
   Julian: *Yes, we have.*

2 Look at this part of a conversation:

   Anna: *Manon is Swiss.*
   David: *No, she's French,* **isn't she?**
   (= I thought she was French, but am I wrong?)

When tag questions really are questions, like David's, the voice goes up at the end.

But when tag questions are not really questions, the voice goes down at the end:

   That was a boring programme, **wasn't it?**
   (= I think that was a boring programme.)

3 Note that the verb we use in the tag depends on the verb used in the statement:

VERB		+ TAG
be:	You're French,	aren't you?
verb:	He plays golf,	doesn't he?
auxiliary verb:	It has arrived,	hasn't it?

Thus, most verbs use **do/does**, while **be** and **auxiliary verbs** use the same verb in the question tag.

4 A positive statement has a negative tag:

POSITIVE	+ NEGATIVE
I'm right,	aren't I? (NOT *am't I?*)
You're 18,	aren't you?
They're getting tired,	aren't they?
They were friendly,	weren't they?
He lives in France	doesn't he?
You speak Spanish,	don't you?
You passed your exams,	didn't you?
She has left,	hasn't she?
You can drive,	can't you?
The bus will come soon,	won't it?

5 A negative statement has a positive tag:

NEGATIVE	+ POSITIVE
It isn't very cheap,	is it?
We aren't going to be late,	are we?
She wasn't angry,	was she?
You don't like this,	do you?
She didn't win,	did she?
She hasn't visited Ireland,	has she?
She can't drive,	can she?
It won't rain today,	will it?

A Complete the conversation by putting in question tags.

Tim: We haven't met before, ◆ *have we* ?
Jo: No, I've just arrived in this country.
Tim: You come from Australia, [1] ?
Jo: Yes, from Sydney.
Tim: It's very hot there, [2] ?
Jo: Most of the time, but not always.
Tim: But it never gets very cold, [3] ?
Jo: No. Well, not as cold as some places.
Tim: They speak English there, [4] ?
Jo: Yes, that's right.
Tim: You haven't been here long, [5] ?
Jo: No, I only got here two weeks ago.
Tim: You're on holiday, [6] ?
Jo: Yes, I'm travelling around for six months.

Sentences and questions

B Complete the sentences by putting in question tags.

♦ The programme starts at seven o'clock, *doesn't it*? ~ Yes, that's right.
1. I can use this ticket on any bus, _____? ~ Yes, you can.
2. The bill won't be very high, _____? ~ No, I don't think so.
3. He wasn't very polite, _____? ~ No, he wasn't.
4. I didn't make a mistake, _____? ~ No, you didn't.
5. It won't be a difficult thing to do, _____? ~ No, I don't think so.
6. That was a lovely meal, _____? ~ Yes, it was delicious.
7. You can't play the piano, _____? ~ No, I can't.
8. They left last week, _____? ~ Yes, that's right.

C Complete the conversation with question tags.

Charles: You're going to Helsinki this week, ♦ *aren't you*?
Marta: Yes, I'm going tomorrow.
Charles: Helsinki is in Finland, ¹ _____?
Marta: Yes, it's the capital.
Charles: You've been there before, ² _____?
Marta: Yes, two years ago.
Charles: But you can't speak Finnish, ³ _____?
Marta: No, I can't.
Charles: But a lot of Finnish people speak English, ⁴ _____?
Marta: Yes.
Charles: Well, I'll see you before you leave, ⁵ _____?
Marta: Yes, I'll see you tonight.

D Use the replies to complete the sentences. Use question tags.

♦ A: *She comes from Italy, doesn't she?*
   B: Yes, she comes from Italy.

1. A: You can _____
   B: Yes, I can speak French very well.

2. A: You haven't _____
   B: No, I haven't heard this story.

3. A: You went _____
   B: Yes, I went to Frank's party.

4. A: It isn't _____
   B: No, it isn't very far from here.

5. A: She won't _____
   B: No, she won't be angry.

6. A: You're not _____
   B: No, I'm not going to leave now.

7. A: You'll _____
   B: Yes, I'll be at home tonight.

37 Short answers

1 Look at this example:

QUESTION +	SHORT ANSWER
Is he at work?	~ **Yes, he is.**
Can I come?	~ **No, you can't.**
Do you like it?	~ **Yes, I do.**
Does she live here?	~ **No, she doesn't.**

We call these 'short answers' because they are not 'full' answers:

Is she sick? { Yes, she is sick. (= full answer)
             { Yes, she is. (= short answer)

We use short answers to reply to 'yes/no' questions (see **Unit 29**):

Are you coming? { Yes, I am.
                { No, I'm not.

2 We form short answers by not using the main verb from the question:
   Have they gone? ~ Yes, they **have** gone.
   Did he go to Paris? ~ Yes, he **did** go.
   Is she waiting? ~ Yes, she **is** waiting.

When the main verb is **be**, we use **be**:
   Are you tired? ~ Yes, I **am**.

When we answer **No**, we use a negative verb:
   Will they win? ~ No, they **won't**.
   Did Paul come? ~ No, he **didn't**.
   Are you cold? ~ No, I'**m not**.

We never use positive short forms in short answers:
   Are you tired? ~ Yes, I am. (NOT Yes, I'm.)
   Is he happy? ~ Yes, he is. (NOT Yes, he's.)

3 We can also use short answers to reply 'yes' or 'no' to statements:

STATEMENT +	REPLY
He's working hard.	~ Yes, he is.
She's at work.	~ No, she isn't.
She loves films.	~ Yes, she does.
He liked the book.	~ Yes, he did.
She can swim fast.	~ Yes, she can.
You've finished.	~ No, I haven't.
She'll enjoy herself.	~ Yes, she will.

4 When we write, we normally put a comma (**,**) after **Yes** or **No** in short answers:
   He lives in London. ~ **No,** he doesn't.

A Make short answers by putting in a 'full stop' (.) and a line (—).

QUESTIONS	ANSWERS
♦ Can you come tonight?	~ Yes, I can**.** come tonight.
1 Will you see Edward tomorrow?	~ Yes, I will see Edward tomorrow.
2 Have you finished your breakfast?	~ No, I haven't finished my breakfast.
3 Do you drive to work?	~ Yes, I do drive to work.
4 Did she come yesterday?	~ No, she didn't come yesterday.
5 Were you tired after the game?	~ Yes, I was tired after the game.
6 Can she sing well?	~ No, she can't sing well.
7 Did Tom have a holiday?	~ Yes, he did have a holiday.
8 Is she studying French?	~ Yes, she is studying French.

Sentences and questions

9 Do you play golf? ~ No, I don't play golf.
10 Did you buy a new table? ~ Yes, I did buy a new table.
11 Are you thirsty? ~ No, I'm not thirsty.
12 Has Jasmine been to Mexico before? ~ Yes, she has been there before.

B Write the correct answers to the questions. Use the phrases from the box.

> Yes, she did.   No, he doesn't.   No, she wasn't.   Yes, he has.   No, I can't.
> Yes, I will.   ~~Yes, they have.~~   Yes, I do.   No, they aren't.

◆ Have they all left? ~ *Yes, they have.*
1 Does Steve work hard? ~
2 Do you like this music? ~
3 Are they listening? ~
4 Did she enjoy her holiday? ~
5 Was Mary at the concert? ~
6 Will you phone this weekend? ~
7 Can you play the guitar? ~
8 Has he gone to bed? ~

C Write positive short answers and then negative short answers for the questions.

		POSITIVE:	NEGATIVE:
◆	Was the film good?	~ Yes, *it was.*	~ No, *it wasn't.*
1	Does he enjoy French food?	~ Yes,	~ No,
2	Can he swim?	~ Yes,	~ No,
3	Will they return tonight?	~ Yes,	~ No,
4	Do you want to buy that shirt?	~ Yes,	~ No,
5	Are they coming in Mike's car?	~ Yes,	~ No,
6	Did you ask Ellie to come?	~ Yes,	~ No,
7	Is your headache better?	~ Yes,	~ No,
8	Were the exams difficult?	~ Yes,	~ No,

D William always says *Yes*. Tom always says *No*. Write their answers.

		WILLIAM:	TOM:
◆	Japanese people eat a lot of fish.	~ *Yes, they do.*	~ *No, they don't.*
1	The sun always shines in England.	~	~
2	New York is busier than London.	~	~
3	Italy will win the next World Cup.	~	~
4	Bananas are delicious.	~	~
5	Cats can sing beautifully.	~	~
6	The English speak very slowly.	~	~

38 So am I, I am too, Neither am I, etc.

1 Look at this:

She is saying that she is also tired.

2 Here are some more examples:

He **was** very angry. ~ So **was** I.

My flat**'s** quite small. ~ So **is mine**.
They **were** waiting. ~ So **was she**.
I**'m** going to have tea. ~ So **am** I.
Anna **has** finished her work and so **has Mary**.
They**'ve** been waiting. ~ So **has she**.
I **work** in an office. ~ So **do** I.
I **enjoyed** the film. ~ So **did** I.
Raphael **will** pass the exam and so **will you**.
He **can** drive. ~ So **can she**.

Note:

▶ we use **so** after a positive statement;

▶ the verb we use after **so** depends on the verb used in the positive statement.

3 Instead of **so am I**, we can say **I am too**, with the same meaning. Here are some examples:

I'm tired. ~ **I am too**.
We've got a small flat. ~ **We have too**.
I work in an office. ~ **I do too**.
William enjoyed the film and **I did too**.
He can drive. ~ **She can too**.

4 We can use expressions like **neither am I** to reply to a negative statement:

I'm not tired. ~ Neither **am** I.
    (= And I'm not tired.)
I haven't seen that film. ~ Neither **have** I.
I don't like this place. ~ Neither **do** I.
I didn't see that play. ~ Neither **did** I.
His sister can't drive and neither **can he**.

5 We can say **I'm not either** to mean the same as **neither am I**:

I'm not tired. ~ **I'm not** either.
    (= And I'm not tired.)
I haven't seen that film. ~ **I haven't** either.
I don't like this place. ~ **I don't** either.
I didn't see that play. ~ **I didn't** either.
His sister can't drive and **he can't** either.

A Complete the sentences with *so*, *too*, *either* or *neither*.

♦ I really enjoyed that meal. ~ *So* did I.
♦ I haven't done the homework. ~ I haven't *either*.
♦ We live in the centre of town. ~ We do *too*.
1 I don't like football. ~ _____ do I.
2 I haven't been to America. ~ _____ have I.
3 My father works in an office. ~ _____ does mine.
4 I haven't seen the news today. ~ _____ have I.
5 I play a lot of different sports. ~ I do _____ .
6 I've been working very hard lately. ~ _____ have I.
7 Anna will be at the party and _____ will Jasmine.
8 My brother can't speak any foreign languages and _____ can my sister.
9 Helen sent me a birthday card and Robin did _____ .
10 George isn't going to the meeting and I'm not _____ .
11 Anthony arrived late and _____ did I.
12 Kathy didn't go to the concert and _____ did I.

Sentences and questions

B Write replies to the sentences using *so* or *neither* and the words in brackets ( ).

- I've got a cold. (I) ~ *So have I.*
- I haven't got much money. (I) ~ *Neither have I.*
1. We're going to the concert. (we) ~
2. My pen doesn't work. (mine) ~
3. I haven't seen Mike today. (I) ~
4. My meal was excellent. (mine) ~
5. I've been ill. (Frank) ~
6. Ron didn't go to the party. (George) ~
7. I can't understand this game. (I) ~
8. I'm not working tomorrow. (I) ~
9. Ruth passed the exam. (John) ~
10. I've eaten enough. (I) ~
11. I'm going to see that film. (we) ~
12. My car is very old. (mine) ~

C Look at the information in the table about four people. Complete the sentences using *so, too, either* or *neither*.

	JULIA	ROBERT	AMBER	PAUL
Lives in:	New York	Chicago	New York	Los Angeles
Speaks:	Spanish	French	Spanish	French
Drives?	Yes	No	No	Yes
Likes:	reading	travelling	travelling	reading
Plays:	basketball	basketball	tennis	tennis

- Julia lives in New York and Amber *does too*.
- Julia lives in New York and *so does* Amber.
1. Robert doesn't live in New York and .... Paul.
2. Robert doesn't live in New York and Paul ....
3. Julia speaks Spanish and .... Amber.
4. Julia speaks Spanish and Amber ....
5. Robert can't speak Spanish and .... Paul.
6. Robert can't speak Spanish and Paul ....
7. Julia can drive and Paul ....
8. Robert can't drive and .... Amber.
9. Julia has passed her driving test and .... Paul.
10. Robert likes travelling and .... Amber.
11. Julia likes reading and Paul ....
12. Julia plays basketball and .... Robert.
13. Amber doesn't play basketball and .... Paul.

Test D: Sentences and questions

A A police officer is asking Raphael some questions. Make questions by putting the words in brackets ( ) in the right order. Complete the short answers.

Police officer: (get – you – did – sir – home – your – before – wife,)
♦ Did you get home before your wife, Sir?

Raphael: Yes, ♦ I did. Half an hour before.

Police officer: (normally – the – home – take – do – bus – you)
1 _____?

Raphael: No, 2 _____. I normally walk. But it was raining yesterday.

Police officer: I see. Shall we sit down, sir?

Raphael: Of course. I'll make you some tea.

Police officer: (wife – soon – is – home – coming – your)
3 _____?

Raphael: Yes, 4 _____. Just like yesterday.

Police officer: (by – travel – she – bus – does)
5 _____?

Raphael: No, 6 _____. She runs.

Police officer: Runs? Even in the rain, sir?

Raphael: That's right. She likes to exercise.

Police officer: (she – was – yesterday – tired)
7 _____?

Raphael: Yes, 8 _____. Sometimes she runs too fast.

Police officer: If she was running and you were on the bus, who was driving your car when it crashed, then?

Raphael: I've no idea, officer. Do you take sugar in your tea?

B Noah is going to ask people in Manchester about their lives and attitudes. Write the first word in each question to complete his questionnaire.

♦ When do you usually go to bed?
♦ Do you play sports?
1 _____ many brothers and sisters have you got?
2 _____ was your childhood like?
3 _____ do you talk to if you need financial advice?
4 _____ you do your shopping in the morning, afternoon or evening?
5 _____ much exercise do you do?
6 _____ type of washing powder do you use?
7 _____ do you enjoy doing on Saturday nights?
8 _____ do English people eat so little fish?
9 _____ your neighbours speak to you?
10 _____ you born in Manchester?
11 _____ is your favourite TV programme?
12 _____ washes the dishes in your house?

Sentences and questions

13 .... you go on holiday in the UK or abroad this year?
14 .... is football so popular in Manchester?

C Joan and her husband agree on everything. Finish Joan's sentences, using *neither* or *so*.

'He won't eat anything yellow, and ♦ *neither will I*. We enjoy walking sometimes, but he prefers sitting in the garden and ¹ .... I can play the piano, and ² .... , so we play together in the evenings. He has been to Egypt, and ³ .... , but we both went there before we met. I don't like long films on the TV, and ⁴ .... We always fall asleep before the end. He had a very lonely childhood, I'm afraid, and ⁵ .... I'll never forget the first time we met, and ⁶ .... We were in a music shop and he began playing my favourite song on the piano. He hasn't stopped playing, and ⁷ .... !'

D Chloe has bought a second-hand yacht. Adam is asking her about it. Complete his questions with three words, using *how* each time.

Adam: It looks fantastic! ♦ *How long is it?*
Chloe: 20 metres. I'm going to sail to the Greek islands next month.
Adam: That sounds nice. ¹ .... that?
Chloe: I'm not sure. About 1,000 kilometres.
Adam: It looks fairly new. ² .... it?
Chloe: Six and a half years. But the last owner didn't use it much. He was too busy working.
Adam: I would use it every weekend, if it was mine. ³ .... you going to use it?
Chloe: At least once a month, probably.
Adam: ⁴ .... you go for?
Chloe: Two or three days at a time, I think. Are you any good at sailing?
Adam: I am actually. But I'm better at standing on the deck in the sun. By the way, ⁵ .... it cost?
Chloe: I can't tell you. I don't want to remember!

E Put the correct question tag at the end of each line.

John: That was an interesting play, ♦ *wasn't it* ?
Paul: You didn't like the main actor, ¹ .... ?
John: Not exactly. He's in that TV programme, ² .... ?
Paul: I think so. He plays the boy's father, ³ .... ?
John: That's right. I couldn't hear him tonight. He hasn't got a very loud voice, ⁴ .... ?
Paul: No, not at all. You just can't hear actors these days, ⁵ .... ?
John: That's because they work in TV, ⁶ .... ?
Paul: I suppose so. More money. He won't earn so much tonight, ⁷ .... ?
John: He was terrible, so he shouldn't earn so much tonight, ⁸ .... ?
Paul: No. You're right. He wasn't great, ⁹ .... ?
John: Anyway, you didn't pay very much for the tickets, ¹⁰ .... ?
Paul: I can't remember. They were free, ¹¹ .... ?
John: That's OK, then, ¹² .... ?

39 Ability: can, can't, could, couldn't

1 We form sentences with **can** like this:

can	+	INFINITIVE
I	can	ski.

POSITIVE
I/He/She/It/We/You/They **can ski**.

NEGATIVE	FULL FORM	SHORT FORM
I/He/She/It/You (etc.)	**cannot ski**.	**can't ski**.

QUESTIONS
Can I/he/she/it/you (etc.) ski?

In spoken English **cannot** is possible, but we normally use **can't**:

*He **can't** swim.*

For short answers (*Can you swim? ~ No, I **can't**.*), see **Unit 37**.

2 We use **can** and **can't** to talk about things we are able to do generally:

*She **can speak** Japanese. (= She is able to speak Japanese.)*
*He **can't ski**. (= He isn't able to ski.)*

We also use **can** and **can't** to talk about things we are able to do at the moment:

*I **can see** the moon. (= I am able to see it now.)*

3 We form sentences with **could** like this:

could	+	INFINITIVE
I	could	ski.

POSITIVE
I/he/she/it/we/you/they **could ski**.

NEGATIVE	FULL FORM	SHORT FORM
I/he/you (etc.)	**could not ski**.	**couldn't ski**.

We use **could** to talk about things we were able to do generally in the past:

*I **could run** 100 metres in 12 seconds when I was young.*
*Lucy **could read** when she was three years old.*

4 We do not normally use **could** for something that happened on a particular occasion in the past. We use **was able to** or **managed to**:

*The boat was in difficulties, but in the end it **managed to** reach the port.* (OR *... it was **able to** reach ...*; NOT *... it could reach ...*)

5 When we talk about a person's ability to do something in the future, we use **will be able to**:

*The baby **will be able to** talk soon.*

A Complete the sentences with *can*, *can't* or *couldn't* and the verbs in brackets ( ).

♦ You don't have to shout. I _can hear_ (hear) you very well.
♦ I _couldn't watch_ (watch) that programme last night because I had to go out.
1 He _____ (play) last week because he was injured.
2 He eats in restaurants all the time because he _____ (cook).
3 I _____ (give) you a lift in my car because it isn't working at the moment.
4 I didn't have a good seat in the theatre, so I _____ (see) the stage very well.
5 John doesn't need a calculator. He _____ (do) very difficult sums in his head.
6 She's very good at music. She _____ (play) three instruments.
7 I _____ (find) my address book. Have you seen it?
8 He spoke very quickly and I _____ (understand) anything he said.
9 We _____ (go) on the trip because we _____ (afford) it. It was very expensive.

Modal verbs

10 I .... (do) any more work because I was very tired, so I stopped.
11 I'm afraid that I .... (talk) to you now. I'm in a hurry. I have to be at work in five minutes.

B Complete the sentences using the words in brackets ( ) and *can*, *can't*, *could* or *couldn't*.

♦ Sarah phoned Jasmine yesterday. (They/not/talk/for a long time, because Jasmine had to go out.)
They couldn't talk for a long time, because Jasmine had to go out.

1 Grandma needs her glasses. (She/not/see/anything without her glasses.)
She ....

2 Mary won her race. (She was so tired after the race that she/not/stand up.)
She ....

3 (Last year, Robert/beat/his younger brother at chess.) But he can't beat him now.
Last year, ...

4 John and Anna have a wonderful view from their hotel room. (They/see/the whole of the city.)
They ....

C Complete these sentences using *managed to* or the correct form of *be able to*.

♦ I *was able to/managed to* get the last ticket for the concert.
1 After waiting for a long time, we .... go into the museum.
2 They .... buy a new carpet yesterday.
3 I .... eat three plates of pasta in the restaurant last night!
4 Our friends .... visit us yesterday afternoon.
5 She .... have a long holiday last year.
6 We .... ski in Scotland last weekend.

D Look at this table and complete the sentences using *can*, *could*, or *will be able to*.

	LAST YEAR	NOW	HOPES FOR THE FUTURE
Joy	swim 100 metres	swim 1000 metres	swim for her club team
Mark	type 15 words per minute	type 30 words per minute	work as an administrator
Anna	speak only a little French	speak French quite well	work as an interpreter
Laura	only cook omelettes	cook quite well	work as a chef
Tom	only play the piano	play the piano and the violin	be a professional musician
Lucy	ride a bike	drive a car	drive a racing car

♦ Last year Joy *could swim 100 metres* .... Now, *she can swim 1,000 metres* ....
♦ At the moment Anna *can speak French* .... quite well, and if she studies hard, perhaps *she'll be able to work* .... as an interpreter.

1 Last year Mark .... Now, ...
2 Last year Anna .... Now, ...
3 At the moment Laura ...., and if she works hard, perhaps ....
4 Last year Tom .... Now, ..., and if he studies hard, perhaps ....
5 Last year Lucy .... Now, ..., and she hopes that one day ....

40 Can/Could I? May I? Can/Could you?

1 We form questions with **can**, **may** and **could** like this:

QUESTIONS		
Can		
May	I/he/she/it/we (etc.)	**wait**?
Could		

2 We use **can**, **may** and **could** to ask for things:

Can (etc.) +	I/we +	**have**	…?
Can	I	**have**	a coffee?

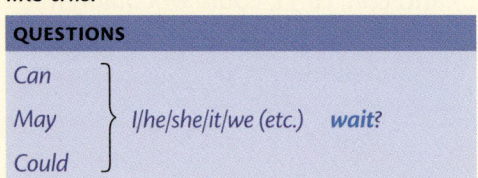

Can we have the menu, please?

Could we **have** two tickets, please?
Can I **have** some sugar?

3 We use **can**, **may** or **could** to ask for permission. **Could I** and **May I** are more formal and polite than **Can I**:

Can/May/Could +	I/WE +	INFINITIVE …?	
May	*I*	*see*	*her?*

Can I borrow your bicycle, please?

Could we **look** at your map, please?
Can I **borrow** your tennis racket, please?

We use **can** or **may** to give permission:
You **can** leave your bag here. (OR … **may** leave …)

If we talk about what is allowed in general, rather than by a particular person, we use **can**:
People **can** drive on the roads when they are 17 years old.

But official notices often use **may**:
BAGS MAY BE LEFT HERE.

4 We use **Can you**, **Could you** and **Would you** (but NOT ~~May you~~) when we ask someone to do something. **Could** and **would** are more formal and polite than **can**.

Can/Could/Would +	YOU +	INFINITIVE	…?
Could	you	help	me?

Could you buy me a newspaper?

A: I'm cold. **Can** you **close** the window?
B: Yes, of course.

A Put the words in brackets ( ) in the right order to make questions.

♦ (have – a return ticket to York – could – please – I – ?)
   Could I have a return ticket to York, please?

1 (please – I – may – a glass of orange juice – have – ?)

2 (we – listen to their new song – can – ?)

3 (your mobile – please – use – I – can – ?)

4 (may – borrow – your camera tomorrow – I – ?)

Modal verbs

5 (please – the menu – pass – you – could – ?)
....

B Ask for permission. Use the words in brackets ( ) and the words from the box.

> use your printer   ~~use your dictionary~~   close the window
> borrow your pen   turn on the TV

♦ SITUATION: You want to find the meaning of a word.
   (may I) *May I use your dictionary?*

1 SITUATION: You want to write down a phone number.
   (can I) ....

2 SITUATION: You want to watch a programme.
   (can I … please) ....

3 SITUATION: You're feeling cold.
   (may I) ....

4 SITUATION: You need to print a document.
   (may I … please) ....

C Ask people to do things. Use the words in brackets ( ) and the phrases from the box.

> ~~buy me a magazine~~   tell me the time   make me a sandwich
> tell me the way to Buckingham Palace   carry one of these cases

♦ PROBLEM: You're sick. You're in bed. You're bored.
   (can you … please) *Can you buy me a magazine, please?*

1 PROBLEM: Your suitcases are very heavy.
   (could you) ....

2 PROBLEM: You're lost in London.
   (could you … please) ....

3 PROBLEM: You've forgotten to put your watch on.
   (can you) ....

4 PROBLEM: You're hungry. You're very tired.
   (can you … please) ....

D Choose the right word from the words in brackets ( ) and put it in the gap.

♦ *Could* .... (May/Could) you give me one of these forms, please?

1 In the street:
   Excuse me, officer, ... (could/may) you tell me how to get to the station?

2 At a railway station:
   A: Let's have our sandwiches here.
   B: .... (Couldn't/Can't) you read? Look at the notice; it says:
      'FOOD .... (MAY/COULD) NOT BE EATEN IN THIS WAITING ROOM.'

3 A: .... (Could/May) you call Jenny about tomorrow's meeting?
   B: I .... (may not/can't/couldn't) call her because she has lost her phone.

4 A: .... (May/Could) someone help me?
   B: What .... (may/can) I do to help you?
   A: We need to move the chairs and to clean this room. Can you help?
   B: I'm afraid I .... (may not/can't) move the chairs because of my bad back.

41 Must, mustn't

1 We use **must** with an infinitive (**do**, **go**, **work**, etc.):

		INFINITIVE	
You	must	work	harder.

Don't use **to** before the infinitive:
NOT ~~You must to work harder.~~

The form of **must** is the same for all persons:

| I/you/he/she/it/we/they | must leave soon. |

2 We use **must** in rules to say that an action is necessary:
  All visitors **must go** to reception when they arrive.

We use **You must …** to give somebody an order:
  Your work is poor – **you must try** harder.
  You must finish this work tomorrow.

We use **I/We must …** to say that we think it is necessary or important that we do something:
  I'm getting tired. **I must go** home now.
  We must get a new car soon.

3 We also use **You must …** to strongly recommend or offer something:
  You must read this book; it's fantastic!
  You must come for lunch at our house.

4 The negative form of **must** is **mustn't** or **must not**:
  You **mustn't park** here – it's not allowed.
  (NOT ~~You mustn't to park here.~~)

5 We use **You mustn't …** (or **You must not**) to say that it is necessary that somebody does NOT do something:
  You **mustn't smoke** in here.
  You **mustn't make** this mistake again.

We use **I/We mustn't …** (or **must not**) to say that we think it is necessary that we do NOT do something:
  I mustn't forget her birthday again.
  We mustn't be late for the meeting.

6 Notice that we can use **must** and **mustn't** (NOT ~~will must~~) to talk about the future:
  I **must** phone Harry tomorrow.
  (NOT ~~I will must phone Harry tomorrow.~~)

To talk about what was necessary in the past, we cannot use **must**; we use a form of **have to** (see **Unit 42**).

We don't generally use **must** in a question form. We use **have to** (see **Unit 42**).

A The Hotel Strict is not a very nice hotel. It has a lot of rules. Read the list of rules and change each one into a sentence using *must* or *must not*.

> **Notice to guests**
> Leave your key at reception when you go out.
> Vacate your room by nine o'clock on the morning you leave.
> Return to the hotel before ten o'clock every night.
> Do not take food into your room.
> Pay for your room when you arrive.
> Do not smoke in the restaurant.

♦ <u>You must leave</u> your key at reception when you go out.
1 You .... food into your room.
2 .... for your room when you arrive.
3 .... your room by nine o'clock on the morning you leave.
4 .... in the restaurant.
5 .... to the hotel before ten o'clock every night.

Modal verbs

B Look at this table of instructions for students in a school. Use the table to make sentences with *must* or *mustn't*.

	Yes	No
Attend all classes.	✓	
Take school books home with you.		✓
Make a noise in the corridors.		✓
Write in school books.		✓
Arrive for lessons on time.	✓	
Bring your own pens and paper.	✓	

♦ You must attend all classes.
1 .... school books home with you.
2 .... a noise in the corridors.
3 .... in school books.
4 .... for lessons on time.
5 .... your own pens and paper.

C Henry wants to make some changes in his life. Look at the pictures and make sentences using the phrases from the box with *must* or *mustn't*.

study after school   run every morning   ~~dress smartly~~   watch TV all day
~~smoke~~   visit my grandmother   sleep in the afternoon   work late at night

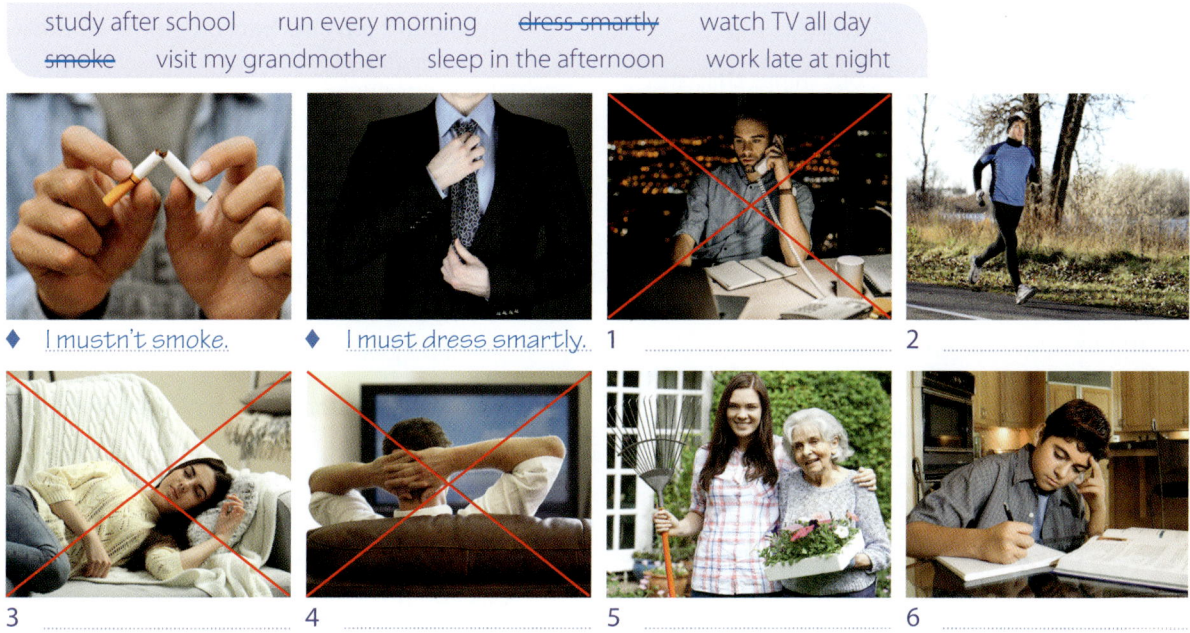

♦ I mustn't smoke.   ♦ I must dress smartly.   1 ....   2 ....
3 ....   4 ....   5 ....   6 ....

D Rewrite the sentences in brackets ( ) using *must* or *mustn't/must not*.

♦ (Have some of this fish. It's wonderful.)
You <u>must have some of this fish</u>. It's wonderful.

1 (Don't tell lies. It's bad.)
You .... It's bad.

2 (Passengers: Do not open the door while the train is moving.)
Passengers .... while the train is moving.

3 (Come for dinner with us one evening next week!)
You .... one evening next week!

4 (All staff: show identity cards when you enter the building.)
All staff .... when they enter the building.

5 (It's bad for you to eat so much unhealthy food.)
You .... so much unhealthy food.

6 (Follow the instructions when using this machine.)
You .... when using this machine.

42 Have to

1 The Present Simple forms of **have to** are:

POSITIVE AND NEGATIVE		
I/you/we/they	have / don't have	to go.
He/she/it	has / doesn't have	

QUESTIONS			
Do	I/you/we/they	have	to go?
Does	he/she/it		

2 We use **have to** to talk about things that are necessary because of rules that other people oblige us to follow:

My brother **has to travel** a lot in his job.
(= It is required by his employer.)
We **have to pay** the rent every month.
(= It is required by the landlord.)

To talk about things that WE think are necessary, we usually use **must** (see **Unit 43**).

3 We also use **have to** for things that are necessary because of the circumstances:

I **have to get** a bus to school. (= It is the only way I can travel there.)
She **has to live** on a small income. (= She only receives a small amount of money to pay for what she needs.)

4 We use **don't have to** to say that something is NOT necessary.

We **don't have to hurry**; we're early.
(= It's not necessary to hurry. We have plenty of time.)
I **don't have to get** up early on Sunday.
(= I can stay in bed if I want.)

5 We can use **have got to** with the same meaning as **have to** to talk about something that is necessary at one particular time (but not in general):

I **have to**/I've **got to make** a phone call now.
You **don't have to**/**haven't got to do** this immediately.

6 The past form of **have to** is **had to**:
I **had to do** a lot of work yesterday.
(See **Unit 48**.)

7 The future form of **have to** is **will have to**:
He'**ll have to look** for another job.
We **won't have to get** tickets in advance.
Will they **have to get** visas?

Note that we cannot use **have got to** in past or future forms:
Yesterday I **had to work** hard. (NOT ~~I had got to work hard.~~)

8 We can use the Present Simple of **have to** to talk about the future:
I **have to do** some shopping tomorrow.
Do you **have to work** next weekend?

A Look at this table about different jobs and use the information to complete the sentences using *have to* or *don't have to*.

	Shop assistants	Bank clerks	Doctors	Teachers
deal with the public	✓	✓	✓	✗
be polite to people	✓	✓	✗	✗
work with money	✓	✓	✗	✗
wear uniforms	✓	✗	✓	✗

♦ Shop assistants <u>have to deal</u> with the public.
1 Teachers .... to people.
2 Bank clerks .... to people.
3 Bank clerks .... with money.
4 Doctors .... with money.
5 Shop assistants often .... uniforms.
6 Teachers .... uniforms.

Modal verbs

B Complete the sentences using the correct forms of *have to* or *have got to* and the words in brackets ( ). Be careful to use the correct tense.

- I have to leave (I/leave) now; I've got an appointment at the dentist's.
- Did you have to study (you/study) literature when you were at school?
- You haven't got to come (You/not/come) with me now if you don't want to.
1. _____ (I/not/work) hard because the job was very easy.
2. _____ (I/do) this work now, or can I do it tomorrow?
3. _____ (I/run) to school because I was late.
4. _____ (I/go) to an important meeting yesterday.
5. _____ (you/show) your passports when you reached the border?
6. _____ (I/pay) in cash next week or can I transfer the money online?
7. I want to be an airline pilot. What qualifications _____ (you/have) to be a pilot?
8. _____ (You/not/decide) today. You can tell me tomorrow.
9. I arrived late yesterday because _____ (I/wait) a long time for a bus.
10. A: _____ (you/work) every weekend?
    B: No, I don't; but _____ (I/work) last weekend.

C Complete the conversations using the words in brackets ( ) and correct forms of *have to* or *have got to*.

A: (Good morning, I'd like to buy a travel card. What/I/do?)
 ♦ Good morning. I'd like to buy a travel card. What do I have to do?

B: (You/fill/in an application form.)
 1 _____

A: (I/give/you/a photograph?)
 2 _____

B: (No, you/not/give/me anything, except the money for the card!)
 3 _____

Dad: (What/you/do/at school today?)
 ♦ What did you have to do at school today?

Sam: (We/do/some/English tests.)
 4 _____

Dad: (How many questions/you/answer?)
 5 _____

Sam: (We/answer/about 40 grammar questions.)
 6 _____

(I/think/about them very carefully.)
 7 _____

Dad: (you/write/a composition?)
 8 _____

Sam: (No, but we/do/one next week.)
 9 _____

43 Must/have to, mustn't/don't have to

1 We use **must** when the speaker thinks it is necessary or important to do an action:
  *You **must** go.* (= It is important that you go.)

We make negatives, questions and short answers like this:
  *You **mustn't** go.*
  ***Must** you go?* ~ *Yes, I **must**.*

2 We use **have to** to talk about an action that is necessary because of rules or laws, or because someone obliges us to do it:
  *Doctors sometimes **have to work** on Sunday.* (It is in the rules of their work.)

We make negatives, questions and short answers with a form of **do**:
  *Teachers **don't have to work** on Sunday.*
  ***Do** you **have to work** today?* ~ *No, I **don't**.*

3 POSITIVE

In positive sentences we can often use **must** and **have to** with little difference in meaning, because many things are important both because we think so and because there are rules:
  *You **must work** hard in order to succeed* (OR *You **have to work** in order to succeed*).

4 NEGATIVE

Note the difference in meaning between **mustn't** and **don't have to**.

In negative sentences we often use **mustn't** to say that something is against the rules or against the law:
  *You **mustn't smoke** on buses.* (= Smoking is against the rules.)
  *In football you **mustn't touch** the ball with your hands.* (= Touching the ball is against the rules.)

We use **don't have to** to say that people are not obliged to do something:
  *In Britain, people **don't have to carry** a passport with them.* (= People are not obliged to carry one.)
  *Nowadays pupils **do not have to learn** Latin at school.* (= They are not obliged to learn it.)

5 QUESTIONS

In questions we usually use **do/does ... have to** (NOT ~~must~~) to ask if something is obligatory or important:
  ***Does** Michael **have to get** up early tomorrow?*
  ***Do** we **have to wait** here?*

A The Stanton Squash Club has decided that it is important for all club members to do these things:

> wear sports shoes and clean clothes   have a shower   pay before you play   finish on time

But these things are not allowed:

> disturb other players   eat or drink outside the bar   take club balls home

Put *have to*, *don't have to* or *mustn't* in the gaps.

♦ You _don't have to_ wear white clothes, but you _have to_ wear sports shoes.
♦ You _mustn't_ disturb other players, but you _don't have to_ be silent.
1 You _____ finish on time, but you _____ start on time.
2 You _____ play with club balls, but if you do, you _____ take them home.
3 You _____ eat or drink outside the bar, but you _____ buy your food in the bar if you don't want to.
4 You _____ have a shower, and you _____ wear clean clothes.

Modal verbs

B Look at the signs and complete the sentences with *don't have to* or *mustn't*.

ANTIQUES
Please feel free to come in.
(No eating inside.)

- You *don't have to* go in.
- You *mustn't* eat inside.

Entry possible **30 minutes** before the concert. No late arrivals allowed.

1 You _____ arrive half an hour early.
2 You _____ arrive late.

All vehicles – **slow**. Drivers of large vehicles, wait for guard before crossing.

3 Small vehicles _____ wait.
4 Drivers of large vehicles _____ cross alone.

STUDENTS!
Please be quiet – 4th-year exam in progress.

5 Students _____ make a noise.
6 Third-year students _____ take the exam.

LIBRARY
No talking.
Please leave books on tables.

7 You _____ talk in the library.
8 You _____ put the books back on the shelves.

SWIMMING POOL
Free swim today.
No eating.
No drinking.

9 Swimmers _____ pay today.
10 Swimmers _____ eat or drink by the pool.

C Put the words from the box in the gaps. Don't add any other words.

> Does she   have to   has   she has   must   mustn't   ~~have~~   does she

Mark: We ♦ *have* to get up early tomorrow.
Rob: Why?
Mark: Have you forgotten? Annie ¹_____ to move to a new flat tomorrow, and I promised we would help her.
Rob: ²_____ have to move out by a particular time?
Mark: No, there's no rush. She doesn't ³_____ leave her old flat before the afternoon, but there are lots of things that ⁴_____ to pack, so we ⁵_____ get there fairly early.
Rob: Why ⁶_____ have to move, by the way?
Mark: She said that I ⁷_____ tell you because she wants to tell you herself, when she sees you tomorrow.

44 Must, can't, may, might, could

1 We use **must**, **can't**, **may** and **could** with an infinitive (e.g. **be, go, come, earn**):

		INFINITIVE	
They	**must**	**earn**	a lot.

2 CERTAINTY

She **must be** rich.

Look at this example with **must**:

Jasmine got top marks in her exams. She **must be** very clever. (= From what we know, we can be certain that Jasmine is very clever.)

We use **must** to say we are certain:

The Greens have two houses and two cars. They **must earn** a lot of money. (= We can be sure that the Greens earn a lot of money.)

A: There's someone outside in an orange car.
B: It **must be** Lucy. She's the only person I know with an orange car.

3 IMPOSSIBILITY

She **can't be** poor.

Look at this example with **can't**:

Mark studied hard for his exams, but he got poor marks; he **can't be** very clever. (= From what we know, we can guess that Mark is **not** very clever.)

We use **can't** to talk about impossibility:

The Browns both have part-time jobs; they **can't earn** much money. (= We can guess that the Browns do NOT earn a lot of money.)

A: There's someone at the door. I think it's William.
B: It **can't be** William. He's in Australia.

4 POSSIBILITY

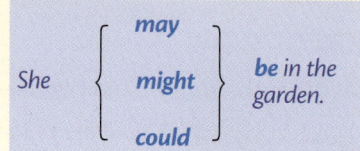

Look at this example with **may**:

A: Eve's not in her room. Where is she?
B: She **may be** in the garden. (= From what we know, **perhaps** she **is** in the garden.)

We use **may**, **might** and **could** for something that is possible but not certain, now or in the future:

My sister **might come** tomorrow. (= From what we know, perhaps she **will** come.)

Now look at this example with **may not**:

A: I've phoned Charlotte, but there's no answer.
B: She **may not** be at home. (OR She **might not be** …) (= Perhaps she is not at home.)

Could not is NOT possible here.

A Complete the sentences using *must* or *can't* and the verbs from the box.

| ~~be~~ | belong | ~~speak~~ | come | spend | have | like | live | want | remember |

♦ Anna lived in America for three years, so she _must speak_ English.
♦ Tom's brother doesn't know anything about medicine, so he _can't be_ a doctor.
1. Jasmine has an incredible number of albums. She _____ music a lot.
2. Peter doesn't speak German, so he _____ from Germany.
3. This jacket _____ to Jessica because it's not her size.
4. That man _____ around here because he doesn't know any of the street names.
5. Jack _____ a lot of clothes. He wears something different every day.
6. Sam's grandmother is almost 100 years old, so she _____ the Second World War.
7. You've got ten cats already. You _____ to get another one.
8. Lucy buys a new dress every day. She _____ a lot of money on clothes.

Modal verbs

B Someone has robbed a bank. The police are sure that the criminal is one of these men. Look at the pictures and complete the sentences using *can't be, could be* or *must be*.

Drake   Hall   Brown   Rogers   Smith

- ♦ A witness says that the robber had short hair. If that's true, then it _can't be_ Drake or Rogers, but it _could be_ Hall.
- ♦ A witness says that the robber had glasses. If that's true, then it _can't be_ Brown or Drake. It _must be_ either Hall or Rogers or Smith.
- 1 A witness says that the robber had black hair. If that's true, then it _____ Hall, but it _____ Brown.
- 2 A witness says that the robber had a moustache. If that's true, then it _____ Rogers but it _____ Drake or Brown.
- 3 A witness says that the robber didn't have a beard. If that's true, then it _____ Drake or Brown but it _____ Hall or Smith.
- 4 A witness says that the robber had a moustache, but no beard. If that's true, then it _____ Drake or Rogers. It _____ Hall.
- 5 A witness says that the robber had black hair and wore glasses. If that's true, then it _____ Rogers. It _____ Hall.
- 6 And if what everyone says is true, then it _____ Smith.

C Complete the dialogues with *must, can't* or *might* and the phrases from the box.

| cost a lot of money | be a soldier | work long hours | go to Portugal |
| come this weekend | take much interest | also be at the shops | be at the gym |

- ♦ Ruth: I think Anna's brother is in the army.
  James: He _can't be a soldier_ ; he's only 15.
- 1 Rob: What are you going to do next summer?
  Lucy: I don't know. We _____, but it's not certain yet.
- 2 Jacob: Mike's new flat is all electric – kitchen, heating, everything.
  Peter: That _____ in electricity bills.
- 3 Sam: Is Mary coming to see us this week?
  Ellie: It depends on her work. She _____ if she finishes the project that she's doing.
- 4 Laura: Have Noah and Kim got any children?
  Tom: Yes, they have two children, but they _____ in them, because they never talk about them.
- 5 Andrew: Do you see your new neighbours very much?
  Sarah: No, they _____, because they are hardly ever at home.
- 6 Paul: Jacob's gone out, hasn't he? Where has he gone?
  Anna: I don't know. He _____ or he _____.

45 Should, shouldn't

1 We use **should** with an infinitive (**do**, **go**, etc.):

I **should**	**do**	some work tonight.
	INFINITIVE	

The form of **should** is the same for all persons:

I/you/he/she/it/we/they **should go**.

2 The negative form is **shouldn't**:

You **shouldn't** sit in the sun all day.
They **shouldn't** spend so much money.

3 We use **I should** or **we should** to say what is a good thing for us to do:

I **should go** home. It's midnight.
We **should invite** them for a meal.

We use **I/we shouldn't** to say that something is a bad thing for us to do:

I **shouldn't** spend so much money.

We use **you should/shouldn't** to give advice:

You **should look** for a better job.
You **shouldn't drive** so fast.

Should is not as strong as **must** or **have to**. Compare:

You **should eat** more fruit. (It's a good idea.)
'You **must eat** more fruit,' said the doctor. (It's very important.)

4 We use the question form **Should I/we** …? to ask for advice:

Should I write my name in this space?

What **should I say** to Helen?
I need a new passport. Where **should I go**?

5 We can say **I think we should**, **I don't think you should**, etc. to give an opinion:

I think we should get a new car.

I **don't think you should believe** everything he says.

We do not usually say:

~~I think you shouldn't …~~

6 We can use **do you think I should** …? to ask for advice:

He hasn't replied to my email. **Do you think I should phone** him?
What **do you think I should give** Tom for his birthday?

A Complete the sentences using the words in brackets ( ) and *should* or *shouldn't*.

♦ <u>You shouldn't work</u> (You/work) so hard. Have a holiday.
♦ I enjoyed that film. <u>We should go</u> (We/go) to the cinema more often.
1 _____ (You/park) here. It's not allowed.
2 What _____ (I/cook) for dinner tonight?
3 _____ (You/wear) a coat. It's cold outside.
4 _____ (You/smoke). It's bad for you.
5 _____ (We/arrive) at the airport two hours before the flight.
6 _____ (I/pay) now or later?
7 Do you think _____ (I/apply) for this job?
8 What do you think _____ (I/write) in this space on the form?
9 _____ (I/eat) any more cake. I've already eaten too much.
10 This food is terrible. _____ (We/complain) to the manager.
11 Which shirt do you think _____ (I/buy)?

Modal verbs

B Henry is cooking a meal. Give him some useful advice. Use the advice from the box and *you should* or *you shouldn't*.

> ~~Don't leave the meat in the oven for more than one hour.~~
> Cut the onions as small as possible.
> Use fresh herbs and fresh vegetables.
> Don't put in too much salt and pepper.
> Wait until the water boils before you put the vegetables into it.
> Heat the oven before you put the meat in.
> Cut the meat into four equal slices.

♦ You shouldn't leave .... the meat in the oven for more than one hour.
1 .... the onions as small as possible.
2 .... fresh herbs and fresh vegetables.
3 .... in too much salt and pepper.
4 .... until the water boils before you put the vegetables into it.
5 .... the oven before you put the meat in.
6 .... the meat into four equal slices.

C Write this conversation between Noah and Joseph using the words in brackets ( ). Use *do* or *should* where required.

Noah: (I want to buy a motorbike. What/you/think/I/do?)
♦ I want to buy a motorbike. What do you think I should do?

Joseph: (You/look/at the advertisements in the papers.)
♦ You should look at the advertisements online.

Noah: (Which website/I/use?)
1 ....

Joseph: (I think/you/go on/the 'What Bike?' website.)
2 ....

Noah: (What/you/think/I/do/before I buy a bike?)
3 ....

Joseph: (I/not/think/you/decide/too quickly.)
4 ....

(You/check/the condition of the bike.)
5 ....

(You/ask/somebody who knows about bikes to look at the bike for you.)
6 ....

(You/not/buy/one simply because it looks nice!)
7 ....

(You/be/very careful.)
8 ....

46 Should, ought to, had better

1 We use **should**, **ought to** and **had better** with an infinitive (e.g. **be**, **go**, **ask**, **wait**):

	INFINITIVE
I **should**	**go**.
You **ought to**	**ask**.
We **had better**	**wait**.

2 We use both **should** and **ought to** to ask for or to give advice, to say what is the correct or best thing to do:

A: *I've got toothache. What **should** I **do**?*
(= What is the best thing for me to do?)
B: *You **should go** to the dentist's.*
(= The best thing for you to do is to go to the dentist's.)

When we are talking about a duty or a law, we usually use **ought to**:

A: *I saw a robbery. What **should** I **do**?*
B: *You **ought to report** it to the police.*
(= It is a person's duty to report it.)

On the other hand, when we are giving a personal opinion, we usually use **should**:

B: *I think you **should** forget about it.*

We use **should** much more than **ought to** in negatives and questions:

*I **shouldn't** go.* (OR *I **ought not to** go.*)
***Should** I go?* (OR ***Ought** I **to** go?*)

3 We can also use **had better** to give advice, to say what is the best thing to do:

*The train is going to leave now. You**'d better** get on it.*

*There'll be a lot of traffic tomorrow. We **had** (OR We**'d**) **better leave** early.*
*I **had** (OR I**'d**) **better** ask the doctor about the pain in my stomach.*

Note that **had** is a past form, but it does not refer to past time here; we use it to talk about present or future time.

We only use **had better** to give advice about a particular thing; when we give general advice, we use **should** or **ought to**:

*When people are in trouble, they **should go** to the police.* (NOT *... they had better go to the police.*)

The negative is **had better not**:

*They **had better not** be late.*

A Complete the sentences using the phrases from the box and *should* or *shouldn't*.

call an ambulance	~~report it to the police~~	move the person yourself
drive home in her car	touch anything	~~do anything about it~~
~~decide for herself~~	give you a new cup	make him do lots of sport
borrow money	leave everything where it is	ask someone to take her
let him eat so much		

♦ A: There is a house near my home where I often hear strange noises.
    B: You *should report it to the police*   .

♦ A: My daughter wants to marry a man I don't like. What should I do about it?
    B: In my opinion, *you shouldn't do anything about it*   .
       Your daughter *should decide for herself*   .

1 A: If someone has a serious accident, what's the right thing to do?
    B: Well, you _____. It's not a good idea to move an injured person.
       Instead, you _____ to take the person to hospital.

Modal verbs

2 A: Last Saturday I bought some coffee cups but one of the handles was broken. What can I expect the shop to do?
   B: They _____.

3 A: My son is 12 years old and he's overweight.
   B: Well, it's important not to eat too much, so you _____.
      Also, you _____.

4 A: If you come home and see that you've been robbed, what's the best thing to do?
   B: Well, you _____. You _____ and call the police.

5 A: Mary can't work because she's feeling sick. How can she get home?
   B: Well, she _____.
      She _____ home.

6 People _____ if they can't pay it back.

B Use the sentences in brackets ( ) to write a reply with *had better* in the following dialogues.

♦ A: I've got a headache.
   B: (You should go and lie down.) You'd better go and lie down.

1 A: The children want to play in the kitchen.
   B: (Well, they should clear everything away when they finish.)
      Well, _____ when they finish.

2 A: I think it's going to rain.
   B: (Yes, we ought to take our umbrellas.) Yes, _____.

3 A: I'm going to go to bed now. We have to get up very early tomorrow.
   B: (Yes, I should go to bed early too.) Yes, _____.

C Complete the dialogues using the correct form of the words in brackets ( ).
Use *to* or *not* if necessary.

♦ A: Should Henry stay in bed?
   B: No, the doctor said he *shouldn't* (should) stay in bed.

1 A: Can we move that cupboard?
   B: No, it's very delicate, so you _____ (ought) leave it where it is.

2 A: Should we change these notices?
   B: No, the show is still on, so we _____ (should) change them until next week.

3 A: You'd better tell the boss about the accident immediately.
   B: No, she's in a bad mod. I _____ (had better) tell her until tomorrow.

4 A: Does the doctor say it's all right for Mrs Bradley to work?
   B: Yes, but she must be careful. She _____ (ought) lift anything heavy, for example.

5 A: Can they come before dinner?
   B: No, we haven't got enough food, so they _____ (had better) come after dinner.

101

47 Need, needn't, needn't have

1 We use the verb **need** to talk about things that we must do. We use **to** + infinitive (e.g. **to do**, **to go**) after **need**:

TO + INFINITIVE	
I **need** **to go**	to the dentist's.

After **he/she/it** we use **needs**:
Mary/She **needs to buy** some white paint.

We make negatives, questions and short answers with a form of **do**:
You **don't need to go** to the doctor's.
Mary **doesn't need to buy** any green paint.
A: **Do** you **need to go** to the dentist's?
B: Yes, I **do**./No, I **don't**.
A: **Does** Mary **need to buy** any brushes?
B: Yes, she **does**./No, she **doesn't**.

2 We can also use **need** to talk about things that we must get. Here we use an object after need:

	OBJECT
Mary **needs**	some white paint.
I **don't need**	a new car.
Does Peter **need**	any help?

3 To talk about what we do not need to do, we can use **needn't**. We use an infinitive (e.g. **go**, **buy**) after **needn't**. **Needn't** has the same meaning as **don't/doesn't need to**:

	INFINITIVE	
You **needn't**	**go**	to the shops. We have enough food.
(OR You **don't need to go** to the shops.)		
Mary **needn't**	**buy**	any paint.
(OR Mary **doesn't need to buy** any paint.)		

We cannot use **needn't** before an object (e.g. your coat); we must use **don't need**:
You **don't need** your coat. It's not cold outside.
(NOT ~~You needn't your coat.~~)

4 We can use **needed to** for past time:
They **needed to clean** everything before they started to paint.

The negative past simple form is **didn't need to**:
The room wasn't dirty so they **didn't need to clean it** before they started to paint it.
(= It was not necessary to clean the room so they didn't clean it.)

We use **needn't have** + past participle to talk about something that was done although it wasn't necessary:
We **needn't have lit** the fire, because it was a warm evening. (= We lit the fire, but it was not necessary to light it.)
You **needn't have bought** any bread, James. There is plenty in the cupboard. (= You bought some bread, but it was not necessary.)

A Use the statements in brackets ( ) to make questions and short answers.

♦ (Tom needs to take some warm clothes.)
<u>Does Tom need to take some warm clothes</u> ? ~ Yes, <u>he does</u>.

♦ (She doesn't need to study hard.)
<u>Does she need to study hard</u> ? ~ No, <u>she doesn't</u>.

1 (Jacob needs a ladder.)
_____ ? ~ Yes, _____.

2 (We don't need to go to the shops.)
_____ ? ~ No, _____.

3 (John doesn't need to leave before lunch.)
_____ ? ~ No, _____.

4 (They need to check the train times.)
_____ ? ~ Yes, _____.

Modal verbs

B Change each sentence in brackets ( ) into a negative sentence using *needn't* where possible. If not possible, write a negative sentence with *doesn't/don't need*.

- (Jasmine needs to pay James today.) Jasmine needn't pay James today.
- (The car needs new tyres.) The car doesn't need new tyres.
1. (We need a lot of red paper.)
2. (Mark needs to get everything ready today.)
3. (Mary needs to leave at six o'clock.)
4. (Anna needs a new bag.)

C When there are exams or competitions at Brightside School, the school provides certain things for all the students, but there are other things that the school does not provide. Use the information in the table to write sentences with *need to bring* or *needn't bring*.

Examinations	The school provides:	The school doesn't provide:
art exams	paint	brushes
maths exams	rubbers	pens and pencils
drawing exams	paper	rulers and pencils
tennis competitions	balls	racquets
football competitions	shirts	shorts and boots

- (art exams/paint) For art exams, students needn't bring paint.
- (tennis competitions/rackets) For tennis competitions, students need to bring rackets.
1. (maths exams/pens and pencils)
2. (football competitions/shirts)
3. (drawing exams/paper)
4. (art exams/brushes)
5. (tennis competitions/balls)
6. (football competitions/shorts and boots)
7. (maths exams/rubbers)
8. (drawing exams/rulers and pencils)

D Rewrite the sentences using *didn't need* or *needn't have* and the correct form.

- The programmes didn't cost us anything. We didn't pay for them.
  We didn't have to pay for the programmes.
- You took your umbrella yesterday but it didn't rain.
  You needn't have taken your umbrella yesterday.
1. Charlotte paid for her holiday in advance, but it wasn't necessary.
   Charlotte _____ for her holiday in advance.
2. My sister spoke to Ellie yesterday, so I didn't phone her.
   I _____ Ellie because my sister had spoken to her.
3. We bought extra food but now John and Mary can't come.
   We _____ extra food because John and Mary can't come.
4. Why did you work during the weekend? We don't have to finish until next week.
   You _____ during the weekend.
5. I didn't take my passport with me because an identity card was enough.
   I _____ my passport with me.

48 Had to do/go, should have done/gone

1 Look at this example:

Jasmine **had to wait** an hour for a bus.

Had to wait means that Jasmine waited because no bus came for an hour.

We use **had to** to talk about something that someone did because it was necessary.

If someone did not do something because it was not necessary, we use **didn't have to**:
I didn't have to work last Saturday. (= I didn't work because it was not necessary.)

The question form is **did ... have to**:
Did you **have to work** last Saturday?

2 Now consider this situation:

Grace's job includes working on Saturday. Last Saturday she was ill, so she didn't work:
Grace **should have gone** to work last Saturday, but she was ill. So she stayed at home.

We use **should have** (**done/gone**, etc.) to say that something which did not happen was the correct or best action. We can also use **should have** to criticize someone. Look at this example:

Peter, a farm worker, didn't close a gate, and the cows got into the wrong field:
Peter **should have closed** the gate.

We use **shouldn't have** (**done/gone**, etc.) to say that something which did happen was not the correct action:
I **shouldn't have got** angry with Jasmine. (= I got angry with Jasmine, but it was not a good thing to do.)
Peter **shouldn't have left** the gate open.

A Complete the dialogues with the words in brackets ( ) and *had to* or *did ... have to*.

♦ **James:** When you had that stomach trouble, _did you have to_ (you) go into hospital?
  Megan: No, _I didn't have to_ (not) go into hospital, but _I had to_ stay in bed for a week.

1 **Oliver:** Was there a translation in the exam?
  Jasmine: No, we _____ (not) translate anything, but we _____ write three essays.

2 **Anna:** I was very busy yesterday.
  William: What _____ (you) do?
  Anna: I _____ prepare everything for today's meeting.

3 **Nathan:** _____ (you) wear uniform when you were at school?
  Abigail: Yes, and we _____ make sure it was always neat and tidy.

4 **Tom:** What _____ (you) do to get your international driving licence?
  Tina: I _____ show the police my national driving licence, but I _____ (not) take another driving test.

5 **Mark:** Our children enjoyed their holiday at the summer camp.
  Mary: _____ (they) help at mealtimes?
  Mark: Well, they _____ (not) make the food, but they _____ (help) with the washing-up.

Modal verbs

B Complete the sentences with *should have* or *shouldn't have* for these situations.

- SITUATION: Raphael didn't take his medicine. Later he got very ill.
  Raphael *should have taken* his medicine.
- SITUATION: Sara drove her car when she was tired and she had an accident.
  Sara *shouldn't have driven* her car when she was tired.
1. SITUATION: Anthony didn't buy any sugar so he couldn't make a cake.
   Anthony _____ some sugar.
2. SITUATION: Ellie had a cold but she still went to the cinema. Later she had to stay in bed.
   Ellie _____ to the cinema.
3. SITUATION: Edward ate a lot of apples. Later he had stomach ache.
   Edward _____ so many apples.
4. SITUATION: Lucy didn't lock the door to her flat when she went to buy a newspaper. While she was away, someone stole her television.
   Lucy _____ the door when she went out.
5. SITUATION: Mary borrowed Tom's camera without asking him.
   Mary _____ Tom's camera without asking him.

C Some of the staff at the Information Office did not go to work last weekend because they were ill. Look at the work timetable and complete the sentences using the words in brackets ( ) and *had to, didn't have to,* or *should have*.

SATURDAY		SUNDAY	
On duty	Comments	On duty	Comments
Jenny	✓	Matt	✓
Noah	ill	Mary	✓
Jasmine	ill	Lewis	ill
Daniel	✓	Laura	ill

- (Jenny/Saturday) *Jenny had to work on Saturday.*
- (Matt/Saturday) *Matt didn't have to work on Saturday.*
- (Laura/Sunday) *Laura should have worked on Sunday* but she was ill.
1. (Matt/Sunday) _____
2. (Jasmine/Sunday) _____
3. (Lewis/Sunday) _____ but he was ill.
4. (Mary/Saturday) _____
5. (Noah/Saturday) _____ but he was ill.
6. (Daniel/Saturday) _____
7. (Jasmine/Saturday) _____ but she was ill.
8. (Lewis/Saturday) _____

Test E — Modal verbs

A Chris is going to Carstairs College in Scotland. Miranda is already studying there. Cross out the incorrect modal verb forms to complete their conversation.

Chris: ✦<u>Can I</u> / ~~Do I can~~ ask you a few questions about Carstairs?
Miranda: Of course. ¹<u>You should</u> / <u>You ought</u> to get as much information as possible before you go.
Chris: Do ²<u>I must</u> / <u>I have</u> to wear a uniform?
Miranda: No, but ³<u>you must</u> / <u>you have</u> dress smartly. You can't wear jeans.
Chris: ⁴<u>Should I</u> / <u>Had I</u> take my laptop with me?
Miranda: No, ⁵<u>you don't ought</u> / <u>you don't need</u> to! You have to write all your essays by hand!
Chris: What? Will ⁶<u>I be possible</u> / <u>I be able</u> to use email?
Miranda: No, I'm afraid not. Carstairs is very old-fashioned. Anyway, when are you leaving?
Chris: ⁷<u>I managed</u> / <u>I could</u> to get a ticket for the train this evening. ⁸<u>I should</u> / <u>I must</u> have reserved a seat, though. ⁹<u>I can</u> / <u>I may</u> have to stand all the way to Scotland.
Miranda: ¹⁰<u>Should I better</u> / <u>Had I better</u> give you a ring later and see how things are going?
Chris: Sure. Can I use my phone at college?
Miranda: Yes, don't worry. But ¹¹<u>you need</u> / <u>you must</u> switch it off during the school day.
Chris: OK. Can you give me any more advice?
Miranda: Yes. ¹²<u>You must</u> / <u>You ought</u> visit the lake near the college. It's beautiful!

B Olivia is emailing Sarah. The numbered words in the box are missing from the text. Put one number only in the text at the right place.

| ¹able | ²have | ³to | ⁴~~should~~ | ⁵managed | ⁶needn't | ⁷ought | ⁸couldn't | ⁹had |

I've had a terrible day! I ✦⁴ have got up early, but I couldn't get out of bed! It was too late to go by bus, so I to get a taxi. Luckily, I to find one quite quickly. Of course, when we arrived outside the office, I didn't have any money, so I pay the driver. Anyway, I was to borrow some from the receptionist. I've paid her back already, but do you think I to give her a present as well? My boss was waiting for me in her office. I should arrived at nine o'clock, and I was half an hour late. I have taken a taxi at all, though! She told me the company was closing, so I had find a new job!

C Mr and Mrs Buck are deciding what to take with them on holiday. Rewrite the sentences using the word in brackets ( ).

Mrs Buck: It's not necessary to take the tent. (need)
✦<u>We don't need to take the tent.</u>
We're not going camping again!

Mr Buck: The hotels will be full, possibly. (might)
The ¹ ....

Mrs Buck: Then it will be necessary to sleep in the car. (have)
Then we ² ....

Modal verbs

Mr Buck: Well, I think we've got everything we need. What's in that paper bag?
Mrs Buck: I'm sure it's the sun cream we got in Brighton. (must)
It ³ _____
Mr Buck: It wasn't necessary to buy it. (needn't)
We ⁴ _____
Mrs Buck: Is it a good idea to take it with us this time? (Should)
⁵ _____ ?
Mrs Buck: It's not possible for us to make the sun shine. (can't)
We ⁶ _____ ?
Mr Buck: The sun's always shining when you're with me, Maddie!
Mrs Buck: Are you feeling OK, George? Maybe you should have a rest. (better)
⁷ _____

D Michael is about to give a presentation. Use the words from the box to complete what he's saying.

| don't need to | should have | better start | ~~Can you~~ | could you pass |
| mustn't forget | might not | should really | Do I need to use | got to finish |

'*Can you* hear me at the back of the hall? ¹ _____ the microphone? Oh dear, it isn't working! You ² _____ move to the front if you can. Excuse me, ³ _____ this information around? Thank you. Have I brought enough copies? I haven't? I'm so sorry. Sir, I can see you don't have a seat, but you ⁴ _____ write anything in my presentation. I'll put everything on my website. I ⁵ _____ to give you the address at the end. Now, I've ⁶ _____ in 30 minutes, so we'd ⁷ _____. I'm sorry, Madam, but you ⁸ _____ be able to see the screen unless you move forward. Anyway, I ⁹ _____ started five minutes ago. Right, where are my notes?'

E Four friends are in a cafe. If the underlined modal verb forms are wrong, correct them. If they are right, put a tick (✓).

Tim: Is that your phone ringing, John?
John: Yes. It <u>can be</u> ◆ *must be* Dave. He said he would ring about now. No, wait a moment, it <u>can't be</u> ◆ ✓ Dave. That's not his number. I wonder who it is.
Phil: You'll <u>have to</u> ¹ _____ answer it if you want to know! Who's that by the window, Tim? Is it Alice?
Tim: It <u>needn't be</u> ² _____. She's in New York. She <u>must</u> ³ _____ go there on business last Monday.
Phil: Then it <u>must be</u> ⁴ _____ her sister or something.
John: That was someone called Louise on the phone. I don't know her …
Phil: But she <u>should have</u> ⁵ _____ your number!
John: … and she says she's in the café with us. By the window.
Tim: Really? Well, she <u>could be</u> ⁶ _____ the girl who looks like Alice.
John: <u>Shall I</u> ⁷ _____ speak to her?
Phil: You <u>don't ought</u> ⁸ _____ to, because she's coming over now.
Louise: Hi, John. I'm Alice's cousin. She gave me your number.
John: Have a seat. <u>Can I</u> ⁹ _____ get you a coffee?

49 Articles (1): a, an or the

1 Compare **a** and **an**:

We use **a** before words which begin with consonants (**b, c, d, f, g, h, j, k, l,** etc.):
   a doctor   **a b**ig car   **a** girl

We use **an** before words which begin with vowels (**a, e, i, o, u**):
   an apple   **an** interesting film

We also use **a** before **u** when it sounds like the word 'you'; and before **eu**:
   university (sound: 'you'): **a** university
   a European city

We also use **an** before words that begin with a silent **h**. Compare **hour** and **house**:
   hour (sound: 'our'): **an** hour
   house: **a** house

2 Compare **a/an** and **the**:

Mary: I bought **a** laptop and a TV yesterday.
Joe: Was **the** laptop expensive?

We usually use **a/an** with a noun to talk about a person or thing for the first time:
   a laptop

We use **the** when we talk about the person or thing again:
   the laptop (= the one that Mary bought)

3 There are some special uses of **a/an** and **the**:

▶ We use **a/an** with prices, frequency and speeds:
   It costs £2 **a** litre.
   I drink about three cups of coffee **a** day.
   You're driving at 150 kilometres **an** hour!

▶ We use **a/an** before **hundred**, **thousand**, and **million**:
   a hundred people   **a** thousand days

▶ We use **a/an** for talking about jobs:
   I'm **a** bank manager.

▶ We use **the** when there is only one of something:
   May I turn on **the** TV? (=There is only one TV in the room.)
   Where's Mary? ~ She's in **the** kitchen. (= There is only one kitchen in the house.)

▶ We use **the** with musical instruments:
   I play **the** guitar. Jasmine plays **the** violin.

A Complete the sentences using *a* or *an*.

♦ I bought _a_ new car yesterday.
1 She's reading _____ interesting book.
2 They've got _____ house in Spain.
3 It's _____ cheap restaurant.
4 He's _____ Italian businessman.

♦ It's _an_ old film.
5 The journey took _____ hour.
6 We've lost _____ black cat.
7 I want to buy _____ umbrella.
8 It was _____ difficult exam.

B Complete the sentences using the phrases from the box and *a* or *an*.

| European country | Indian river | ~~American director~~ |
| university town | Japanese city | English airport | German car |

♦ Steven Spielberg _is an American director_.
1 Tokyo is _____
2 Heathrow is _____

3 The Ganges is
4 Oxford is
5 A Mercedes is
6 Spain is

C Owen wants to take out an insurance policy so Mike Cox, an agent from the insurance company, is asking him some questions. Complete their conversation using *a*, *an*, or *the*.

Mr Cox: Hello, my name is Mike Cox. I am from ♦ *an* insurance company. I have ♦ *a* form with some questions. Your name is Owen Brent. Do you have ¹ _____ middle name?

Mr Brent: Yes, my full name is Owen Marcus Brent.

Mr Cox: All right. Now, where do you live, Owen?

Mr Brent: I live in ² _____ house in Peckham.

Mr Cox: Peckham, I see. And what is your job?

Mr Brent: I'm ³ _____ scientist. I work for ⁴ _____ government.

Mr Cox: Do you work in ⁵ _____ laboratory or in ⁶ _____ office?

Mr Brent: I work in ⁷ _____ small office in ⁸ _____ centre of London.

Mr Cox: And how do you get to ⁹ _____ office from Peckham?

Mr Brent: I usually take ¹⁰ _____ underground.

Mr Cox: What is your salary, Owen?

Mr Brent: Well, I earn almost £50,000 ¹¹ _____ year.

Mr Cox: Now, your family. You're married, aren't you?

Mr Brent: Yes, and we have two children, ¹² _____ girl and ¹³ _____ boy. ¹⁴ _____ girl is 16 and ¹⁵ _____ boy is 14.

Mr Cox: Fine. And you want to take out ¹⁶ _____ insurance policy for £100,000. Is that right?

Mr Brent: Yes, that's right.

Mr Cox: Well, that's all. Can you sign ¹⁷ _____ form here at ¹⁸ _____ bottom? Thank you.

D There are some mistakes in these sentences. If the underlined words are wrong, correct them. If they are right, put a tick (✓).

♦ I'm not sure what she does, but I think she's <u>a</u> ✓ doctor.
♦ I saw <u>the</u> *a* thousand different things when I was on holiday.
1 Be careful! That perfume costs £180 <u>a</u> _____ bottle.
2 We must invite him to the party. He plays <u>a</u> _____ piano and <u>a</u> _____ guitar.
3 A: What does John do?
   B: I'm not sure, but I think he is <u>the</u> _____ teacher in a school.
4 She likes to drive at <u>the</u> _____ hundred miles an hour.
5 I play <u>the</u> _____ violin in an orchestra. They pay me £300 <u>the</u> _____ day!
6 I've got <u>the</u> _____ hundred jobs to do before we leave.
7 A: Is my handbag in the living room?
   B: No, it isn't. I saw it in <u>a</u> _____ kitchen.

50 Articles 2: a/an, the or no article

1 We use **a/an** with singular nouns:
   He was reading **a** book.
   I saw **an** interesting film yesterday.

2 Look at this example:
   When I arrived, John was reading **a** book.

   We use **a/an** when it isn't necessary to make clear which particular thing we are talking about. There are lots of books; John was reading one of them.

   We use **a/an** to talk about people's jobs:
   James is **an** engineer. (= There are lots of engineers; James is one.)

   We use **a/an** to describe things or people:
   They have **a** beautiful house. (= There are lots of beautiful houses; they have one.)
   John is **an** old friend of mine.

3 We use **the** with singular or plural nouns:
   the book   **the** books

   We can use **the** with uncountable nouns (e.g. **music, water, food, education**):
   The water is in the fridge.

   Note:
   ▶ uncountable nouns do not have a plural (NOT two musics, three waters).
   ▶ we do not use **a/an** with uncountable nouns (NOT a music, a water).
   (See Unit 53.)

4 We use **the** when it is clear which person or thing we are talking about:
   Abigail was reading **a** book. She closed **the** book. (= She closed the book that she was reading.)
   Anna likes music, but she doesn't like **the** music that John plays.
   Mike's gone to **the** shops. (= the local shops)
   She's in **the** kitchen. (= the kitchen in this house)
   I must go to **the** bank. (= my bank, where I keep my money)
   the centre/**the** station/**the** airport (in a city)
   the River Thames (there is only one)
   the government (in my country)

5 We do not use **the** before plural nouns (e.g. **vegetables**) or uncountable nouns (e.g. **education, music**) when we are talking about something in general:
   Do you like **vegetables**? (= any vegetables)
   I think **education** is very important.

6 We do not use **a** or **the** before names of languages, meal names, the names of cities, most countries and most streets, and the names of airports, stations, single mountains or lakes:
   She speaks **Spanish**.
   She lives in **Montpellier** in **France**. (But we say **the** U.S.A., **the** United Kingdom.)
   What time will **lunch** be?
   from **Heathrow Airport** to **Oxford Street**

A Complete the sentences with *a*, *an* or *the* if required. Leave the gaps empty if nothing is required.

♦ I want to put some money into my bank account, so I'm going to _the_ bank this afternoon. It's in Midland Street.
1. I had _____ sandwich for _____ lunch today.
2. We flew to _____ Dusseldorf Airport in _____ Germany.
3. It was _____ long flight, but eventually we arrived in _____ U.S.A.
4. I'm trying to learn _____ Japanese. I'm having _____ lesson tomorrow.
5. He made _____ angry speech against _____ government.
6. She is _____ famous actor and she is appearing in _____ popular TV series.
7. They live in _____ Paris in _____ area near to _____ River Seine.
8. They've bought _____ small flat in _____ Park Street.

Articles, nouns, pronouns, etc.

B Complete the sentences with *a*, *an* or *the* if required. Leave the gaps empty if nothing is required. (Note that the following words in this exercise are uncountable nouns: *music, fuel, education, fish, food, coffee, exercise*.)

♦ She read _the_ emails that had arrived that morning.
1. It was a nice day, so we had _____ lunch in _____ garden of my house.
2. I'm just going to _____ shops. I'll be back in a few minutes.
3. We phoned for _____ taxi to take us to _____ airport.
4. I like listening to _____ music when I come home.
5. Without _____ fuel, _____ cars don't work.
6. John was at home. He was reading _____ magazine in _____ living room.
7. His parents believe that _____ education is a very important thing.
8. Jasmine doesn't like _____ fish; she never eats it.
9. After _____ dinner, I washed _____ plates and glasses.
10. Did you like _____ food at _____ party yesterday?
11. A: Where's _____ coffee?
    B: It's in _____ cupboard next to _____ sink.
12. Doctors say that _____ exercise is good for everybody.

C Complete this conversation with *a*, *an* or *the* if required. Leave the gaps empty if nothing is required.

Mike: Is Maria ♦ _a_ student at your college?
Rosie: No, she's ¹_____ old friend of mine. We were at school together.
Mike: What does she do now?
Rosie: She's ²_____ computer programmer. She's not English, you know. She comes from ³_____ Brazil, but she's living in ⁴_____ U.S.A. at the moment.
Mike: Has she got ⁵_____ job there?
Rosie: Yes, she's working for ⁶_____ big company there.
Mike: Do you send ⁷_____ emails to each other?
Rosie: Yes, and I had ⁸_____ long email from her yesterday.
Mike: What did she say in ⁹_____ email?
Rosie: She said that she was living in ¹⁰_____ nice apartment in ¹¹_____ centre of ¹²_____ Chicago.

D Complete the story with *a*, *an* or *the*.

Yesterday I was sitting on ♦ _the_ six o'clock train when I saw ¹_____ strange man walking along the platform. He came into the carriage of ²_____ train where I was sitting, and he sat in the seat opposite mine. He opened ³_____ newspaper and started reading it. On ⁴_____ front page of ⁵_____ newspaper, there was ⁶_____ picture of ⁷_____ bank robber. The words under ⁸_____ picture were: 'Wanted by the police'. It was ⁹_____ same man!

51 Plural nouns; one and ones

1 We normally form plural nouns by adding **-s**:

SINGULAR		PLURAL
a cup	→	some cups
one student	→	three students
the cat	→	the cats

2 **one** and **ones**

Sometimes we use **one** instead of repeating a singular noun:

I'm going to buy **a drink**. Would you like **one**?
Our **house** is the **one** with the red door.

Or, we use **ones** instead of a plural noun:

Shall I buy the red **apples** or the green **ones**?
These **biscuits** are cheaper than those **ones**.

3 We often use **Which one ...?** and **Which ones ...?** in questions:

Shop assistant: **Which one** would you like, the black dress or the pink one?
Mary: I'd like the black one, please.

James: I like the black and white photographs. **Which ones** do you like? The black and white ones or the colour ones?
Lucy: I prefer the colour ones.

4 But we form some plural nouns differently:

MAN	→	MEN	+ -ES		
woman	→	women	bus	→	buses
child	→	children	kiss	→	kisses
person	→	people	wish	→	wishes
foot	→	feet	watch	→	watches
tooth	→	teeth	match	→	matches
sheep	→	sheep	box	→	boxes
mouse	→	mice	potato	→	potatoes
fish	→	fish	tomato	→	tomatoes

-Y	→	-IES	-F/-FE	→	-VES
family	→	families	loaf	→	loaves
city	→	cities	wife	→	wives
country	→	countries	knife	→	knives

(For more information plural nouns, **see Appendix 1**, page 242.)

A Complete the picture labels with plural nouns.

♦

Some *boxes*

1

Some ....

2

Two ....

3

Some ....

4

Four ....

5

Some ....

6

Some ....

7

Four ....

8

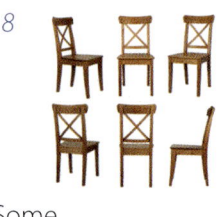

Some ....

9

Some ....

10

Two ....

11

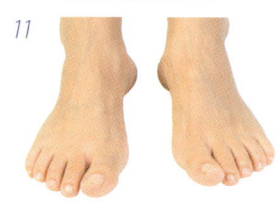

Two ....

Articles, nouns, pronouns, etc.

B Tick (✓) the correct plural forms and cross out the incorrect ones.

- knives ✓
- ~~matchs~~
- countries
- wishes
- wives
- mans
- tooths
- citys
- potatoes
- tomatos
- potatos
- mice
- matches
- cities
- teeth
- mouses
- countrys
- knifes
- wishs
- men
- familys
- wifes
- tomatoes
- families

C Replace one of the nouns in the sentences in brackets ( ) with *one* or *ones*.

- He's just bought a new suit.
  (It's a blue suit.) It's a blue one.
- A: Who is your favourite actor?
  B: (The actor that I like best is Joe Late.) The one that I like best is Joe Late.

1. I'm going to buy an orange juice.
   (Would you like an orange juice?)
2. The chocolate cakes are popular.
   (But the strawberry cakes are nicer.)
3. A: Which house do you like?
   B: (I like the house with the red door.)
4. I bought a blue carpet last time.
   (This time I want a green carpet.)
5. English is a difficult language.
   (There isn't an easy language.)
6. A: Where did you put the photos?
   B: (Do you mean the photos that we took in Turkey?)

D Elliot and Ellen are buying things for their new apartment. Complete their conversation with *one* or *ones*.

Ellen: Here's the china department. We need some cups.
Elliot: Do we want large ◆ ones or small [1] ____ ?
Ellen: Small [2] ____ are best.
Elliot: But I like tea in a large cup.
Ellen: OK, put six small cups and a large [3] ____ in the basket.
Elliot: What about a teapot? There's a metal [4] ____ and a nice china [5] ____. Which [6] ____ do you like?
Ellen: I prefer the china [7] ____.
Elliot: It's similar to the little cups but it's not like my big [8] ____.
Ellen: Well, it doesn't have to be exactly the same. Now, we also need knives.
Elliot: Can't we use the [9] ____ that my mother gave us?
Ellen: Well, I suppose the big [10] ____ for bread is all right, but we certainly need some little [11] ____ for vegetables and a sharp [12] ____ for meat.
Elliot: All right. Where are the knives?

52 This, that, these, those

1 Look at these examples:
- **This** exercise is difficult.
- **These** are very expensive!
- What is **that**?
- Did you eat **those** sandwiches?

2 Here are the singular and plural forms:

SINGULAR		PLURAL
this car	→	**these** cars
that car	→	**those** cars

We use **this**, **that**, **these**, and **those** with nouns (e.g. **painting**, **apple**):
- I like **this painting**.
- **Those apples** are delicious.

We use **this**, **that**, **these**, and **those** without a noun, when the meaning is clear. For example:

A student has just finished his homework, and he says to his friend:
- **That** was easy! (= the homework)

Mike meets his mother at the station. He picks up her suitcases, and he says:
- **These** are heavy! (= the cases)

3 We use **this** and **these** for things which are near to us, and **that** and **those** for things which are not near. Look at these pictures:

Look at **this**.

Look at **those**.

4 Things which are happening now are near to us in time, so we use **this** and **these**:

John (at a concert):
- Some of **these** songs are beautiful.

Things which are finished are not near to us, so we use **that** or **those**:

John (after leaving the concert):
- Some of **those** songs were beautiful.

A Put *this* or *these* in the gaps.

♦ I'd like to buy **this** book, please. How much is it?
1. Could you tell me where _____ bus goes, please?
2. _____ questions are difficult. Could you help me?
3. _____ sandwiches are mine. Yours are on the table.
4. _____ is wonderful! I love a hot bath after work.
5. Have you got some cheaper pens? _____ are very expensive.

Put *that* or *those* in the gaps.

6. Look at _____ clouds. I'm sure it's going to rain.
7. Did you enjoy _____ film? I thought it was boring.
8. Let's cross the road. _____ taxi is free.
9. _____ apartments are all very expensive, because they're in the centre of town.
10. _____ was delicious! I was so hungry.

Articles, nouns, pronouns, etc.

B You are at the greengrocer's. Ask how much the fruit and vegetables are. Use *How much …?*, the words from the box, and *these* or *those*.

THERE: ~~cucumbers~~   pineapples   lemons   bananas   tomatoes

HERE: ~~oranges~~   pears   cabbages   potatoes   melons

♦ How much are those cucumbers?
♦ How much are these oranges?
1
2
3
4
5
6
7
8

C Complete the dialogue with *this*, *that*, *these*, or *those*.

James: It's very pleasant to sit here on ♦ this _____ terrace in the middle of ¹_____ mountains.
Anna: Yes, and the food is good. ² _____ grapes are delicious.
James: Delicious, yes, but ³ _____ one's bad. What are ⁴ _____ people over there eating?
Anna: Oh, ⁵ _____ is fondue. It's made with cheese. You see, they take one of ⁶ _____ little pieces of bread and then dip it in ⁷ _____ pot with the cheese in it.
James: We can try ⁸ _____ if we come again.
Anna: All the local restaurants serve it. So if we don't come back here, we can have it at ⁹ _____ little restaurant in the village.
James: Yes, but in the village you don't have ¹⁰ _____ wonderful view of the mountains.

53 Countable and uncountable nouns

1 Most nouns have singular and plural forms:

house/houses   dog/dogs   man/men

We call these nouns countable nouns, because we can count them:

one house   two dogs   three men

We can use **a**, **some** and **the** with countable nouns:

	SINGULAR	PLURAL
a:	a house	–
some:	–	some houses
the:	the house	the houses

2 Some nouns have only one form. We call these uncountable nouns, because we cannot count them:

water   bread   petrol
golf   tennis rain

Look at these pictures:

rain (uncountable)   cars (countable)

We do not use **a** or **one**, **two**, **three**, etc. before uncountable nouns, but we can use **some** or **the**:

a: We need to buy bread and sugar.
some: Let's stop the car. We need some petrol.
the: Look at the rain!

3 Here is a list of common uncountable nouns and some of the words we use in front of them:

a	glass / bottle	of	water / milk
a	cup	of	tea / coffee
a	spoonful	of	sugar / coffee
a	slice / piece	of	cake / bread / toast / cheese
a	piece	of	information / luggage / news / advice / homework
some			money / petrol / snow

We can use **some** with all these words. We also use **grams**, **kilos**, **litres**, etc. in shops:

Can I have two **litres** of **milk**, please?

4 Some nouns can be countable or uncountable:

UNCOUNTABLE:
I like **tea**.
Her **hair** is red.
I haven't got **time**.
I always have **sugar** in my tea.

COUNTABLE:
I'll have **two teas**, please. (= cups of tea)
There's **a hair** in my tea.
We had **a good time**.
Three sugars in my tea, please.

A Put a circle around the uncountable nouns below.

house	cat	cheese	car	coat	snow	lemon
(advice)	clock	table	tea	ball	museum	apple
painting	petrol	news	cigar	teacher	film	rain
holiday	office	bed	pen	sugar	homework	watch
tennis	doctor	cinema	luggage	chair	banana	information
cup	coffee	shoe	shirt	money	exam	hour

Articles, nouns, pronouns, etc.

city	park	toast	sock	nose	water	school
bread	book	jumper	cloud	milk	bike	television

B Choose the correct word in brackets ( ) to complete the sentences.

♦ (slice/piece/cup) I'd like a *cup* of coffee, please.
1 (glass/slice/spoonful) Would you like a .... of cheese on your toast?
2 (pieces/cups/bottles) My father gave me two .... of advice.
3 (slice/bottle/piece) Could you buy a .... of milk at the shops?
4 (spoonful/piece/cup) That was a difficult .... of homework!
5 (glass/piece/slice) Would you give me a .... of water, please?
6 (slices/cups/pieces) How many .... of luggage do you have?
7 (spoonfuls/glasses/cups) I normally take three .... of sugar in my tea.
8 (pieces/slices/litres) I've just put 40 .... of petrol in the car.
9 (piece/slice/glass) I need a .... of information.
10 (piece/kilo/slice) I'd like half a .... of coffee, please.

C Put a tick (✓) if the sentence is correct, and a cross (✗) if it is incorrect.

♦ We live in a flat. ✓
♦ I have some moneys. ✗
1 The car needs a petrol. ....
2 She takes a milk in her tea. ....
3 Mary likes tea; I prefer coffee. ....
4 He's got some new games. ....
5 Two glasses of water. ....
6 A table and two chairs. ....
7 Give me two toasts. ....
8 A snow comes in winter. ....
9 Give me some cup of tea. ....
10 Tim doesn't eat meat. ....
11 Two coffees, please. ....
12 Please buy some sugar. ....
13 Two kilos of a bread. ....
14 We have two homeworks. ....
15 I need some information. ....
16 We need some bananas. ....
17 Have we got a butter? ....
18 I like some egg for breakfast. ....
19 I can see some young women. ....
20 Can you see the moon? ....

D Complete the sentences with the words from the box.

| a (x2) | bottle | cartons | cup (x2) | pieces | slice (x2) | some (x4) | the (x4) | two (x2) |

♦ My father has *a* motorbike.
1 After school I have a .... of bread with .... butter on it.
2 Tom has got three .... of luggage.
3 Lucy always has a .... of coffee after lunch.
4 For this experiment we need a glass .... with .... water in it.
5 We want .... coffees, please – one white and one black.
6 We must stop at a garage and put .... petrol in .... car.
7 How much is .... bottle of Coke at .... supermarket?
8 There are two .... of milk in .... fridge.
9 Can I have a .... of tea and a .... of cake, please?
10 There are .... hairs in .... bath. Both are long and blond.

54 A, some, any, no

1 Look at these pictures:

a pen   *some pens*   *some food*   *no food*

2 We use **a** with singular countable nouns (e.g. **pen**, **car**, **friend**):
- I bought **a pen** yesterday.
- Do you have **a car**?
- He doesn't have **a friend**.

(For countable and uncountable nouns, see **Unit 53**.)

3 We use **some** or **any** with plural countable nouns (**pens**, **friends**, **books**):
- I bought **some** new pens yesterday.
- John doesn't have **any** friends.
- Do you have **any** books about Africa?

4 We use some or any with uncountable nouns (e.g. **money**, **information**, **advice**, **news**, **music**, **coffee**, **milk**, **toast**, **bread**, **food**, **water**, **snow**):
- I haven't got **any** money.
- Did the teacher give you **any** advice?
- I would like **some** coffee, please.

5 POSITIVE

We normally use **some** in positive sentences:
- She took **some photos**.
- I'd like **some information**, please.

But we sometimes use **any** like this:
- You can leave at **any** time. (= It doesn't matter when you leave.)
- Take **any** book. (= It doesn't matter which book you take.)

6 NEGATIVE

We usually use **any** in negative sentences:
- I did**n't** see **any** good **films** last year.
- We have**n't** got **any food**.

We sometimes use **no** instead of **not ... any**:
- I'm sorry, there are **no** buses to the museum.
- The shops are shut, and we've got **no** food.

7 QUESTIONS

We use **any** in questions:
- Do you speak **any** Russian?

But we use **some** in requests:
- Can you give me **some information**?

We also use **some** when we offer something:
- Would you like **some coffee**?

A Put the words in brackets ( ) in the correct order to make sentences.

♦ A: Can I help you, sir?
B: (to buy – for my living – room. – furniture – I'd – some – like)
   Yes, please. I'd like to buy some furniture for my living room.

1 A: Shall we go into town this afternoon?
B: Why? (shops open today. – any – There – aren't)

2 A: (Can I – cheese, please? – some – have)

B: Of course. How much would you like?

3 A: (any – in Cambridge? – museums – Are there)

B: I don't know. We can find out at the Tourist Information Centre.

Articles, nouns, pronouns, etc.

4 A: I'd like to go to Bristol, please.
   B: Certainly, madam. (any – You – train from platform 9. – can take)

5 A: I'd love to go to South America.
   B: Really? (you speak – Spanish? – Do – any)

6 A: I'm hungry! We haven't eaten all day. Look at that wonderful restaurant!
   B: Wait a moment! (money – with us. – We haven't – any – brought)

B Make the following statements negative. Use *not … any*.

♦ We've got some photos of our holiday.
We haven't got any photos of our holiday.

1 She gave me some advice.

2 There are some good films at the cinema this week.

3 You'll find some cake in the cupboard.

4 Maria had some heavy luggage with her at the airport.

5 There are some letters for you today.

6 We saw some snow on the mountains this morning.

C Tom and Tina are writing a shopping list. Complete their conversation with *a, some, any* or *no*.

Tom: We haven't got ♦ *any* eggs so we need to buy ♦ *some*.
Tina: No, no. There are ¹ .... in the fridge, but there's ² .... cheese.
Tom: OK, cheese. Now, we've got ³ .... fruit in the sitting room but we haven't got enough for the weekend so we need to buy ⁴ .... more. What else?
Tina: We want to have ⁵ .... salad for lunch, I think.
Tom: Yes, of course. So we need ⁶ .... lettuce. Oh, and ⁷ .... tomatoes because there aren't ⁸ .... in the kitchen.
Tina: We must buy ⁹ .... bottle of oil as well.
Tom: OK, and I want to buy ¹⁰ .... newspaper because there's ¹¹ .... football match on TV this afternoon and I want to know what the reporters are predicting.
Tina: But there are ¹² .... football matches today because the weather is so bad. We can go and see ¹³ .... film instead.
Tom: Oh, all right. Anyway, are there ¹⁴ .... more things to put on the list?
Tina: No, I think that's everything. I hope you've got ¹⁵ .... money because I haven't got ¹⁶ ....
Tom: OK. Put ¹⁷ .... coat on and get ¹⁸ .... shopping bag and we're ready.

55 I and me (subject and object pronouns)

1 Look at this:

SUBJECT +	VERB +	OBJECT
Mary	saw	Peter and Paul.
She	saw	them.

Note that we can use **she** (subject pronoun) instead of **Mary**, and **them** (object pronoun) instead of **Peter** and **Paul**.

2 Here are the subject and object pronouns:

		SUBJECT		OBJECT
Singular	1	I	9	me
	2	you	10	you
	3	he	11	him
	4	she	12	her
	5	it	13	it
Plural	6	we	14	us
	7	you	15	you
	8	they	16	them

We must always have a subject in English:
They are coming. (NOT ~~Are coming.~~)

3 Look at the subject and object pronouns (1–16) in this conversation:

A: [1]**I** saw Michelle yesterday, but [4]**she** didn't see [9]**me**.
B: Are [2]**you** going to see [12]**her** tomorrow?
A: No, I'm meeting Steve. [6]**We**'re playing golf.
B: [7]**You**'re both beginners! [5]**It** isn't an easy game. I played [13]**it** last year and I was terrible!
A: Why don't you come with [14]**us**? We can help [10]**you**.
B: I would like to play with [15]**you** both tomorrow, but my brother is leaving in the afternoon. [3]**He** is catching the two o'clock train, and we're taking [11]**him** to the station. He's spending a month with our aunt and uncle. [8]**They** live in Scotland. I stayed with [16]**them** last year.

4 We use **it** for things and for the weather, time, days, dates, distances, and for animals:
I'm studying economics. **It**'s a difficult subject.
It's hot today.
It's four o'clock.
It's Tuesday. **It**'s the third of April.
It's 200 miles to York.
Look at that bird! **It**'s eating the bread.

A Rewrite these sentences using subject and object pronouns instead of the underlined words.

♦ John and I saw Peter yesterday. He bought John and me a cup of coffee.
We saw Peter yesterday. He bought us a cup of coffee.

1 David and Mike are arriving today. I'm meeting David and Mike at the station.
....

2 I'm looking for Mary. Have you seen Mary? Mary isn't at home.
....

3 John and I saw a film called *The Tiger* yesterday. Have you seen *The Tiger*?
....

4 Come to the swimming pool with Joanna and me. Joanna and I are leaving now.
....

5 George and Jasmine are meeting Paul today. Paul is having lunch with George and Jasmine.
....

6 There's Jack! Jack's got a heavy suitcase. Shall we help Jack?
....

Articles, nouns, pronouns, etc.

B Look at the pictures and put pronouns in the gaps.

♦   I   him
1   I   her
2   she   it
3   we   you
4   they   him
5   it   them
6   you   us
7   I   you

♦   I   saw him   , but he   didn't see me   .
1   ____ saw ____ , but ____ didn't see ____ .
2   ____ saw ____ , but ____ didn't see ____ .
3   ____ saw ____ , but ____ didn't see ____ .
4   ____ saw ____ , but ____ didn't see ____ .
5   ____ saw ____ , but ____ didn't see ____ .
6   ____ saw ____ , but ____ didn't see ____ .
7   ____ saw ____ , but ____ didn't see ____ .

C James is talking about himself and his family. Put subject pronouns (*I*, *you*, etc.) in the gaps.

Hi! ♦ I _____ am James and ¹ _____ live in Australia. ² _____ 've got two brothers. ³ _____ 're called Pete and Mike. My mother works at the hospital. ⁴ _____ is a doctor. My father works in a sports shop. ⁵ _____ works very hard. The shop makes a lot of money, and ⁶ _____ 's always full of people.

Now put object pronouns (*me*, *you*, etc.) in the gaps.

On Saturdays I work for my father. I help ⁷ _____ in the shop, and he gives ⁸ _____ some money. On Sundays we go to the beach. We have two dogs, and we take ⁹ _____ with us. We also take a ball and they play with ¹⁰ _____ on the beach while we swim in the sea.

Now put object or subject pronouns in the gaps.

At the moment I'm at university. I'm studying Business. ¹¹ _____ 's an interesting subject. Two of my schoolfriends are at university with ¹² _____ . Our teachers are good but ¹³ _____ give ¹⁴ _____ a lot of work to do. Next week ¹⁵ _____ are all taking our first exams. I want to get good marks in ¹⁶ _____ .

56 There or it/they

1 Look at these sentences:
   There is a big market near the river; **it is** very good for fruit and meat.
   There are two buses on Sunday; **they** both go to the station.

We use **there is/are** when we talk about something for the first time in a conversation, and when we say where it is or when it is. We do not use **there** to talk about the same thing again; we use singular **it** (here meaning 'the big market') or plural **they** (here meaning 'the two buses'). Here are some more examples:
   There are two schools here; **they** are both new.
   There's a good programme on Sunday; **it** gives all the sports news.

2 We use **there** with different forms of **be**:
   There weren't any laptops 50 years ago.
   A: **Have there been** any problems this year?
   B: Yes, **there have**.
   There used to be a park here. (= There was a park here but it isn't here now.)
   There may be some eggs in the fridge. (= It is possible that there are some eggs.)

3 We also use **there is/are** etc. to talk about the number of people or things in a place. Look at these questions and answers:
   A: How many people **were there** at your party?
   B: **There were** about 12.
      (NOT ~~We were about 12.~~)
   A: **Are there** many restaurants here?
   B: Yes, **there must be** ten or more.
      (NOT ~~They must be ten.~~)

We can use **of us**, **of them**, etc. after the number:
   There were about 12 **of us**.

4 For the weather, we use **it** with a verb or adjective, but **there** with a noun:

> **it** + verb: It **rained/snowed** a lot last winter.
> **it** + adjective: It was **foggy/sunny/windy/cloudy**.
> **there** + noun: There was a lot of **fog/cloud**.

5 Notice these examples with **it takes**:
   It takes seven years to become a doctor.
   A: How long **does it take** to make bread?
   B: **It takes** several hours (to make bread).

These sentences describe the time that is necessary to do something.

A Complete the sentences using *there is*, *there are*, *it is* or *they are*.

♦ _There are_ two cinemas in our town; _they are_ both near my flat.
1 _____ one train on Sundays; _____ an express train.
2 _____ two national holidays this month, and _____ both on a Friday.
3 _____ several trees in our garden, but _____ not very tall.
4 _____ a big lake in the park; _____ very deep.

B Write answers to the questions using *There were ... of* and the words in brackets ( ).

♦ A: How many people were there at your party?
  B: (20/us) _There were 20 of us._
1 A: How many of you were there in the car?
  B: (five/us) _____
2 A: How many sailors were there in the boat?
  B: (six/them) _____
3 A: How many people were there at the supper?
  B: (12/us) _____

Articles, nouns, pronouns, etc.

C Rewrite the sentences using the words in brackets ( ) and *it* or *there*.

♦ There's a lot of snow in December.
(snows a lot) It snows a lot in December.

♦ It's quite cloudy this morning.
(quite a lot of cloud) There's quite a lot of cloud this morning.

1 There's a lot of rain in April.
(rains a lot)

2 It's foggy on the motorway this morning.
(fog on the motorway)

3 There are a lot of clouds in the mountains.
(very cloudy)

4 It's very windy on the west coast.
(a lot of wind)

D Complete the sentences using *there* and the words from the box. Use each word from the box once.

| have been | is | may be | used to be | was | will be |

♦ There is an accident on this road almost every day.

1 Last year .... a terrible fire at that factory.
2 Next Monday at seven o'clock .... a meeting of the committee.
3 When I was young, ... a lot more cinemas than there are now.
4 Since 1900 .... two world wars.
5 .... a late-night bus, but I'm not sure if there is.

E Look at the times needed to prepare certain foods, then write a statement or a question and answer.

bake bread – about three hours	~~prepare a salad – about ten minutes~~
cook a stew – about two hours	cook an omelette – a few minutes
~~boil an egg – about three minutes~~	make tea – about five minutes.
make a cake – about an hour.	

♦ It takes about three minutes to boil an egg.

♦ A: How long does it take to prepare a salad?
  B: It takes about ten minutes.

1 It .... an omelette.

2 A: How long .... tea?
  B: ....

3 It .... bread.

4 A: How long .... stew?
  B: ....

5 It .... a cake.

123

57 My, your; mine, yours

1 Look at these sentences:

This car belongs to **me**. It's **my** car. It's **mine**.

2 Now look at this table:

OBJECT PRONOUN	POSSESSIVE ADJECTIVE	POSSESSIVE PRONOUN
me	my	mine
you	your	yours
him	his	his
her	her	hers
it	its	its
us	our	ours
you	your	yours
them	their	theirs

3 **my**, **your**, etc.

▸ We use **my**, **your**, etc. with nouns:
  my book   **his** hands   **their** house

▸ We say:
  Anthony and **his** wife. (NOT ... ~~her wife~~.)
  Sara and **her** husband.
  (NOT ... ~~his husband~~.)

▸ We use possessive adjectives with parts of the body:
  Her hair is red.   **My** hands are cold.

4 **mine**, **yours**, etc.

▸ We use **mine**, **yours**, etc. instead of **my book**, **your keys**, etc:
  My flat is in the centre of town. Where's **yours**? (yours = your flat)

▸ We often use possessive pronouns in comparative sentences:
  Our cat is smaller than **theirs**.
  (theirs = their cat)
  Your house is older than **mine**.
  (mine = my house)

▸ We use **a/some** + **noun** + **of** + **possessive pronoun** to talk about one of a number of people or things:
  I went to the club with **a friend of mine**.
  (= one of my friends)

5 We do NOT use **a/an** or **the** with possessive adjectives or pronouns:
  It's ~~a~~ my bag. They're ~~the~~ ours.

6 **'s** or **s'**

▸ We use **'s** with singular nouns or names:
  When is the team**'s** next game?
  I went to Sam**'s** house.

▸ We use **s'** with plural nouns that end with **-s**:
  She borrowed her parents**'** car.

▸ We use **'s** with plural nouns that do not end with **-s**:
  Many people**'s** jobs are difficult.

▸ Remember that **its** and **it's** are different:
  I've got a new dog. **Its** name is Pluto.
  (Its = possessive adjective)
  It's cold today. (It's = It is)

(See **Unit 35**.)

A Complete the sentences using possessive adjectives (*my*, *your*, etc.) and possessive pronouns (*mine*, *yours*, etc.)

♦ This car belongs to me. This is *my* car. It's *mine*.
1 That ticket belongs to you. That's _____ ticket. It's _____.
2 These shoes belong to her. These are _____ shoes. They're _____.
3 This house belongs to them. This is _____ house. It's _____.
4 Those books belong to him. Those are _____ books. They're _____.
5 That bag belongs to me. That's _____ bag. It's _____.
6 This key belongs to her. This is _____ key. It's _____.
7 Those coats belong to us. Those are _____ coats. They're _____.
8 These pens belong to me. These are _____ pens. They're _____.
9 That watch belongs to him. That's _____ watch. It's _____.

Articles, nouns, pronouns, etc.

B Look at the pictures and complete the sentences. Use *my*, *your*, etc. and *mine*, *yours*, etc.

me   you   him

us   them   her

♦ Those are his   keys.
1 That book is _____ .
2 These pens are _____ .
3 That's _____ money.
4 This bike is _____ .
5 That ruler is _____ .

6 This is _____ car.
7 Those are _____ sandwiches.
8 Is this bag _____ ?
9 Those apples are _____ .
10 This is _____ phone.
11 Is this _____ watch?

C If the underlined words are correct, put a tick (✓). If they are wrong, write the correct words.

♦ Look at the sky! <u>Its</u> going to rain.   It's
♦ Is that <u>Erica's</u> car?   ✓
1 Those photos on the table are <u>the mine</u>.
2 I met <u>a friend of me</u> at the shops.
3 The <u>childrens'</u> toys were on the floor.
4 I can't do this exercise. <u>Its</u> very difficult.
5 I like all of that <u>writers'</u> books.
6 <u>People's</u> opinions often change.
7 The <u>workers'</u> wages are very low so they are very unhappy.
8 They were talking about the <u>world's</u> problems.
9 Shall we give the cat <u>it's</u> food?
10 She stayed with <u>some relatives of hers</u> in Spain.

D Replace the words in brackets ( ) with possessive pronouns (*mine*, *yours*, etc.).

♦ My car is faster than (your car).   yours
1 Her house is bigger than (my house).
2 Your watch is more expensive than (his watch).
3 My exams are more difficult than (their exams).
4 Their garden is more beautiful than (our garden).
5 Your son is younger than (her son).
6 My husband is stronger than (your husband).
7 Her job is harder than (his job).

58 Myself, yourself, etc.; each other

1 Look at this table:

SUBJECT PRONOUNS	OBJECT PRONOUNS	REFLEXIVE PRONOUNS
I	me	myself
you (singular)	you	yourself
he	him	himself
she	her	herself
it	it	itself
we	us	ourselves
you (plural)	you	yourselves
they	them	themselves

We use **myself**, **yourself**, **herself**, etc. to refer to the subject:

Be careful. **You** might hurt **yourself**.

I bought **myself** a new shirt.
He taught **himself** to swim.
They enjoyed **themselves** at the concert.

2 Compare these sentences:

Jenny made Jo a cup of coffee.
(= Jenny made the coffee for Jo.)

Jenny made **herself** a cup of coffee.
(= Jenny made the coffee for herself.)

3 We also use **myself**, **yourself**, etc. to emphasize that the subject did the action, not another person:

He built the whole house **himself**.
(= He built it alone; nobody helped him.)

4 We use **each other** like this:

Tom and Lucy were talking to **each other**.
(= Tom was talking to Lucy, and Lucy was talking to Tom.)
We like **each other** very much.
(= I like her and she likes me.)

Compare **themselves** and **each other**:

Oliver and Ruth took these photographs **themselves**. (= They took them, not another person.)
Oliver and Ruth took photographs of **each other**. (= Oliver took a photograph of Ruth, and Ruth took a photograph of Oliver.)

A Fill the gaps with *myself, yourself*, etc.

♦ I cooked _myself_ a meal and then I watched television.
1 I'm sure he'll enjoy _____ on his trip.
2 I cut _____ while I was preparing the vegetables.
3 We amused _____ by playing cards while we were waiting for the plane.
4 She put the plates on the table and told them to help _____ to the food.
5 Tom hurt _____ when he was playing football.
6 Oliver cooked _____ a snack when he got home.

B Complete the sentences with the correct verb tenses and *myself, yourself*, etc. in the correct place.

♦ (you/cut) Be careful with that knife or _you'll cut yourself_ _____ .
1 (enjoy/very much) It was a very nice trip and we _____ .
2 (burn) I _____ while I was taking the dish out of the oven.
3 (He/teach) He didn't have lessons. _____ .

Articles, nouns, pronouns, etc.

4 (I think I/buy) .... a new coat tomorrow.
5 (She/make/a sandwich) .... and ate it in the kitchen.

C Complete the sentences with *myself, yourself,* etc.

♦ Did you paint the room _yourself_ ? ~ Yes, it took me three days to do it.
1 If you won't help me, I'll have to do it all ....
2 She fixes her car ....
3 The students organized the concert ....
4 We painted the whole house ....
5 He makes all his clothes ....

D Complete the sentences using the words in brackets ( ) and *myself, yourself,* etc. at the end of the sentence.

♦ (She is a very successful singer. She/write/all her songs/.)
   She is a very successful singer. _She writes all her songs herself._
1 Could you send this parcel for me? ~ (No, I'm sorry, I won't have time. You/have/to send it/.)
   No, I'm sorry, I won't have time. ....
2 (Nobody helped us, so we/carry/all our luggage/.)
   Nobody helped us, so ....
3 (This is an excellent photograph./you/take it/?)
   This is an excellent photograph. ....
4 (She was wearing a dress that she/make/.)
   She was wearing a dress that ....
5 (I hope you like the present. I/choose/it/.)
   I hope you like the present. ....
6 (Do you like this meal? I/invent/the recipe/.)
   Do you like this meal? ....

E Complete the sentences with *each other, ourselves, yourselves* or *themselves*.

♦ They spent the whole evening arguing with _each other_ .
♦ Their house is very beautiful; they designed it _themselves_ .
1 Mary met John in April, but they didn't see .... again until July.
2 They're not friends; in fact, they don't like .... at all.
3 Don't ask me to help you. You must do it ....
4 We didn't buy it .... A friend bought it for us.
5 I could hear two people shouting at ....
6 We're working in the same office now, so Ron and I see .... every day.

59 Direct and indirect objects

1 Look at this example:

(i) She gave **her friend** the book.
(ii) She gave the book **to her friend**.

In both sentences **a book** is the thing which is given, and **her friend** is the person who receives it.

2 Here are other sentences like (i):

	+ PERSON (indirect object)	+ THING (direct object)
She **gave**	her brother	a shirt.
He **sent**	me	an email.
I **showed**	him	my passport.
Jasmine **lent**	Frank	some money.
I'll **offer**	her	a job.
I'll **cook**	them	a meal.
I **fetched**	her	a plate.
I'll **get**	you	a magazine.
I'll **buy**	you	a coffee.

3 Here are some other sentences like (ii):

	+ THING (direct object)	+ PERSON (to + object)
She **gave**	a shirt	**to** her brother.
I **sent**	postcards	**to** my friends.
I **showed**	my card	**to** the clerk.
She **lent**	some money	**to** her friend.
He **offered**	the chocolates	**to** the others.

Note that we use **to** + object after these verbs which express the idea of giving or showing something to somebody:

   give   send   show   lend   offer

But we use **for** + object after verbs which express the idea of doing something for another person:

   cook   fetch   buy   get (= 'fetch' or 'buy')

	+ THING (direct object)	+ PERSON (for + object)
We **cooked**	a meal	**for** everybody.
He **fetched**	the newspaper	**for** his father.
I'll **get**	your book	**for** you.
She **bought**	some toys	**for** them.

A Put the words in brackets into the correct order to make sentences.

♦ (He – lent – his car – Mark – .)
He lent Mark his car.

1 (a sweet – James – She offered – .)

2 (Mary – his holiday photographs – He showed – .)

3 (them – an invitation – Have you sent – ?)

4 (a birthday present – Did you buy – her – ?)

5 (I – some of my books – a friend – gave – .)

6 (When you go to the pharmacy, – some tissues – me – could you get – ?)

Articles, nouns, pronouns, etc.

B Now write the sentences from Exercise A again, but using *to* or *for*.

- ♦ He lent his car to Mark.
- 1 She offered
- 2 He showed
- 3 Have you sent
- 4 Did you buy
- 5 I gave
- 6 When you go to the pharmacy, could you get

C Write sentences, putting the words in brackets ( ) in the correct place.

- ♦ She wrote a card. (me) — She wrote me a card.
- 1 They sent an invitation. (us)
- 2 Michelle gave a present. (to Mike)
- 3 I made a sandwich. (her)
- 4 Tom bought a new phone. (for Ellie)
- 5 My uncle sold his camera. (me)
- 6 She left a message. (for you)
- 7 Mary sent some flowers. (them)
- 8 Did you take the money? (to the bank)

D Tim and Lucy went to a restaurant last night for a meal. Make sentences about what happened while they were there. Write two sentences. Use the words in brackets ( ).

- ♦ (The waiter/give/the menu)
  (her) The waiter gave her the menu.
  (to Lucy) The waiter gave the menu to Lucy.
- 1 (The waiter/fetch/some wine)
  (them)
  (for them)
- 2 (The waiter/show/the bottle)
  (her)
  (to Lucy)
- 3 (The chef/cook/a special meal)
  (them)
  (for them)
- 4 (The waiter/give/the bill)
  (Tim)
  (to Tim)
- 5 (Lucy/lend/some money, because he didn't have enough to pay the bill)
  (Tim)
  (to Tim)

60 Much, many; how much/many; more

1 Look at these examples with **much** and **many**:

*There weren't **many** people in the restaurant.*

*I don't have **much** money.*

We use **much** and **many** to talk about quantity.

We normally use **much** and **many** in negative sentences:
A: I'm so hungry.
B: I'm sorry, I do**n't** have **much** food in the house. Shall we go out to a restaurant?
I have**n't** bought **many** games this year.

We also use **much** and **many** in questions:
Do **many** tourists come here?
Is there **much** snow in the mountains?

We can use **how much** and **how many** in questions:
How much luggage have you got?
How many times have you been to London?

2 We also use **more** to talk about quantity:
John did two exams yesterday and he is doing two **more** exams today.
We have some food, but we will need **more** food for the party tonight. Shall we go to the shops?

We often say **some more** or **any more**:
A: Would you like **some more** toast?
B: No, thanks. I don't want **any more**. But could I have **some more** orange juice?

3 We use:
▶ **much** with uncountable nouns:
   much food   **much** luggage   **much** snow
   much time   **much** money
   (For uncountable nouns, see **Unit 53**.)
▶ **many** with plural nouns:
   many things   **many** books
   many games
   many people   **many** tourists
   many times
▶ **more** with uncountable and plural nouns:
   more toast/juice   **more** glasses
▶ **much/many/more** without a noun:
   How **much** did that coat cost?
   A: That cake was delicious.
   B: Would you like some **more** (cake)?

A If the sentences are correct put a tick (✓). If they are incorrect, put a cross (✗).

- I don't have much food in the house.   ✓
- I don't have many food in the house.   ✗
1. We don't have many information about this machine.
2. We must buy some more apples.
3. How much people can you see?
4. Older students have more exams.
5. Is there many news this week?
6. We don't have much juice.
7. Do you have many luggage?
8. Grace doesn't earn much money.

Articles, nouns, pronouns, etc.

B Write *much* or *many* in front of these nouns.

- How _much_ money?
- How _many_ films?
- Not _many_ people.
1. How _____ snow?
2. How _____ tables?
3. How _____ cats?
4. How _____ petrol?
5. How _____ advice?
6. How _____ balls?
7. How _____ sugar?
8. How _____ buses?
9. How _____ books?
10. How _____ food?
11. How _____ cups?
12. How _____ watches?
13. How _____ homework?
14. How _____ times?
15. How _____ information?
16. How _____ toast?
17. Not _____ news.
18. Not _____ exams.
19. Not _____ luggage.
20. Not _____ children.
21. Not _____ museums.

C Complete the dialogues using *much*, *many*, *more*, *how much* or *how many*.

- A: How _many_ albums has your sister got?
  B: She hasn't got _many_. I've got _more_ than she has.

1. A: Is there _____ cheese in the fridge?
   B: No, and there aren't _____ eggs, either.

2. A: _____ money do you earn?
   B: Not _____, but I earn _____ than my brother.

3. A: Do you have _____ homework?
   B: Yes, because there aren't _____ days before the exams.

4. A: _____ food do we need?
   B: We haven't got _____ vegetables, so we need to buy some _____.

5. A: Is there _____ luggage in the coach?
   B: There aren't _____ big suitcases, but there are a lot of small ones.

6. A: _____ toast do you want? _____ pieces?
   B: Two please, and without _____ butter.

7. A: _____ spoonfuls of sugar do you take?
   B: No sugar thank you. I don't usually eat _____ sugar.

D Complete the dialogue with *many*, *much* or *more*.

Jenny: I had a terrible Sunday. I met a friend at the airport, because he wanted some help with his luggage. But his plane was late, and he didn't have ♦ _much_ luggage! What about you?

Steve: I went into town to buy some books. I spent £50!

Jenny: How ¹ _____ books did you buy?

Steve: Only three! In fact, I want to buy some ² _____ books tomorrow.

Jenny: I don't have ³ _____ time to read at the moment. We're so busy at the office.

Steve: How ⁴ _____ hours a day do you work?

Jenny: I do eight hours at the office, and then I do two ⁵ _____ hours at home!

Steve: Do you get ⁶ _____ money for that?

Jenny: No, I don't get much, but I enjoy the work.

Steve: Why don't you ask your boss for some ⁷ _____ money?

Jenny: I don't have ⁸ _____ opportunities. She's always in America on business.

Steve: I see. Listen, do you want some ⁹ _____ advice?

Jenny: OK.

Steve: Look for a new job!

61 A lot of, lots of, a little, a few

1 Look at this example with **a lot of**:

She's got **a lot of** luggage.
(*a lot of* = a big amount or number)

We use **lots of** with the same meaning:
She's got **lots of** luggage.

In spoken English, we usually use **a lot of**/**lots of** in positive sentences:
There's **a lot of**/**lots of** information in this book.
(NOT *There's much information in this book.*)
I bought **a lot of**/**lots of** new books today.
(NOT *I bought many new books today.*)
A lot of/**Lots of** students work in the holidays.

But in written English, we often use **much** and **many** in positive sentences:
There are big problems in **many** parts of the world.

2 We use **a lot of**/**lots of**:
▶ with uncountable nouns:
   a lot of luggage   **lots of** information
▶ with plural nouns:
   a lot of books   **lots of** students

3 Use a singular verb with an uncountable noun:
There **is** a lot of **information** in this book.
(NOT *...are...*)

Use a plural verb with a plural noun:
A lot of **students work**. (NOT *...works.*)

4 Look at these examples with **a few** and **a little**:

She has **a few** bags.
She has **a little** luggage.
(*a few* and *a little* = a small number or amount)

We can use **a few** and **a little** with **more**:
Would you like **a little more** coffee?
I should have had **a few more** hours' sleep.

5 We use:
▶ **a little** with uncountable nouns:
   I have **a little money**, but I don't have much.
▶ **a few** with plural nouns:
   Can you wait **a few minutes**, John?

We can use **a few** and **a little** without a noun:
A: Have you got any money?
B: Sorry. I only have **a little** (money).
A: How many of his albums have you got?
B: I'm not sure exactly. **A few** (albums).

6 Here are some common uncountable nouns:

coffee	milk	cheese	information
water	bread	money	advice
sugar	news	luggage	homework

A Complete the dialogues using the words in brackets ( ) and *a lot of* or *lots of*.

♦ A: Are you going to the cinema tonight?
  B: (No, I have homework to do.) No, I have a lot of/lots of homework to do.

1 A: Are you hungry?
  B: (No, I ate cake in town.) _____

2 A: Do you want some help?
  B: (Yes, please. I have luggage.) _____

3 A: Did you enjoy the party?
  B: (Yes, I met interesting people.) _____

4 A: Can you pay for our plane tickets?
  B: (Yes, I have money at the moment.) _____

Articles, nouns, pronouns, etc.

5 A: Is William coming?
   B: (No, he isn't. He has things to do.)

6 A: Did she help you?
   B: (Yes, she gave me good advice.)

B What do you see in the pictures? Write your answers. Use *a lot of/lots of*, *a few* or *a little*.

♦
a few pens

1

2

3

4

5

6

7

C A friend is visiting you. Rewrite the questions you ask your friend, using *a few* or *a little* instead of *some*.

♦ Would you like some coffee? Would you like a little coffee?
1 Would you like some biscuits?
2 Shall I make you some sandwiches?
3 Would you like some cheese?
4 Can I bring you some cake?
5 Would you like some milk in your coffee?
6 Would you like some more sugar in your coffee?

D Tick (✓) the underlined words if they are correct. Rewrite them if they are incorrect.

♦ There is are_____ a lot of tall buildings in New York.
♦ I bought a few ✓_____ presents today.
1 A lot of people travels_____ to work by car.
2 She only has a little_____ luggage with her.
3 We need a little_____ tomatoes for this meal.
4 There are_____ a lot of news on TV in Britain.
5 My father gave me a little_____ advice before I went to university.
6 Could you give me a few_____ water, please?
7 Lots of_____ children use computers in school.
8 Are you hungry? Shall I make you a little_____ sandwiches?

62 Something, anybody, nothing, etc.

1
something/anything = a thing
somebody/anybody = a person
someone/anyone = a person
somewhere/anywhere = a place

2 We usually use **something**, **somebody**, **someone** and **somewhere** in positive sentences:
   Something is burning. (= I can smell burning. I don't know what is burning.)
   I'm going to have **something** to eat. (= I'm going to eat; I don't know what I'm going to eat.)
   Somebody told me that it was a good film. (= A person told me it was a good film. I can't remember who told me.)
   She lives **somewhere** in the north.

3 We usually use **anything**, **anybody**, **anyone** and **anywhere** in negative sentences, and in questions:
   I didn't know **anyone** at the party. (= There were no people at the party who I knew.)
   I couldn't find my bag **anywhere**. (= I couldn't find my bag in any place.)
   Did you understand **anything** she said?

4
nothing = not anything
nobody/no one = not anybody/not anyone
nowhere = not anywhere

We use **nothing**, **nobody**, **no one** and **nowhere** before or after positive verbs:
   Nothing makes Joe unhappy. (= There isn't anything that makes Joe unhappy.)
   There's **nothing** I want to watch on TV.
   Nobody was there when I arrived.
   There is **nowhere** that I would prefer to live than here. (= There isn't anywhere …)

5
everything = all things
everybody/everyone = all people
everywhere = all places

We use **everything**, **everybody**, **everyone** and **everywhere** before or after positive verbs:
   Everyone likes music.   I've done **everything** I can.

6 Note that we use a singular verb after all these words:
   Nothing is wrong.   **Everyone was** friendly.

7 We can use **else** after **something**, **anybody**, **nowhere**, **everyone**, etc.:
   Let's talk about **something else**.
   (= Let's talk about a different subject.)
   I didn't tell **anybody else**.
   (= I didn't tell another person.)
   There is **nowhere else** I can look for it.

8 We can also use an adjective (e.g. **wrong**, **nice**) after **something**, **anything**, etc.:
   Have I said **something wrong**?

A Complete the sentences with the words from the box.

   ~~anything~~   nobody   everything   somebody (x2)   somewhere
   nothing   everywhere   something   anyone   everyone

♦ She didn't say _anything_ about her job when I spoke to her.
1 _____ phoned you today, but he didn't tell me his name.
2 I'm sure you'll find it _____ in the house if you keep looking.
3 I had to go to the cinema on my own because I couldn't find _____ to go with me.
4 She said that _____ was fine and she was very happy.
5 Can I speak to you for a moment? I want to discuss _____ with you.
6 Unfortunately, I couldn't help. There was _____ I could do about the problem.
7 I looked _____ but I couldn't find it.
8 She married _____ she met when she was a student.
9 _____ was out of the office so there was _____ to answer the phone.

Articles, nouns, pronouns, etc.

B Choose the correct verb form in brackets ( ) to complete the sentences.

- I'm afraid I _don't know_ (know/don't know) anything about this subject.
- I rang the doorbell but nobody _was_ (was/wasn't) in.
1. I asked a lot of people, but nobody _____ (knew/didn't know) the answer.
2. I _____ (have seen/haven't seen) anything so lovely before in my life!
3. I _____ (ate/didn't eat) anything for lunch yesterday.
4. Nothing interesting _____ (has happened/hasn't happened) since the last time I spoke to you.
5. He loves football. Nothing else _____ (is/isn't) important to him.
6. She _____ (said/didn't say) anything about her plans for the future.

C Rewrite these sentences using the words in brackets ( ) with the underlined adjectives or *else*.

- A <u>strange</u> thing happened yesterday. (something)
  Something strange happened yesterday.
- Let's listen to some <u>different</u> music. (something)
  Let's listen to _something else_.
1. Is there an <u>interesting</u> programme on TV tonight? (anything)
   Is there _____ on TV tonight?
2. You won't find better food in any <u>other</u> place. (anywhere)
   You won't find better food _____.
3. Is there a <u>cheap</u> place we can go for lunch? (anywhere)
   Is there _____ we can go for lunch?
4. Let's sit in a <u>different</u> place. (somewhere)
   Let's sit _____.
5. I'd like a <u>hot</u> drink. (something)
   I'd like _____ to drink.

D Put the right form of a word beginning with *some-*, *any-*, *no-* or *every-* into the conversation.

Dennis: Have you read ♦ _anything_ interesting lately?
Sarah: Yes, ¹_____ lent me a novel last week and I really enjoyed it.
Dennis: What was it about?
Sarah: It was about ²_____ who goes to visit Australia. She likes to go ³_____ alone. While she's travelling around on her own, ⁴_____ terrible happens to her. She loses ⁵_____ – including her passport and all her money. She doesn't know ⁶_____ who can help her, and she's got ⁷_____ to stay.
Dennis: What happens then?
Sarah: I'm not going to tell you ⁸_____ else! You should read the book yourself.
Dennis: It sounds like a very depressing book! I'd prefer to read ⁹_____ funny.
Sarah: No, read it. It's great fun. And ¹⁰_____ wonderful happens at the end.

63 Every/each; one/another/other/others

1 We use **every** and **each** to talk about all people or things in a group or series. In many contexts, both **every** and **each** are correct:
> The letter has been sent to **every**/**each** member of staff.
> We checked **every**/**each** item before we sent it.

We use **every**/**each** + singular noun + singular verb:
> **Every**/**Each** student has to fill in this form.

We can use **each** (but not **every**) + **of** + **the**/**possessive** + **plural noun**:
> I put **each of the documents** into the correct place.

We can use **each** (but not **every**) on its own as a subject or between a subject and a main verb:
> Tickets are now available and **each** costs the same.
> Tickets (will) **each** cost the same.

2 Sometimes we can only use **every**; at other times we can only use **each**. We use **every** to talk about a group or series of people or things in general, with the meaning 'all of them':
> **Every** ticket had been sold.

We use **each** to talk about all individual things or people in a group or series:
> **Each** ticket costs £20.

3 We use **one** + **of** + **the**/possessive + plural noun to talk about one person or thing when there are several or many:
> **One of the students** in my class was off sick today.
> He is staying with **one of his relatives**.

We can use **one** + singular noun:
> **One flight** leaves at five o'clock and the other is at nine o'clock.

We can use **one** + singular verb:
> There are two flights. **One leaves** at five o'clock and the other leaves at nine o'clock.

(See **Unit 51**.)

4 We use **another** + singular noun with the meanings 'one more' or 'a different one':
> Would you like **another drink**?
> Let's go to **another restaurant** for a change.

Notice that we do not use **another** with **one** and a singular noun (NOT *another one drink*).

Notice also that we do not use **another** with a plural noun (NOT *I met another people*).

5 We use **the**/possessive/quantifier + **other** + plural noun with the meanings 'different ones' or 'ones that have not been mentioned':
> **The other hotels** were more expensive.
> Ray agreed with me but **my other friends** said I was wrong.
> For **all other enquiries**, phone this number.

We use **the**/possessive + **other** + singular noun with the meaning 'the one that has not already been mentioned':
> One of his sisters lives in France and **his**/**the other sister** lives in Australia.

We use **the other (one)** to talk about a person or thing that has not already been mentioned:
> He's got two homes – one is in London and **the other (one)** is in Florida.

6 We use **others** with the meaning 'other people or things':
> Some people like sport and **others** aren't interested in it at all.

We use **the others** with the meaning 'the other people or things (in a set or group)':
> We arrived first and **the others** came later.

A Decide whether the underlined parts of the sentences are correct or not. Put a tick (✓) next to the sentences that are correct and rewrite the underlined parts of the sentences that are not correct.

♦ I've told <u>every of my friends</u> about this.   *each of my friends*
♦ <u>Each room has</u> its own private bathroom.   ✓

Articles, nouns, pronouns, etc.

1 Every house in the street is exactly the same.
2 Each assignment on the course have to be completed on time.
3 Each candidate for the job was interviewed separately.
4 We couldn't park because every car park were full.
5 We each paid £5 towards the cost of the food.
6 There are three tests and every lasts for one hour.

B Complete these questions using *another*, *other* or *others*.

♦ Could I ask you *another* question?
1 What time is the _____ flight that day?
2 What will the _____ say when I tell them about this?
3 Do you know any _____ clubs that are as good as this one?
4 Will you have _____ chance to take the exam?
5 Could we change our meeting to _____ date?

C Complete this article about a film star using *one*, *another*, *other* or *others*.

Walter Richards had a remarkably successful film career. ♦ *One* reason for his success was that he had such a relaxed acting style that he never really seemed to be acting. ¹_____ reason was of course his good looks. No ²_____ actor looked quite like him and his image was used on posters and all sorts of other goods. In a film career spanning 60 years, he won two Oscars and many ³_____ awards. He first came to fame playing an ambitious musician in *The Path To Glory* and he played a similar character in ⁴_____ film shortly afterwards – *High Hat*. ⁵_____ roles quickly followed and he was soon a household name. Many people felt that, although he made over 100 films, most of the ⁶_____ weren't as good as the first two. Nevertheless, he continued to have a highly successful career, and was working on ⁷_____ film when he died, aged 85.

D Complete these dialogues using *one*, *another*, *other*, *the other*, *others* or *the others*.

♦ A: All their flights are fully booked.
   B: Well, we'll have to use *another* airline. Lots of airlines fly there.
1 A: Do you like this writer?
   B: I'm not sure. I really enjoyed one of her books but I haven't enjoyed any of _____ books she's written.
2 A: Have you been to any _____ cities in Britain apart from London?
   B: Yes, on my _____ visit to this country last year, I went to Birmingham.
3 A: Are you on your own?
   B: Yes, but _____ are on their way. They'll be here soon.
4 A: Is the company you work for big?
   B: It has two main offices. _____ office is in Lisbon and _____ is in Paris.
5 A: Can we make a decision now?
   B: No, I think we should have _____ discussion about the subject later.

64 All, most, some, none

1 We use

all/**most**/**some** + NOUN (e.g. **most cities**)

to talk about things or people in general:
- She thinks that **all sports** are boring.
  (= She thinks that every sport is boring.)
- **Most cities** have a lot of shops.
  (= Almost every city has a lot of shops.)
- In **some countries** life is very hard.
  (= In a number of countries in the world, but not all or most …)

We do not say **all**/**most**/**some** + **of** + noun:
- **Most people** take exams during their lives.
  (NOT Most of people …)

2 We can also use **all** with **morning**/**afternoon**/**evening**/**night**/**day**/**week**/**year** (e.g. **all afternoon**) to mean 'the whole', 'from the beginning to the end of':

- They've been working hard **all day**.
- I waited for the phone call **all morning**.

3 We use

all/**most**/**some**/**none** + of + **the**/**my**/**her** + NOUN
(e.g. **all of my books**)

to talk about particular things or people:
- He spent **all of his money**.
- **Most of my friends** are interested in sport.
- I knew **some of the people** at the party.
- **None of the shops** were open.

Notice that we use a positive verb with **none**.
We can leave out **of** after **all** (but not after **most**, **some**, **none**):
- He spent **all his money**.

4 We can use

all/**most**/**some**/**none** + of + **it**/**them**

when we have already mentioned the noun that **it** or **them** refers to:
- It was lovely food, but I couldn't eat **all of it**.
  (it = the food)
- I phoned a number of hotels, but **most of them** were full. (them = the hotels)
- That cake looks nice. Can I have **some of** it?
  (it = the cake)

A Look at the exam results for four people. Complete the sentences using *all of, some of, most of* or *none of*. Sometimes you will need *the* (e.g. *some of the*).

STUDENT	EXAM 1	EXAM 2	EXAM 3	EXAM 4	EXAM 5	EXAM 6
Alice	PASS	PASS	FAIL	PASS	PASS	PASS
William	PASS	PASS	PASS	PASS	PASS	PASS
Laura	FAIL	PASS	PASS	PASS	FAIL	FAIL
David	FAIL	FAIL	FAIL	FAIL	FAIL	FAIL

♦ Alice passed _most of the_ exams.
1. William passed _____ exams.
2. William failed _____ them.
3. Laura passed _____ exams.
4. Laura passed _____ them.
5. Laura failed _____ them.
6. David passed _____ them.
7. David passed _____ exams.
8. David failed _____ exams.

Articles, nouns, pronouns, etc.

B Complete the sentences with the phrases from the box. Use the phrases more than once.

 all   all the   none of the   some   some of the

- All _____ European children have to go to school.
- The classroom is empty because *some of the* _____ children are outside.
1. We can't buy anything today because _____ shops are closed.
2. We like that restaurant. _____ food is expensive, but everything is very good.
3. _____ people say he's the best tennis player in the world, but I don't agree.
4. That's a terrible shop. _____ assistants are very helpful.
5. William's very lazy. He watches films online _____ afternoon.
6. _____ drinks machines here are working. Where can I get a coffee?
7. It's a wonderful trip. You have _____ day to see the sights.
8. IMPORTANT NOTICE: _____ passengers must have a valid ticket.
9. If _____ students can answer the teacher's questions, she explains the point again.
10. We can't sit down. _____ chairs are wet.
11. _____ cars use petrol and others use diesel.
12. This light works _____ time, but not always.

C Write full sentences using *all*, *most*, *some* or *none*. Use *them* or *it* when possible and include *of* or *the* if necessary.

- 100% – sports – physical and – 20% – dangerous.
  All sports are physical and some of them are dangerous.
- 80% – Hepworth's art – abstract and – 25% – difficult to understand
  Most of Hepworth's art is abstract and some of it is difficult to understand.
1. 80% – professional footballers – well off and – 20% – very rich.

2. 80% – sea – very salty and – 0% – fresh water.

3. 30% – pop music – very pleasant but – 20% – terrible.

4. 75% – Indian food – spicy and – 15% – very spicy.

5. 100% – my relatives – slim and – 0% – very tall.

6. 75% – my friends – students but – 0% – very clever.

7. 80% – Nepal – mountainous and – 0% – flat.

8. 75% – the Earth – inhabited but – 10% – desert.

Test F: Articles, nouns, pronouns, etc.

A This is an advertisement in a music shop. In the numbered lines cross out one *or* two of the words *a*, *an* or *the*.

- ♦ It's ~~a~~ time to change your life!
1. Would you like to learn to play the a piano?
2. All you need is half a an hour a day and a the simple book!
3. What's the name of the a book? *Bob Bryant's Big Piano Book*!
4. The friends are great, but the music will be your partner forever!
   Don't just stand there! Buy this book today!
5. You'll also get the a free download of piano music from around a the world!

B William and Michelle are going on holiday with their children, Chloe and Dan. Complete their conversation with the words from the box. One of the words is not needed.

| everywhere | anybody | someone | everyone |
| ~~anywhere~~ | somewhere | nothing | nobody |

William: Has anyone seen the big blue beach ball? I can't find it ♦ anywhere.
Chloe: Have you looked in the cupboard under the stairs?
William: Yes, there's [1] .... there. Only a box.
Chloe: And did you look in the box?
William: Of course. I've looked [2] ....
Chloe: Well, it must be [3] ....
Dan: Come on, [4] .... , let's help Dad find the blue beach ball!
Michelle: But [5] .... could find it last year, or the year before.
William: Surely [6] .... has seen it?
Chloe: Do you know what I think? I think we've never had a blue beach ball.

C Read this dialogue about the British Museum. Put *a*, *an*, *the* or nothing (–) in the gaps.

Cathy: Have you been to ♦ the British Museum yet?
Alice: I don't even know where it is, I'm afraid.
Cathy: It's in [1] .... street near Tottenham Court Road.
Alice: What's the name of [2] .... street?
Cathy: Russell Street. The mummies from Ancient Egypt are on [3] .... first floor.
Alice: I'd love to see [4] .... Egyptian mummy. People say that when kings died, the ancient Egyptians gave them [5] .... food and [6] .... water to take to the next world.
Cathy: That's right. And have you heard about the Elgin Marbles?
Alice: Yes. They were part of [7] .... Parthenon in Athens, and Lord Elgin brought them back to London 200 years ago. Now they're in the British Museum, but [8] .... Greek Government wants them back in Athens. What do you think about that?
Cathy: I'm not sure. If we send [9] .... Marbles back to [10] .... Greece, we'll have to send everything back in the end, won't we?

Articles, nouns, pronouns, etc.

Alice: Why not?
Cathy: So all [11]............ paintings by Picasso in museums around the world would go back to Spain?
Alice: Yes. I think it's [12]............ good idea. Everyone would have to travel to [13]............ countries that made these famous things.

D Two students are in a cafe, talking about going home to Mexico. If the underlined phrases are correct, put a tick (✓) in the space provided. If they're incorrect, rewrite them.

Federico: How many sugar do you take in your coffee? ♦ How much sugar
Maria: Half a spoonful, please. I only like a little. ♦ ✓
Federico: So, how many bags have you packed? [1]............
Maria: Two. Why? How many luggage have you got? [2]............
Federico: Too much. I'll have to post some of it. [3]............ How much costs it to post things? [4]............ Is it very expensive?
Maria: I don't know. I'm OK at the moment, but I haven't bought some presents yet. [5]............ I'm waiting for my Dad to send me any more money! [6]............
Federico: How many presents are you going to buy, then? [7]............
Maria: A lot! [8]............ I've got a big family. What about you?
Federico: Me? I'm only going to get a little things. [9]............ I've only got a little cash left, I'm afraid. Can you give me an advice? [10]............
Maria: Well, you could get a lot of [11]............ small presents, I suppose, or just a little, big ones. [12]............
Federico: Do you want some more coffee? I think there's a few more in the pot. [13]............
Maria: No thanks, I haven't got a lot of time. [14]............ I've had three cups already.

E John and Steve used to share a house, but John left this morning to live in a different house. Steve is sending him an email. Put the words from the box in the gaps.

| me | mine | one | ones | some | that | them |
| them | there | there's | ~~your~~ | yours | yourself | |

Hi John,

Are you sure that you've taken all ♦ your things? I'm sure [1]............ green football on top of the wardrobe isn't mine, and [2]............ an expensive black fountain pen on the table which is [3]............. And did you give [4]............ the book on fishing, or did you buy it for [5]............? I can't remember. There are [6]............ purple socks with Mickey Mouse on [7]............. Are those the [8]............ you bought at the market? Also, [9]............ are no sheets left on your bed. But the sheets were [10]............, weren't they? I lent [11]............ to you, and I want them back! Finally, I'm sure I bought two big cakes yesterday. You haven't taken [12]............, have you?

Steve

65 Adjectives (order)

1 We use adjectives to describe people and things. Here are some examples:

old small friendly rich cheap

Look at these sentences:
I've bought an **old** table for my kitchen.
My home town is **small** and **friendly**.
We had lunch in a **cheap** restaurant.

2 The form of adjectives never changes:
a **rich** man   a **rich** woman   two **rich** men

3 We put an adjective before a noun:

ADJECTIVE	+	NOUN
I saw a	beautiful	cat.

We put an adjective after **be**:

BE	+	ADJECTIVE
They	are	hungry.

We sometimes use these verbs instead of **be**:

look feel taste smell sound

Here are some examples:
She **looks happy**.
This cheese **tastes wonderful**.
I **feel cold**.

4 When we use two adjectives before a noun, we put in a comma (,):
He's a **nice, old** man.

When we use two adjectives without a noun, we use **and**:
You look **tired** and **hungry**.

5 When we use more than one adjective, there is a general guide to the correct order:

SIZE + AGE + COLOUR + NATIONALITY + MATERIAL

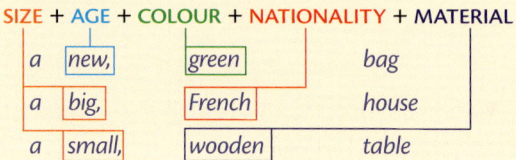

We often use materials as adjectives:
a **cotton** shirt   a **silver** ring   a **plastic** bag

6 Here are some common nationality adjectives:

American	German	Portuguese
Australian	Greek	Russian
Chinese	Indian	Turkish
Dutch	Italian	South African
English	Japanese	Spanish
French	Polish	Swedish

A There are 13 adjectives in this story. <u>Underline</u> them.

My ♦<u>favourite</u> picture is one of a large, square room by a Dutch artist. An elegant man sits on a wooden bench in a corner. He has a small black dog at his feet. The dog looks sleepy. Through the open window you can see bright sunshine. When I look at this picture I feel warm and happy.

B Complete this text using the adjectives from the box.

busy   careful   ~~enjoyable~~   free   good   late   long   old   tall   valuable

142

Adjectives and adverbs

C Complete the sentences using the correct forms of the words from the box.

> look (x2)   feel   ~~taste~~   sound (x2)   smell

- ♦ _Taste_ these apples. I've already eaten two. They're delicious!
- 1 That music _____ terrible. What group is playing?
- 2 Those flowers look nice and they _____ good too. What are they?
- 3 I saw Jasmine yesterday, but I didn't speak to her. She _____ tired.
- 4 Could you close the door, please? I _____ cold.
- 5 That new picture will _____ wonderful in your dining room.
- 6 Do you know where that song comes from? It _____ Spanish.

D Look at these sentences. If the underlined adjectives are in the wrong order, cross them out and write in the correct order. If you think the order is correct, put a tick (✓).

- ♦ She lost a ~~gold small~~ _small gold_ ring at the party last night.
- ♦ I have an old Italian ✓ painting in my living room.
- 1 I'm looking for my cotton green _____ shirt and my brown leather _____ shoes.
- 2 George has a Spanish modern _____ villa near the sea. He goes there every summer.
- 3 I live in an old white _____ house near the river. I've got a black large _____ dog!
- 4 I had an interesting talk with a Polish young _____ student last week.
- 5 We are having lunch in a big Japanese new _____ restaurant in the centre of town.
- 6 I left all my books in a red plastic _____ bag on the bus. I was so stupid!

E Complete the sentences with a name and a nationality from the box.

NAMES			NATIONALITIES		
Salamanca	Vincent van Gogh	A Volkswagen	Dutch	Italian	German
Alfred Nobel	Sherlock Holmes	Chang	French	English	American
Audrey Tautou	pizza	Batman Forever	Spanish	Swedish	Chinese

- ♦ _Batman Forever_ is an _American_ film.
- 1 _____ is a _____ car.
- 2 _____ was a _____ artist.
- 3 _____ is an _____ detective.
- 4 _____ is a _____ actor.
- 5 _____ is an _____ food.
- 6 _____ was a _____ chemist.
- 7 _____ is a _____ surname.
- 8 _____ is a _____ city.

66 Adjectives: -ed or -ing

1 Compare **frightened** and **frightening**:

We can use adjectives that end with **-ed** to describe people's feelings:

frightened

SUBJECT

Joshua was very **frightened**.

The subject of the sentence (e.g. *Joshua*) is the person who has the feeling.

We use an adjective that ends with **-ing** (e.g. frightening) to talk about a thing or person that makes us have a feeling:

frightening

SUBJECT

The ghost was very **frightening**.

The subject of the sentence (e.g. *the ghost*) causes the feeling.

2 Here are some more examples to compare:

We are all **surprised** by the news. (= We feel surprised.)	The news is **surprising**. (= The news makes us feel surprised.)
I was very **tired** at the end of the journey. (= I felt tired.)	The journey was very **tiring**.* (= The journey made us feel tired.)
He was **excited** by the way the game ended.	The end of the game was **exciting**.
I'm **interested** in your idea.	Your idea is **interesting**.
The students were **bored** during the lesson.	The lesson was **boring**.
Were you **disappointed** by the film?	Was the film **disappointing**?
I wasn't nervous before the exam; I was **relaxed**.	I went for a **relaxing** walk.
The children were **entertained** by three clowns.	The clowns were very **entertaining**.
Jack was totally **convinced** by Anna's explanation.	Anna's explanation was totally **convincing**.

*Note that we can say:
The journey was very **tiring**.
OR: It was a very **tiring journey**.

A Choose the correct adjective in brackets ( ) to complete the sentences.

♦ It was a terrible play and I was *bored* (bored/boring) from start to finish.
1 I'm very _____ (excited/exciting) because I'm going to New York tomorrow.
2 Are you _____ (surprised/surprising) or were you expecting this news?
3 I'm reading a very _____ (interested/interesting) book at the moment.
4 I've had a very _____ (tired/tiring) day at work today and I want to go to bed.
5 Most people were _____ (surprised/surprising) that he won the championship.
6 I'm _____ (bored/boring). Let's go out for a cup of coffee somewhere.
7 Visit our _____ (excited/exciting) new shop!

144

Adjectives and adverbs

8 His speech was very long and very _____ (bored/boring).

B Complete the sentences using the words from the box.

| bored | interested | surprising | amusing | confused |
| boring | amused | confusing | surprised | ~~interesting~~ |

♦ Your idea is very _interesting_. Tell me more about it.
1 He told me a very _____ story. I laughed and laughed.
2 This is a terribly _____ book. Nothing happens in it.
3 She's _____ in politics and often talks about it.
4 The map was _____ and I got lost.
5 She was _____ because she had nothing to do all day.
6 Everyone else thought it was funny, but she wasn't _____.
7 Could you repeat that, please? I'm a bit _____ because it was very complicated.
8 It is _____ that she failed the exam, because she's a good student.
9 Everyone was _____ by the sudden noise.

C Complete the dialogue using the words from the box.

| bored | boring | confusing | convinced | convincing | disappointed | ~~entertained~~ |
| entertaining | frightened | interesting | relaxed | surprised | surprising | |

Sebastian: What sort of films do you like?
Liz: When I go to the cinema, I like to be ♦_entertained_.
Sebastian: And what sort of films do you find ¹_____?
Liz: Well, I like films that tell a good, ²_____ story. And I mean a story that you can follow, not the sort that goes backwards and forwards in time. I find those very ³_____. And I'm ⁴_____ when I watch a horror film. I usually close my eyes when the horror starts.
Sebastian: Yes, but if the story is too simple, surely you get ⁵_____ because you know exactly what's going to happen.
Liz: I don't mean that. If something is intelligible, it's not necessarily ⁶_____. Often good stories have ⁷_____ events or endings – things that you can't possibly know at the beginning.
Sebastian: For me the most important thing is that the actors must be ⁸_____ so that you really believe that they are the person they are acting.
Liz: If that's true, I imagine that you are ⁹_____ most of the time because, well, for example, Harrison Ford is always Harrison Ford. I'm never ¹⁰_____ that he's somebody else.
Sebastian: Yes, but it's often not important in his films because they're escapist – if you're feeling tense about work or something, you have a good laugh and you come out feeling ¹¹_____ and happy with the world.
Liz: I'm ¹²_____ that you like his films. Although the special effects are good, the story is always terribly simple.
Sebastian: He's not my favourite, but his films are not bad.

67 Cardinal and ordinal numbers

1 Look at these examples:
   Three students were late.
   She lives on the **third** floor.

Three is a cardinal number.
Third is an ordinal number.

2 Now look at the table:

CARDINAL NUMBERS		ORDINAL NUMBERS	
1	one	1st	first
2	two	2nd	second
3	three	3rd	third
4	four	4th	fourth
5	five	5th	fifth
6	six	6th	sixth
7	seven	7th	seventh
8	eight	8th	eighth
9	nine	9th	ninth
10	ten	10th	tenth
11	eleven	11th	eleventh
12	twelve	12th	twelfth
13	thirteen	13th	thirteenth
14	fourteen	14th	fourteenth
15	fifteen	15th	fifteenth
16	sixteen	16th	sixteenth
17	seventeen	17th	seventeenth
18	eighteen	18th	eighteenth
19	nineteen	19th	nineteenth
20	twenty	20th	twentieth
21	twenty-one	21st	twenty-first
22	twenty-two	22nd	twenty-second
30	thirty	30th	thirtieth

3 cardinals (40 to 4,000,000)
   40 forty   60 sixty   80 eighty
   50 fifty   70 seventy 90 ninety

   100 one hundred
   101 one hundred and one
   1,000 one thousand
   1,000,000 one million
   200 two hundred
   210 two hundred and ten
   3,000 three thousand
   $4,000,000 four million dollars

4 Look at how we say these dates:

13 or 13th June: The **thirteenth** of June.
June the **thirteenth**.
1994: Nineteen ninety-four.
26 or 26th March 1995 (26.3.95):
The **twenty-sixth** of March, nineteen ninety-five.

A Look at the numbers in brackets ( ). Cross out the wrong form and tick (✓) the right form for each one.

♦	(116)	~~one hundred sixteen~~	one hundred and sixteen ✓
1	(49)	fourty-nine	forty-nine
2	(600)	six hundred	six hundreds
3	(4th)	fourth	forth
4	(12th)	twelfth	twelfth
5	($2,000)	two thousand dollars	two thousands dollars
6	(23rd)	twenty-three	twenty-third
7	(78)	eighty-seven	seventy-eight
8	(8th)	eightth	eighth
9	(17)	seventeen	seventeenth
10	(5th)	fiveth	fifth
11	(7,000,000)	seven million	seven millions
12	(9th)	ninth	nineth
13	(30th)	thirteenth	thirtieth
14	(395)	three hundred and ninety-five	three hundred ninety-five

Adjectives and adverbs

B Write out the numbers in brackets ( ).

- (211)   two hundred and eleven
1. (462)
2. (20th)
3. (1st)
4. (12th)
5. (9,000,000)
6. (310)
7. (8th)
8. (111)
9. (14)
10. (2nd)
11. (5,000)
12. (68)
13. (34th)
14. (150)
15. (3rd)
16. (25th)
17. (19th)

C Look at where these people live in the block of flats and complete the sentences.

- John lives in flat forty on the fourth floor.
1. Charles lives in flat
2. Maria
3. Diana
4. Michael
5. Peter
6. Jasmine
7. Anna
8. Oliver

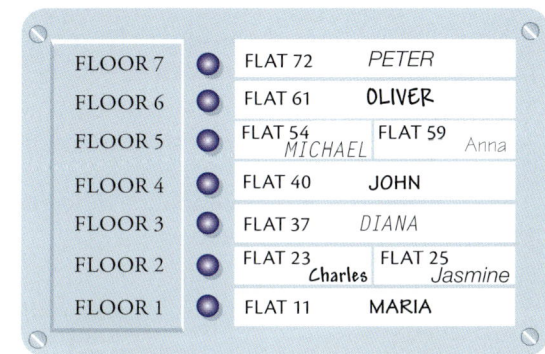

FLOOR 7	FLAT 72	PETER	
FLOOR 6	FLAT 61	OLIVER	
FLOOR 5	FLAT 54 MICHAEL	FLAT 59	Anna
FLOOR 4	FLAT 40	JOHN	
FLOOR 3	FLAT 37	DIANA	
FLOOR 2	FLAT 23 Charles	FLAT 25	Jasmine
FLOOR 1	FLAT 11	MARIA	

D Write the dates and years in words in this interview using the information in brackets ( ).

A: When were you born?
B: I was born on (13.10.90) ♦ the thirteenth of October, nineteen ninety.
A: When did you go to secondary school?
B: In (2001) ¹
A: And when did you leave secondary school?
B: Seven years later. My final exam was on (16.6.08) ²
A: Did you start university in the same year?
B: Yes, on (29 September) ³
A: Did you spend three or four years there?
B: Well, I left in (2012) ⁴   . That's four years.
A: And your first job? When was that?
B: I started work in an office on (10.1.13) ⁵
A: Did you enjoy it? How long did you stay?
B: It was terrible! I left two months later, on (9 March) ⁶
A: What did you do then?
B: I went to America. I spent two years in New York. I returned to England in (2015) ⁷

68 Comparison: (not) as ... as

1 We use as + **adjective** + as (e.g. **as old as**) to say that two things or people are the same in some way:

The chair is **as expensive as** the table.
You're **as old as** me. (= We are the same age.)

Note that we say **as me/as him/as her/as us/as them**, and not **as I/as he/as she**, etc:
She's as strong as **him**. (NOT ... as he.)
I'm as fast as **them**. (NOT ... as they.)

We use **not as ... as** to talk about a difference between two things or people:

The two-star hotel is**n't as big as** the four-star hotel.
I'm **not as clever as** her. (= She is cleverer than me.)

2 We can also use **as** + **adverb** + **as** (e.g. **as well as**):
Abigail cooks **as well as** Tom. (= Abigail and Tom are both good cooks.)
He couldn't run **as quickly as** Maria. (= Maria ran more quickly than him.)

3 We use **as many** + **plural noun** + **as** (e.g. **as many friends as**) to say that the numbers of two things are equal:
Jasmine has got **as many friends as** Mary.

We use **not as many ... as** to say two things are not equal:
I don't have **as many books as** you.

4 We use **as much** + **uncountable noun** + **as** (e.g. **as much money as**) to compare two things. Uncountable nouns are words for things that we cannot count, and so they do not have a plural form (e.g. **money**, **work**, **luggage**, **traffic**):
Helen earns **as much money as** Matt.
Jack doesn't do **as much work as** me.
They aren't carrying **as much luggage as** us.

(See also **Unit 53**.)

A Complete each sentence so that it means the same as the one above it. Use *as* + adjective/adverb + *as*.

♦ Sweden is bigger than Britain.
   Britain isn't *as big as Sweden*.
1 The other students learn more quickly than me.
   I don't learn _____ the other students.
2 You're very angry and I'm very angry also.
   I'm _____ you.
3 The seats at the front are more expensive than the seats at the back.
   The seats at the back aren't _____ the seats at the front.
4 Central Park in New York is bigger than Hyde Park in London.
   Hyde Park in London isn't _____ Central Park in New York.
5 Her last film was very good and her new film is also very good.
   Her new film is _____ her last film.
6 The other students work harder than him.
   He doesn't work _____ the other students.

Adjectives and adverbs

B Look at the pictures and complete the sentences using *as … as* and a word from the box.

long   clean   fast   fresh   tall   big   ~~cheap~~   strong   wide   full

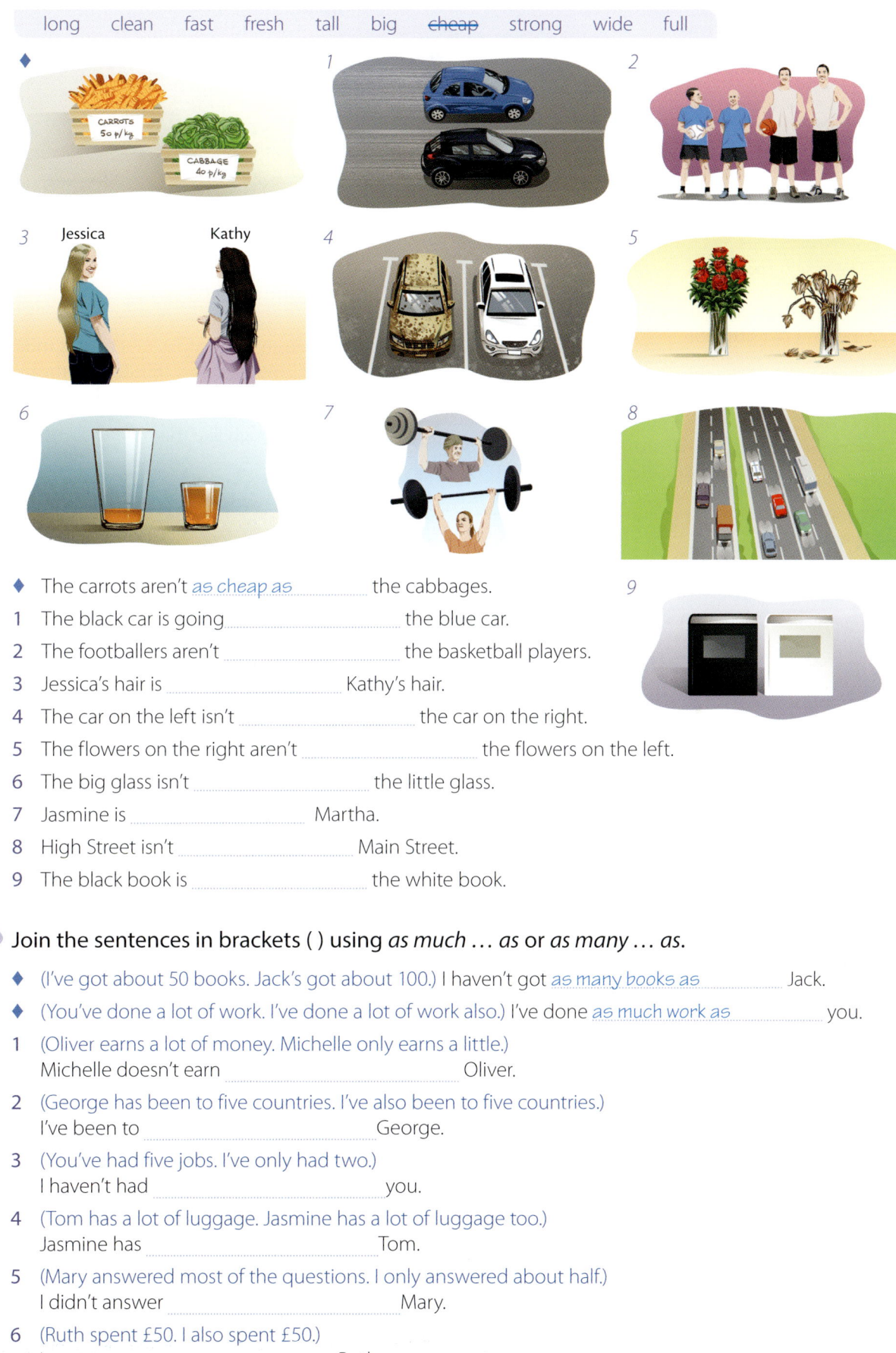

- ♦ The carrots aren't *as cheap as* the cabbages.
- 1 The black car is going _____ the blue car.
- 2 The footballers aren't _____ the basketball players.
- 3 Jessica's hair is _____ Kathy's hair.
- 4 The car on the left isn't _____ the car on the right.
- 5 The flowers on the right aren't _____ the flowers on the left.
- 6 The big glass isn't _____ the little glass.
- 7 Jasmine is _____ Martha.
- 8 High Street isn't _____ Main Street.
- 9 The black book is _____ the white book.

C Join the sentences in brackets ( ) using *as much … as* or *as many … as*.

- ♦ (I've got about 50 books. Jack's got about 100.) I haven't got *as many books as* Jack.
- ♦ (You've done a lot of work. I've done a lot of work also.) I've done *as much work as* you.
- 1 (Oliver earns a lot of money. Michelle only earns a little.)
  Michelle doesn't earn _____ Oliver.
- 2 (George has been to five countries. I've also been to five countries.)
  I've been to _____ George.
- 3 (You've had five jobs. I've only had two.)
  I haven't had _____ you.
- 4 (Tom has a lot of luggage. Jasmine has a lot of luggage too.)
  Jasmine has _____ Tom.
- 5 (Mary answered most of the questions. I only answered about half.)
  I didn't answer _____ Mary.
- 6 (Ruth spent £50. I also spent £50.)
  I spent _____ Ruth.

69 Too and enough

1 Look at this example:

The case is **too heavy**. He can't carry it.

We use **too** to mean 'more than is good or suitable in the situation'.

2 We can use **too** like this:

> **too** + ADJECTIVE:
> I don't want to go out. I'm **too tired**.
>
> **too many** + PLURAL NOUN:
> I couldn't find her at the concert because there were **too many people** there.
>
> **too much** + UNCOUNTABLE:
> (e.g. **too much** work/money/food/noise/salt/ information/time/bread)
> Our teacher gives us **too much work**.

3 We can use **too** with **to** + infinitive to explain why someone cannot do something:

> She's **too young to drive**. (= She can't drive because she's too young.)

4 Now look at this example:

This case is **big enough**. I can put all my clothes into it. The small case is**n't big enough**.

We use **enough** to mean 'as much or as many as we need'. We use **not ... enough** to mean 'less than we need'.

5 We can use enough like this:

> ADJECTIVE + **enough**:
> Is your room warm **enough**?
>
> **enough** + PLURAL NOUN:
> I've got **enough potatoes**, thanks.
>
> **enough** + UNCOUNTABLE NOUN:
> I can't talk to you now. I haven't got **enough time**.

6 We can also use **not ... enough** + **to** + infinitive to say why someone cannot do something:

> She is**n't old enough to drive**. (= She can't drive because she isn't old enough.)

A Complete the sentences using *too* or *enough* and the word in brackets ( ).

♦ I can't eat this soup because it's _too hot_ (hot).
♦ We couldn't buy the tickets because we didn't have _enough money_ (money).
♦ We didn't buy the car because it wasn't _big enough_ (big).
1 I couldn't see her because it was .... (dark).
2 I can't decide what to do because I haven't got .... (information).
3 You can't change the situation now. It's .... (late).
4 Have you had .... (food), or would you like some more?
5 He did badly in the exam because he was .... (nervous).
6 Slow down! You're driving .... (fast).
7 He shouldn't play in the team because he isn't .... (good).
8 I haven't got .... (clothes). I must buy some more.
9 Robert didn't go to work because he didn't feel .... (well).
10 I couldn't lift the suitcase because I wasn't .... (strong).
11 We didn't go swimming because the water was .... (cold).
12 Mary couldn't post all the packages because she didn't have .... (stamps).

Adjectives and adverbs

B Complete the sentences using *too much*, *too many* or *enough* and the word in brackets ( ).

- I'm not enjoying my job at the moment because they're giving me *too much work* (work).
- Is your coffee *sweet enough* (sweet)?
1. Shall we have another coffee? Have we got .... (time)?
2. I couldn't finish the exam because there were .... (questions).
3. We didn't go for a walk because it wasn't .... (warm).
4. I couldn't eat the meal because there was .... (salt) in it.
5. Mary passed the test because she answered .... (questions) correctly.
6. I didn't enjoy the party because there were .... (people) there.
7. Is that chair .... (comfortable) or would you like to sit here?
8. George couldn't work because the others were making .... (noise).
9. We can't play that game because we haven't got .... (players).
10. Shall I make some sandwiches? Have we got .... (bread)?
11. Her work isn't very good. She makes .... (mistakes).

C Join the sentences using *too* or *enough* with *to* + infinitive (e.g. *to do*, *to go*).

- Clare couldn't sleep. She was too worried.
  Clare was too worried to sleep.
- I can't go on holiday. I haven't got enough money.
  I haven't got enough money to go on holiday.
1. I can't do any more work. I'm too tired.

2. Julia won't pass the exam. She isn't good enough.

3. Clive can't play basketball. He's too short.

4. His girlfriend couldn't go to the party. She was too ill.

5. David couldn't pay the bill. He didn't have enough money.

6. Shall we go to the beach? Is it hot enough?

7. I can't see you tonight. I'm too busy.

8. I don't want to go home. It's too early.

9. Chris couldn't repair the car. He didn't have enough tools.

10. I didn't visit all the museums. I didn't have enough time.

70 So and such

1 We use **so** and **such** to intensify adjectives. Compare:

*Helen got all the answers right. She is **so** clever.* (= She is very clever.)

*Helen got all the answers right. She is **such a** clever person.* (= She is a very clever person.)

We use **so** before adjectives that do not have a noun after them, and before adverbs:

ADJECTIVE	
This tea is **so**	sweet!
Tom's feet are **so**	big!

ADVERB	
They get up **so**	late.
Maria sang **so**	beautifully!

We use **such a/an** before an adjective + singular noun (e.g. **person**).
We use **such** before a plural noun (e.g. **feet**) or an uncountable noun (e.g. **food**):

ADJECTIVE + NOUN	
It was **such an**	amazing car!
He has **such**	big feet!
That was **such**	excellent food.

(For uncountable nouns, see **Unit 53**.)

2 We can use **so** with **many** and **much**:

▶ **so many** + plural noun:
   *There were **so many** people in the shop.*

▶ **so much** + uncountable noun:
   *We had **so much** work to do.*

We can use **such** with **a lot of**:

▶ **such a lot of** + plural noun:
   *There were **such a lot of** people in the shop.*

▶ **such a lot of** + uncountable noun:
   *We had **such a lot of** work to do.*

3 Sentences with **so** and **such** can also describe the result of something:

	RESULT	
It was **so** dark	**that** we didn't see him.	
He arrived **so** late,	he missed his plane.	

	RESULT	
It was **such a** dark night	**that** we didn't see him.	
It was **such a** lovely day,	we went to the beach.	

A Complete the sentences with *such* or *so*.

♦ Tom is very handsome. He has <u>such</u> beautiful eyes.
♦ It was a very pleasant trip because the guide was <u>so</u> nice.
1 My birthday was wonderful. I got .... lovely presents.
2 It was difficult to drive because there was .... much snow.
3 I like Tom. He is .... a nice person.
4 We couldn't play tennis because it was .... windy.
5 Jack loves his children. He is .... a wonderful father.
6 Nobody listens to Jasmine because she says .... silly things.
7 The nurses are wonderful here. They are .... helpful.
8 Look at the stars. They are .... bright tonight.

Adjectives and adverbs

B Complete the sentences with *such*, *such a* or *such an*.

- Edinburgh is <u>such a</u> wonderful city.
1. Motorbikes are _____ dangerous machines.
2. I love skiing. It's _____ exciting sport. But it's a dangerous sport, too.
3. My cousin had _____ terrible accident. He almost died.
4. I like these new dresses. They have _____ pretty colours.
5. We had _____ wonderful meal. The food was excellent.
6. Susan Strange is _____ interesting writer.

C Write sentences using *so*, *such*, *such a* or *such an* and the words in brackets ( ). Put the verbs in the correct tense.

- I can't believe that Tom is only 13 years old. (He/have/grow/tall!)
  <u>He has grown so tall!</u>
- I never believe those boys. (They/be/always/tell/stupid lies!)
  <u>They are always telling such stupid lies!</u>
1. I enjoy John's cooking. (He/be/wonderful cook.)

2. I can't hear anything. (Those people/be/make/much noise.)

3. Jacob won three prizes. (He/be/lucky.)

4. Sara always looks lovely. (She/wear/pretty clothes.)

5. We had three ice creams. (They/be/delicious.)

6. I don't smoke. (It/be/unhealthy habit.)

7. I enjoyed that test. (It/be/easy.)

D For each sentence, write another sentence with a similar meaning. Use *so … that*.

- We decided not to call them because it was very late.
  It was <u>so late that we decided not to call them</u>.
1. Ellie didn't finish the exam because she worked very slowly.
   She worked _____
2. We didn't buy the sofa because it was very expensive.
   The sofa was _____
3. Paul didn't go out because he was very tired.
   Paul was _____
4. Peter couldn't see the holes because they were very small.
   The holes were _____
5. I couldn't finish the food because there was too much of it.
   There was _____

71 Comparative adjectives

1 Look at the way we compare things:

£100 per night   £50 per night

The Plaza Hotel is **cheaper than** the Excelsior.
The Excelsior Hotel is **bigger than** the Plaza.
The Excelsior is **more expensive than** the Plaza.
The Plaza Hotel is **smaller than** the Excelsior.

2 **Cheaper** and **more expensive** are comparative adjectives. We form them like this:

▶ short adjectives (one syllable):

ADJECTIVE	COMPARATIVE
old	older
long	longer
nice	nicer
new	newer
slow	slower
fat	fatter
hot	hotter
big	bigger

▶ long adjectives (two syllables or more):

ADJECTIVE	COMPARATIVE
famous	more famous
difficult	more difficult
careful	more careful
expensive	more expensive

▶ adjectives ending with **-y**:

| happy | happier |
| hungry | hungrier |

▶ irregular adjectives:

| good | better |
| bad | worse |

(For more information, see **Appendix 4**, page 245.)

3 To compare things, we use a comparative adjective + **than**:
Tom is **richer than** Paul.
Paris is **more beautiful** than London.
My new car is **better than** my old one.

A Write the comparative form of these adjectives.

♦ cold — *colder*
1. big
2. careful
3. expensive
4. good
5. fat
6. famous
7. new
8. modern
9. young
10. cheap
11. delicious
12. rich
13. long
14. hungry
15. nice
16. happy
17. difficult
18. old
19. beautiful
20. friendly
21. hot
22. wonderful
23. bad
24. small
25. sad

Adjectives and adverbs

B Write comparative sentences about the pictures using *than* and the words in brackets ( ).
Use the Present Simple.

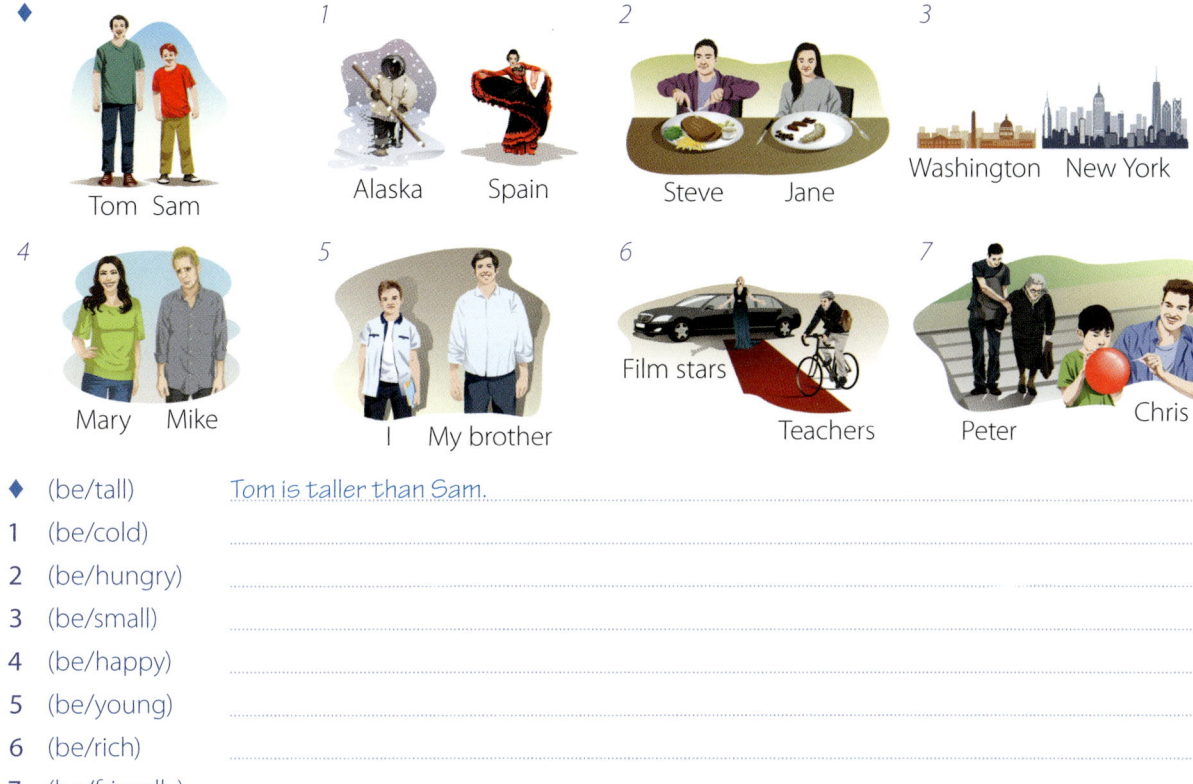

- (be/tall) <u>Tom is taller than Sam.</u>
1 (be/cold) ....
2 (be/hungry) ....
3 (be/small) ....
4 (be/happy) ....
5 (be/young) ....
6 (be/rich) ....
7 (be/friendly) ....

C Look at the information about two boats, the Queen Anne and the King John.

BOATS	LENGTH	AREA	TOP SPEED	YEAR MADE	PRICE
Queen Anne	14 metres	40 metres²	35 knots	2005	£9,000
King John	9 metres	23 metres²	30 knots	1997	£3,500

Now put words from the box in the sentences.

| King John (x2) | ~~bigger~~ | slower | is | than |
| Queen Anne (x2) | longer | expensive | more | |

- The Queen Anne is <u>bigger</u> than the King John.
1 The King John is smaller .... the Queen Anne.
2 The Queen Anne is .... modern than the King John.
3 The King John .... older than the Queen Anne.
4 The .... is faster than the ....
5 The Queen Anne is more .... than the King John.
6 The King John is .... than the Queen Anne.
7 The .... is cheaper than the ....
8 The Queen Anne is .... than the King John.

72 Superlative adjectives

1 We use superlatives in the following way:

The **most expensive** seats are at the front of the theatre.
The **cheapest** seats are at the back.
The **least expensive** seats are at the back.
He is **the worst** player in the team.
It was **the happiest** day of their lives.

We can use the superlative without a noun:
The seats at the back are **the cheapest**.

2 Look at these tables:

▶ short adjectives (one syllable):

ADJECTIVE	SUPERLATIVE
warm	the warmest
tall	the tallest
low	the lowest
big	the biggest
hot	the hottest
wet	the wettest

▶ long adjectives (two syllables or more):

ADJECTIVE	SUPERLATIVE
famous	the most/least famous
difficult	the most/least difficult
careful	the most/least careful
expensive	the most/least expensive

▶ adjectives ending with **-y**:

easy	the easiest
happy	the happiest

▶ irregular adjectives:

good	the best
bad	the worst

(For more details see **Appendix 4**, page 245.)

3 We usually use **the** before the superlative:
London is **the biggest** city in England.
The Taj Mahal is **the most beautiful** building in the world.

Note that we use **in** (not **of**) for places after the superlative:
… the **richest** man **in** Europe.
(NOT … ~~of Europe~~.)

We do not always use a noun after a superlative adjective:
George and Mary have three children. Mike is **the oldest**.
A: Which table did you buy?
B: **The most expensive**.

4 We often use the Present Perfect with ever after the superlative:
That was the **best** film **I've ever seen**.
A: How was your holiday?
B: Fantastic! Iceland is the most beautiful country **I've ever visited**.

A Put the words in brackets ( ) in the right order to make sentences.

♦ (the world – Antarctica – coldest – is – place – the – in – .)
  <u>Antarctica is the coldest place in the world.</u>

1 (city – the – Manchester – in England – is – friendliest – .)
  ....

2 (in New York – expensive – restaurant – The Manhattan – the – is – most – .)
  ....

3 (is – river – Africa – the – The Nile – longest – in – .)
  ....

156

Adjectives and adverbs

4 (town – most – in Spain – Granada – beautiful – is – the – .)

5 (painting – The Mona Lisa – the – famous – in – is – most – the world – .)

6 (the – Europe – mountain – in – highest – Mont Blanc – is – .)

B Complete the sentences using the superlative form of the adjective in brackets ( ).

♦ Anna is _the youngest_ (young) person in the class.
1 We stayed in _____ (bad) hotel in the whole city.
2 People say that it is _____ (funny) film of the year.
3 What is _____ (tall) building in the world?
4 Her teachers say that she is _____ (good) student in the school.
5 Many people say that Venice is _____ (beautiful) city in the world.

C Look at the information about three boats and complete the sentences using the correct superlative form of the adjectives in brackets ( ).

BOATS	LENGTH	TOP SPEED	PRICE
Queen Anne	14 metres	35 knots	£9,000
Red Devil	6 metres	72 knots	£23,000
Jolly Jim	4 metres	28 knots	£6,000

♦ (long) The Queen Anne is the longest _____ boat.
1 (short) _____ boat.
2 (fast) _____ boat.
3 (slow) _____ boat.
4 (expensive) The Red Devil is _____ boat.
5 (expensive) The Jolly Jim is _____ boat.

D Write sentences using the words in brackets ( ). Use *the* + superlative, and the Present Perfect + *ever*.

♦ (It's/cold/place/I/visit) _It's the coldest place I've ever visited._
1 (It's/big/ship/I/see)
2 (He's/rich/man/I/meet)
3 (It's/difficult/exam/I/do)
4 (It's/sad/film/I/see)
5 (She's/happy/person/I/meet)
6 (It's/modern/flat/I/see)
7 (It's/hot/country/I/visit)
8 (It's/small/dog/I/see)

73 Adverbs (1): adjectives and adverbs

1 Here are some adjectives and adverbs:

ADJECTIVE	ADVERB
quick	quickly
careful	carefully
easy	easily

2 Compare adverbs and adjectives:

ADVERBS

We use adverbs to describe how someone or something does an action:

Peter plays the violin beautifully.

(*Beautifully* describes how Peter plays.)

ADJECTIVES

We use adjectives to describe people or things.
We use adjectives before nouns, or after **be/seem/get**:

Look at that beautiful violin!
That violin is beautiful.

3 We form most regular adverbs by adding **-ly** to the adjective:

slow → slowly	bad → badly

The whole team played very badly.

If an adjective ends with **-y**, the adverb ends with **-ily**:

happy → happily	easy → easily

We solved the problem easily.

If an adjective ends with **-ble**, the adverb ends in **-bly**:

comfortable → comfortably

4 Some adverbs are irregular; they do not end with **-ly**:

good → well

He's a good guitar player. (*good* = adjective)
He plays the guitar well. (*well* = adverb)

Fast and **hard** are both adjectives and adverbs:

fast → fast   hard → hard

Maria is a fast learner. (*fast* = adjective)
Maria learns fast. (*fast* = adverb)
James is a hard worker. (*hard* = adjective)
James works hard. (*hard* = adverb)

5 We form the comparative of regular adverbs with **more** or **less**:

carefully → more/less carefully

You should do your work more carefully.
She does her work less carefully than other people.

The comparative of **well** is **better**:

She speaks Arabic better than me.

The comparatives of **fast** and **hard** are **faster** and **harder**:

Could you walk faster? We're in a hurry.
You will have to work harder in future.

6 We form the superlative of regular adverbs with **the most/the least**:

more efficiently → the most efficiently / the least efficiently

In the office, Oliver does his work the most efficiently and Ellie does her work the least efficiently.

The superlative of **well** is **the best** and the superlative of **badly** is **the worst**:

Which member of the team played the best and who played the worst?

The superlatives of **fast** and **hard** are **the fastest** and **the hardest**:

They decided to find out who could run the fastest.
Who works the hardest in your class?

A Choose the correct adjective or adverb in brackets ( ) to complete the sentences.

♦ The train was very _slow_ (slow/slowly) and I arrived late.
1 The journey took a long time because the train went very _____ (slow/slowly).
2 Mrs Green went _____ (quick/quickly) back to her office.
3 I'm afraid I can't give you an _____ (immediate/immediately) answer.

Adjectives and adverbs

4 The work that the builders did for us was very .... (bad/badly).
5 The builders did the work for us very .... (bad/badly).
6 She organized the party very .... (good/well), and everybody enjoyed it.

B Complete the sentences using the adverb form of the adjective in brackets ( ).

♦ She read the message *quickly* (quick).
1 Read the instructions .... (careful).
2 He looked at her .... (angry), but he didn't say anything.
3 She passed all her exams .... (easy).
4 I ran as .... (fast) as I could.
5 He thinks that he did the test .... (bad) and that he'll fail.
6 She was working .... (busy) when I arrived.
7 He was playing .... (happy) when I came into the room.

C Complete the dialogues with the adverb form of the adjectives from the box.

slow   fast   hard   good (x2)   ~~easy~~   bad

♦ A: Were the questions difficult?
  B: No, I answered them *easily* .
1 A: Does she speak English .... ?
  B: No, she only knows a few words.
2 A: Hurry up! I'm waiting!
  B: Just a minute. I'm coming as .... as I can.
3 A: Did you lose at tennis again?
  B: Yes, I played .... and I lost.
4 A: Have you been working .... today?
  B: No, I've done nothing all day!
5 A: Have you finished that book yet?
  B: No, I always read very .... It takes me a long time to finish a book.

D Complete the sentences using the comparative or superlative adverb form of the adjectives in brackets ( ).

♦ You must do your work *more carefully* (careful) in future.
1 He has run the 100 metres .... (fast) than any other athlete in the world this year.
2 Everyone else did the test .... (good) than me, because they'd worked .... (hard) than me.
3 You can travel .... (cheap) at certain times of the year.
4 He plays .... (confident) than he did in the past because he has got .... (good) at the game.
5 You could eat .... (expensive) if you didn't buy so many takeaways.
6 You will be able to sit .... (comfortable) in this chair.

74 Adverbs (2): adverbs of frequency

1 Look at how often Jasmine does things in a year:

She has a cup of tea at breakfast.	365
She goes to the cinema.	10
She walks to work.	0
She goes swimming.	52
She goes on holiday.	2

We can say:
  She **always** has a cup of tea at breakfast.
  She **sometimes** goes to the cinema.
  She **never** walks to work.
  She goes swimming **every week**.
  She goes on holiday **twice a year**.

2 We use these adverbs to talk about how often we do things:

| always | usually | normally | often |
| sometimes | rarely | hardly ever | never |

We put **always**, **usually**, etc. after **be** or an auxiliary (e.g. **have**, **must**):
  He **is always** late.
  I'**ve often** been to Spain for my holidays.
  You **must never** swim after a big meal.

But we put **always** etc. before main verbs:
  I **usually walk** to work.
  She **hardly ever drinks** coffee.

3 We can compare the meaning of these adverbs like this:

0%	never	100%	always
5%	hardly ever	90%	usually
10%	rarely	80%	normally
30%	sometimes	70%	often

(We usually say the word **often** without pronouncing the letter **t**.)

4 If we want to say exactly how often we do things, we use these expressions:

| every … | once a … | twice/two times a … |
| three times a … | | four times a … |

We put these expressions at the end of sentences. Here are some examples:
  I run round the park **every day**.
  I play tennis **once a week**.
  She drinks coffee **three times a day**.
  I go skiing **once a year**.
  He drives to London **twice a month**.

A Rewrite the sentences, putting the words in brackets ( ) in the correct place.

♦ I work late at the office.
  (often) I often work late at the office.

1 You must lock the front door when you leave.
  (always)

2 Steve and Charlotte play golf.
  (twice a month)

3 I eat a sandwich for lunch.
  (usually)

4 I go to jazz concerts at the weekend.
  (sometimes)

5 My teacher gives me a lot of homework.
  (every day)

6 We see our Mexican friends.
  (hardly ever)

7 They go to Morocco for their holidays.
  (often)

8 William and Marie go to the theatre.
(four times a year) ....

9 They are at home in the evening.
(rarely) ....

B Look at the table and write sentences comparing Liz and Nathan.
Use adverbs from the table in Section 3 (opposite).

			10%	20%	30%	40%	50%	60%	70%	80%	90%	100%
♦	walk to work	Liz	▨	▨	▨							
		Nathan										
1	get up early	Liz	▨	▨								
		Nathan	■	■	■	■	■	■	■	■	■	■
2	watch TV	Liz	▨	▨	▨	▨	▨	▨	▨			
		Nathan	■	■	■							
3	take a taxi	Liz	▨									
		Nathan										
4	have supper at home	Liz	▨	▨	▨	▨	▨	▨	▨	▨	▨	
		Nathan	■	■	■	■	■	■				

♦ Liz sometimes walks to work. Nathan never walks to work.
1 ....
2 ....
3 ....
4 ....

C Look at the table about John's activities and write sentences using the words in brackets ( )
and the Present Simple.

	DAY	WEEK	MONTH	YEAR
swimming		2		
French	1			
his mother			3	
a shower	2			
broad				1
sister				3
tennis		4		

♦ (He/go/swimming)   He goes swimming twice a week.
1 (He/practise/French)   ....
2 (He/phone/his mother)   ....
3 (He/have/a shower)   ....
4 (He/go/abroad)   ....
5 (He/visit/his sister)   ....
6 (He/play/tennis)   ....

75 Adverbs (3): place, direction, sequence

1 We use **here** with the meaning 'in or to this place/the place where the speaker is':
> I've been living **here** for three years.
> Come **here**, I want to speak to you.

We use **there** with the meaning 'in or to that place/another place, away from where the speaker is':
> Stay **there**, I'll come and get you.
> Go and stand **there**, I'll take a picture of you.

We also use **there** with the meaning 'in or to a place previously mentioned':
> I lived in France for a year and I made a lot of friends while I was **there**.

We often use **over here** and **over there** when we are speaking informally:
> Come **over here** and sit down.

2 Some common adverbs describing a place or a movement in a particular direction are:

> *abroad* (= in/to another country)
> *ahead*
> *away*
> *back*
> *downstairs/upstairs*
> *in/out*
> *inside/outside* (= in or out of a building)
> *nearby*
> *forward(s)/backward(s)/sideways*

> Mary is **abroad** but she's coming back soon.
> She ran **downstairs** and opened the front door.
> He walked **out**, saying that he couldn't stay.
> The queue slowly moved **forward(s)**.

Notice that we use **out** with the meaning 'not at home/work, etc. for part of a day or a day' and **away** with the meaning 'not at home/work, etc. for more than a day':
> Mr Butler is **out** at the moment. He'll be back at around 12 o'clock.
> My wife is **away** this week. She's at a three-day conference.

3 We often use these adverbial phrases when giving someone directions to a place:

> *straight on/ahead*
> *turn left/right*
> *on the left/right* (to say where something is)
> *to the left/right* (for movement)
> *as far as*

> Go **straight on**. When you come to the traffic lights, **turn right**. The first road **on the left** is the one you want.

4 When we talk about a number of actions or events that happen one after the other, we can indicate the order with these adverbs and adverbial phrases:

> *first(ly)/first of all*
> *second(ly)*
> *third(ly)*, etc.
> *last(ly)*
> *finally*

Instead of using **second**(ly), **third**(ly), etc., we often use the following adverbs and adverbial phrases to link actions or events in a sequence:

> *then*
> *next*
> *afterwards*
> *after that*

> To make this dish, **first** you chop the tomatoes, **then** you add the garlic ...
> First of all I went to Paris, **after that** I spent some time in Switzerland, **then** I travelled round Germany and **finally** I went to the Netherlands.

Adjectives and adverbs

A Complete the sentences with the correct adverb in brackets ( ).

- Jess lived *abroad* (abroad/away) for several years, mostly in the US.
1. We had to wait .... (out/outside) until the club opened.
2. I'm going .... (out/away) now and I'll be back in about an hour.
3. Fortunately there was a hospital .... (nearby/nearly).
4. I went .... (upstair/upstairs) and looked for the bathroom.
5. The queue of traffic slowly moved .... (forwards/out).
6. We're going .... (out/away) for the weekend.
7. George has gone .... (out/away) until the end of the week.
8. Would you like to live .... (away/abroad)?

B Complete the directions from the station to Tom's house using the adverbial phrases from the box.

> on the right   turn left   straight ahead   turn right   ~~turn right~~

- Come out of the station and *turn right*.
1. .... at the first junction.
2. Go .... until you reach the traffic lights.
3. .... into my road.
4. You'll find my house ....

C Look at this sequence of events and put them in the correct order. Link the events using suitable adverbs or adverbial phrases. More than one answer is possible.

> **How I found an apartment to rent:**
> I agreed with the landlord that I would rent it.
> I made a list of apartments I could afford.
> I signed the contract.
> I went to see some of the apartments.
> ~~I looked through the adverts online.~~
> I moved into the apartment.
> I paid the first month's rent as a deposit.
> I decided which apartment to rent.

- *First of all/First(ly) I looked through the adverts online.*
1. ....
2. ....
3. ....
4. ....
5. ....
6. ....
7. ....

163

76 Adverb + adjective; noun + noun; etc.

1

It was cold.   It was **very** cold.

We can use an adverb (e.g. **very**) before an adjective (e.g. **cold**) to make the adjective stronger. Some common adverbs we use in this way are:

| very | extremely | really |

We were **very tired** after the trip.
I felt **extremely nervous** before the exam.
I'm **really angry** with you. (= very angry)

We can also make an adjective weaker with these adverbs:

| fairly | quite | rather |

Our car is **fairly old**. (= It's old, but it isn't very old.)
The meal was **quite nice**. (= It was nice but not wonderful.)
It was **rather late** when we finally arrived. (= It was late but not very late.)

2

When we use two adjectives together, we order them like this:

▶ We use 'opinion' adjectives (e.g. **wonderful**, **nice**, **pleasant**, **strange**) before any other adjective (e.g. **new**):

	OPINION	
a	wonderful	new product
a	lovely	warm day
a	beautiful	little cottage
an	horrible	green shirt

▶ We use 'size' adjectives (e.g. **big**, **tall**) before an adjective that gives other information, for example its age (**new**, **old**), its colour, its shape (**thin**, **round**):

	SIZE	
a	big	new building
a	small	red mark
a	huge	black cloud
an	large	round stone

3

We can use two nouns together. The first noun is like an adjective and gives information about the second noun:

	NOUN +	NOUN
a	cardboard	box
a	coffee	pot
a	laundry	basket
an	office	building

A Complete these sentences using *really* or *quite*.

◆ The film was _really_ good. I enjoyed it a lot.
1 It's _____ cold outside, but not very cold.
2 It isn't a wonderful book, but it's _____ good.
3 The tickets were _____ expensive – they cost much more than I expected.
4 This series is _____ popular in my country; millions of people watch it.
5 He's _____ good at his job, but he sometimes makes bad mistakes.
6 The meal was _____ nice, but it wasn't very good.
7 It's _____ dangerous to drive so fast in such terrible weather conditions.
8 I'm not a brilliant tennis player, but I am _____ good.
9 They're all _____ intelligent students, and they will all pass their exams easily.
10 The company that I work for is _____ big, but it's not enormous.

Adjectives and adverbs

B Put the words in brackets ( ) into the correct order.

- (a – town – beautiful – little) a beautiful little town
1. (a – day – pleasant – sunny)
2. (a – smile – big – nice)
3. (a – large – coffee – black)
4. (a – old – coat – horrible)
5. (a – large – building – white)
6. (a – bird – big – grey)
7. (a – woman – thin – tall)
8. (a – small – car – blue)
9. (a – story – little – strange)

C Match the words in box A and box B to describe what you can see in each picture.

A		
~~table~~	tennis	paper
rubbish	door	soup
road	picture	key
coat	coffee	light

B		
cup	court	pot
handle	sign	hanger
ring	bowl	~~lamp~~
bulb	frame	bin

a table lamp

1

2

3

4

5

6

7

8

9

10

11

77 Position of adverbs in a sentence

1 There are four possible positions for adverbs:

- before the subject:
  Sometimes she gets very tired.
- between the subject and the verb:
  I **sometimes** read biographies.
- between a modal or auxiliary and the main verb:
  I can **sometimes** play this game very well.
- at the end of a clause or sentence:
  He makes me angry **sometimes**.

However, not all adverbs can go in all four positions.

2 We use adverbs of certainty (**probably**, **certainly**, **definitely**) in these positions:

- between the subject and a positive verb:
  Jasmine **probably** knows the answer.
- after a positive auxiliary/modal:
  They'll **probably** win.
- before a negative auxiliary/modal:
  Jasmine **probably** doesn't know the answer.
  They **probably** won't win.

3 We use adverbs of completeness (**almost**, **nearly**, etc.) in these positions:

- between the subject and the verb:
  He **almost** died.
- after an auxiliary/modal:
  I've **nearly** finished.

4 We use some adverbs that emphasize a statement (**even**, **just** (= simply), **only**, **also**) in these positions:

- between the subject and the verb:
  She was rude and she **even** laughed at me.
  I don't know why, I **just** like jazz.
- after an auxiliary/modal:
  I can't **even** understand a word.
  I'm **only** joking.

Notice that we use **just** before a negative modal or auxiliary:
I **just** don't understand why it happened.

5 Note that all these adverbs go after **be**:
She is **probably** at work now.

For the positions of adverbs related to time (**just**, **already**, **yet**) see **Unit 15**.

6 We use **too** and **either** at the end of a sentence. We use **too** after two positive verbs and **either** after two negative verbs:

George earns a lot and he spends a lot **too**.
I don't like dogs and I'm not keen on cats **either**. (See also **Unit 103**.)

7 We usually use adverbs of manner (those that describe how something is done, e.g. **well**, **badly**, **quickly**, **carefully**) in these positions:

- after the verb:
  Please drive **carefully**.
- after an object:
  I read the letter **carefully**.

8 We use adverbial phrases of time (e.g. **in the morning**, **last Saturday**, **during the holidays**) at the beginning or end of a sentence or clause:

Last Saturday I had a great time.
I had a great time **last Saturday**.

We usually use other adverbial phrases (e.g. those describing place or manner) after the object:

He put his suitcase **on the floor**.
She opened the letters **with a knife**.

9 When there is more than one adverb or adverbial phrase in a sentence, we normally use them in this order:

manner → *place* → *time*

He was working hard in his office last night.

Adjectives and adverbs

A Rewrite the sentences using the adverb in brackets ( ) in the correct place.

♦ (probably) They will take the train.   They will probably take the train.
1 (definitely) She comes from Leeds.
2 (nearly) The meal is ready.
3 (even) He lent me some money.
4 (certainly) She works very hard.
5 (only) There were two tickets left.

B These sentences are taken from a newspaper's sports section but they are all incorrect. Rewrite them so that they are correct.

♦ He will play definitely in Saturday's game.
   He will definitely play in Saturday's game.
1 Tickets for the game almost have sold out.

2 They won't probably become champions.

3 He scored a penalty and he created also two goals.

4 They didn't just play well enough to win.

5 They won nearly but they were unlucky at the end.

C These sentences are taken from film reviews. Put the adverbs in brackets ( ) into the correct position in the underlined parts of the sentences.

♦ This film will be a big hit with the public. (definitely)   will definitely be
1 Many of the characters and events are unbelievable. (almost)
2 This film doesn't create any interest or excitement. (just)
3 The plot isn't very interesting and the performances aren't very good. (either)
4 Although the film was released last week, it has earned a lot of money. (only)
5 This film has attracted a lot of publicity. (certainly)
6 She can act very well and she can sing very well. (also)

D Put the words in brackets ( ) in the correct order to make sentences.

♦ (hard–worked–yesterday– .)
   Lucy worked hard yesterday.
1 (all day–have–well–worked– .)
   They
2 (after lunch–in the sea–swam– .)
   The children
3 (during the night–rained–heavily– .)
   It
4 (before supper–did–in my room–my homework– .)
   I
5 (better–last week–played– .)
   Our team

Test G Adjectives and adverbs

A Complete the conversation between two neighbours using the comparative or superlative form of the adjective or adverb in brackets ( ).

Sam: I'm pretty sure my house is a bit ♦ _bigger_ (big) than yours.
Pete: Really? I thought mine was ¹ _____ (big) in the street.
Sam: Oh. Anyway, my daughter Jo is ² _____ (bright) girl in her class.
Pete: That reminds me. I saw you and Jo pushing your car last week. I must say my car works ³ _____ (good) than yours.
Sam: Really? What's ⁴ _____ (far) you've ever driven? We've crossed America from coast to coast in my car.
Pete: Your wife didn't enjoy the journey, though, did she? You know, I think I've been ⁵ _____ (happy) married than you.
Sam: I'm not surprised. You've bought your wife ⁶ _____ (expensive) presents in the world, haven't you?
Pete: Well, I've got enough money. I suppose I work ⁷ _____ (hard) than you, don't I, and earn money ⁸ _____ (quick)?
Sam: I think we'd have a fight if you weren't ⁹ _____ (tall) man in town.

B Jasmine has just arrived in a small town in Italy. She's emailing her friend Mia in England. Choose the correct words in brackets ( ) to complete the email.

Hi Mia,
I arrived about three hours ago. I'm sitting in the living room on the ♦ _third_ (three/third) floor of the house. I was ¹ _____ (excited/exciting), of course, on the way here, but the journey was ² _____ (tired/tiring). It's ³ _____ (so/such) a beautiful house! I'm a bit ⁴ _____ (worried/worrying), though. Life here for the next six months is going to be very ⁵ _____ (quietly/quiet). On the ⁶ _____ (16/16th) of June, there's a festival in the village, but that's the only thing this year! I hope you will email me. I will be ⁷ _____ (disappointed/disappointing) if I don't get a message now and again. I met my neighbour just after I arrived. She was ⁸ _____ (so/such) helpful! She got married last month, and it's her ⁹ _____ (28/28th) birthday tomorrow. She speaks English ¹⁰ _____ (good/well), and she sings ¹¹ _____ (beautifully/beautiful) – I can hear her now! Anyway, you know I'm going to try to write a book about my father, so I won't be ¹² _____ (boring/bored) here. I'm a ¹³ _____ (slowly/slow) writer, but I think it will be an ¹⁴ _____ (interesting/interested) story in the end.
Speak soon,
Jasmine

C Tom, Ingrid, Raphael and Hilary are talking about their children. Rewrite the underlined part of the conversation.

Tom: I'm worried, Ingrid. <u>Paul is quicker at schoolwork than Joanna.</u> ♦ _Joanna_ isn't as _quick at schoolwork as Paul_.
Raphael: Kids work too hard at school these days in my view, Tom. <u>Our son Andy didn't watch the football match with me on Saturday. He was too tired!</u>
¹ _____ too tired to _____ !

Adjectives and adverbs

Ingrid: But you need to work hard to get a job with good pay. Our oldest boy, Sam, is 25 now. <u>He can't buy a house. He hasn't got enough money.</u>
² _____ enough money to _____.

Hilary: But everything costs so much these days! We took Andy to a cycle shop to see a new bike yesterday. <u>We didn't buy it because it was really expensive.</u>
³ _____ so expensive that _____.

Tom: I know! We looked at a new car. <u>I've never seen a more beautiful machine!</u>
⁴ It's the _____ I've ever seen!

Ingrid: <u>And you drive wonderfully, Tom!</u> ⁵ And you're _____!

Tom: Thank you, darling. <u>I'm not as fast as Raphael.</u> ⁶ Raphael _____.

Hilary: Tom! Don't say things like that! <u>Raphael is the worst driver I've ever met!</u>
⁷ I've never _____.

Raphael: How do you know? <u>You don't open your eyes in the car. You're too frightened.</u>
⁸ _____ too frightened to _____.

Hilary: <u>I'm not going to argue with you. I haven't got enough time.</u>
⁹ _____ enough time to _____.
Boys and their cars! Why don't you spend more time in the garden, Raphael?

D Put the words in brackets ( ) in the correct order to complete the text about Bath.

Bath is ♦ <u>an interesting English city in the South West.</u> (in the South-West/an/English/interesting/city). Tourists ¹ _____ (for four or five days/stay/usually/there). Most people will visit ² _____ (the/Roman/old/amazing/Baths), and then they ³ _____ (probably/will/a bus/up to the Royal Crescent/take). After that they ⁴ _____ (beautiful/parks/in one of Bath's/green/can either relax) or have tea in ⁵ _____ (the/18th-century/elegant/very/Pump Rooms). There's a festival once a year, and ⁶ _____ (to get/tickets/difficult/always/it's) because it's so popular. Outside Bath, you can visit ⁷ _____ (American/unusual/the/really/Museum), or the lions at Longleat, or you ⁸ _____ (can/peacefully in the countryside/drive around/just).

E Esther is leaving a voicemail message. Complete her message with the words from the box.

| as far as | garden | on the left | ~~at home~~ | upstairs | away |
| crates | fairly | sideways | address | table | outside |

'Hi there Helen! I thought you'd be ♦ <u>at home</u>. Oh dear. Anyway, I'm going ¹ _____ for a few days. I'm leaving the car ² _____, though. It's ³ _____ old, like me, and the garage is full of old ⁴ _____. I've lost my ⁵ _____ book, but I think I know the way to The Grange. You take the train ⁶ _____ Little Hollow, and then it's ⁷ _____ when you leave the station. Anyway, the weather looks good, so if you want to borrow my ⁸ _____ chairs while I'm away, go ⁹ _____, turn left and they're in that little cupboard. You'll have to go into the cupboard ¹⁰ _____, I'm afraid, because it's full of old ¹¹ _____ legs and things like that! Anyway, I'd better go. Bye for now!'

78 Prepositions of place and movement

1 **In**, **on** and **at** are used to talk about places:

- We use **in** with enclosed spaces (e.g. rooms, buildings) and limited areas (e.g. towns, parks, countries, continents):
  in my pocket   **in** her car   **in** Germany

- We use **on** with surfaces (e.g. walls, floors, shelves) and lines (e.g. paths, coasts, the equator):
  on the grass   **on** the sea
  on the line   **on** the third floor

- We use **at** with a point (e.g. **at** the bus stop), and **at** with a building, when we mean either inside or outside:
  A: Let's meet **at** the cinema.
  B: OK. Shall we meet **in** the cinema itself or **on** the pavement outside?

There is a woman **in** the car.
There are people **outside** the cinema.
The people are **on** the pavement.
There is a clock **above** the cinema entrance.
The cinema entrance is **under** the clock.
The bank is **next to/beside** the cinema.
The letter box is **opposite** the cinema.
The bank is **between** the cinema and the cafe.
There is a hill **behind** the town.
The car is **in front of** the bank.

2 Look at the illustration and read the sentences:

3 **Into**, **onto**, and **to** are used to talk about movement:
  We moved the chairs **into** my bedroom.
  The actor ran **onto** the stage.
  They walked **to** the next town.

The opposites are **out of**, **off** and **from**:
  We moved the chairs **out of** my bedroom.
  The actor ran **off** the stage.
  We drove **from** London to Edinburgh.

Here are other prepositions of movement:
  They ran **across** the field to the road.
  James cycled **along** the road to the next town.
  I walked **up** the hill and ran **down** the other side.
  The bus went **past** the bus stop without stopping.
  The train goes **through** three tunnels.

A These sentences describe the picture. Look at the picture and change the underlined words which are wrong. Tick (✓) the underlined words which are correct.

- There is a TV <u>under</u> on_____ the table.
- There is a dog <u>on</u> ✓ _____ the floor.
1. The dog is <u>under</u> _____ the table.
2. The cat is <u>next to</u> _____ the flowers.
3. The keys are <u>next to</u> _____ the flowers.
4. The flowers are <u>in</u> _____ the vase.
5. There is a big book <u>in front of</u> _____ the flowers.
6. There is a picture <u>on</u> _____ the TV.
7. The cat is <u>above</u> _____ the table.
8. There is a bird <u>on</u> _____ a cage.

Prepositions

B Complete the sentences with *in*, *on* or *at*.

- Peter lives _in_ Turkey.
1. There were some beautiful pictures _____ the walls of their sitting room.
2. The children are playing _____ the grass _____ the park.
3. Does this bus stop _____ the railway station?
4. I live in a flat _____ the fifth floor.
5. Ecuador is _____ South America; it lies _____ the equator.
6. There is a queue of people _____ the bus stop.

C Complete the sentences using the words from the box.

> into (x3)   onto (x2)   ~~to~~   out of   off

- The march started in the park. From there we marched _to_ the Town Hall.
1. The tiger escaped from its cage and jumped _____ the lake. It took a long time to get it _____ the lake and back _____ its cage.
2. Stupidly, Simon drove his car _____ the beach and then he couldn't move it, because the wheels sank _____ the sand. In the end he needed eight people to push it _____ the beach and back _____ the road.

D Look at this picture of a town showing the route for a race and complete the text using the words from the box.

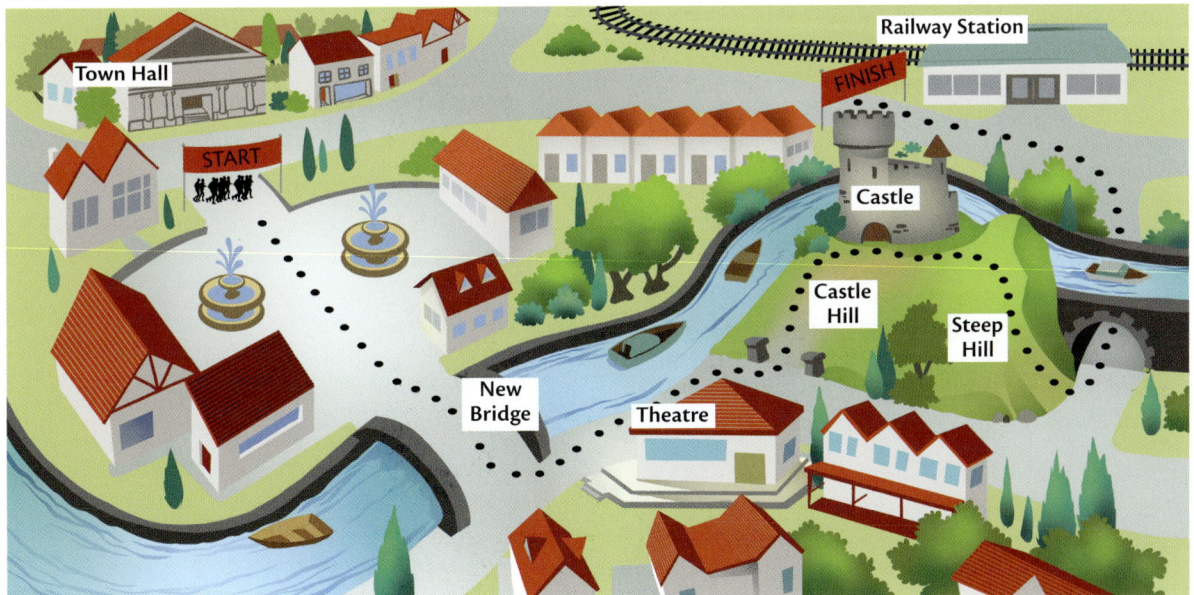

> across   along   ~~at~~   down   in front of   past   from   under   through   up

The race starts ♦ _at_ the Town Hall. The runners start ¹ _____ the Town Hall and run ² _____ the main square, to the river. Then they run over New Bridge and go ³ _____ the road beside the river for about 200 yards. They go ⁴ _____ the theatre and ⁵ _____ Castle Hill. They turn right ⁶ _____ the castle, and they go ⁷ _____ Steep Hill. Then they go ⁸ _____ the tunnel ⁹ _____ the river, and they finish at the station.

79 Prepositions of time

1 When we talk about time we often use the prepositions **in**, **on** or **at**.

▶ We use **in** with parts of the day, and with months, seasons and years:

  in the morning, **in** the afternoon, **in** the evening
  in January, **in** February, **in** March
  in the spring, **in** the summer, **in** the autumn, **in** the winter
  in 1542, **in** 1868, **in** 2016

▶ We use **on** with days and dates:

  on Wednesday, **on** Thursday evening, **on** Christmas Day, **on** her birthday
  on 9th April (We say **On** April the ninth or **On** the ninth of April.)

▶ We use **at** for times of the day, and with meals and mealtimes:

  at 11 a.m., **at** three o'clock
  at breakfast, **at** lunchtime, **at** teatime, **at** dinner

We also say:
  at night, **at** the weekend
  at Christmas, **at** Easter

2 The following words can replace **in**, **on** and **at**:

  this   next   last   every

  I'm going home   **in** April.
                        this April.
  I'm playing tennis   **on** Wednesday.
                        next Wednesday.
  She left   **at** the weekend.
                        last weekend.
  He visits Jasmine   **on** Saturdays.
                        every Saturday.

3 We can use from ... to to talk about time:

THE FRICK COLLECTION

OPENING HOURS
10.00 – 6.00

The museum is open **from** 10 a.m. **to** 6 p.m.

Here are some more examples:
  She's staying here **from** Sunday **to** Tuesday.
  We have a tea break **from** three-thirty **to** four o'clock.

Sometimes, we use **from** on its own:
  I will be in Paris **from** Wednesday.

MONDAY	TUESDAY	WEDNESDAY
		in Paris →

A Complete the sentences with *in*, *on* or *at*.

  ♦ I went to Turkey _in_ July.
  1 We must leave _____ five o'clock.
  2 We'll have a break _____ the afternoon.
  3 She's arriving _____ Monday.
  4 It's very cold here _____ night.
  5 I was born _____ 1992.
  6 I never work _____ the weekend.
  7 We can play tennis _____ the summer.
  8 School starts _____ 5th September.
  9 I'll see you _____ lunchtime.

B Complete this conversation using words from the box.

  two o'clock   ~~summer~~   2015   winter   weekend   Saturday   birthday

Anna: Are you going on holiday in the ♦ _summer_ ?
Tom: No, but I went skiing in Italy in the [1]_____, and I'm going to America at the [2]_____. I'll be in New York on [3]_____; then I'm travelling south to Texas. What about you? Are you going away this year?
Anna: Yes. In fact, I'm flying to Morocco at [4]_____ tomorrow.
Tom: Really? It's a wonderful country. I was there in [5]_____.
Anna: Just think! I'll be on a Moroccan beach on my [6]_____!

Prepositions

C In these sentences there are some mistakes. Sometimes the underlined prepositions are wrong. Sometimes the prepositions are not necessary. Cross out the prepositions which are wrong and replace them if necessary. Put a tick (✓) if the preposition is correct.

- I normally go to the south of France ~~on~~ in _____ the winter. I usually go in ✓ December, but ~~in~~ – _____ last December I couldn't go because my wife was ill.
1. We'll leave at _____ eleven o'clock in _____ Saturday morning.
2. Shall we visit George in _____ Spain in _____ next April?
3. I always drink two cups of coffee on _____ breakfast. In _____ the afternoon I drink tea. I drink hot milk in _____ night before I go to bed.
4. They play golf on _____ every Tuesday in _____ the summer.
5. I gave her a painting on _____ her birthday at _____ June.

D Look at the table with your arrangements for the next few days (*today, this week*), and for the next few months (*in December, next year*). Use the information in the table to write sentences using the Present Continuous (*I'm doing*), and a preposition (*in, on,* etc.) if necessary.

- ~~(play/golf)~~ → ~~the afternoon~~
1. (meet/Steve) → Wednesday morning
2. (go/to the bank) → ten o'clock on Friday
3. (go/sailing) → the weekend
4. (start/a new job) → next Monday
5. (visit/Egypt) → December
6. (sell/my house) → 10th January

- I'm playing golf in the afternoon.
1. I
2. I
3.
4.
5.
6.

E Complete the sentences using the information in brackets ( ).

- (two o'clock → three o'clock) The shop is closed *from two o'clock to three o'clock.*
- (Friday →) She will be on holiday *from Friday.*
1. (June → August) The beach is busy
2. (ten o'clock) I'll be at the sports centre
3. (March →) The new motorway will be open
4. (Monday → Friday) We work
5. (2009 → 2012) He lived in Kenya
6. (January →) She will be in Hong Kong

80 As/like; as if/as though

1 We use **as** + noun:
- to talk about someone's job or role:
  She works **as an assistant** in a laboratory.
  He came to fame **as the main character** in a successful film.
- to talk about the function or use of something:
  I lent him some money **as a favour**.
  You can use this sofa **as a bed**.

2 We use **as** in phrases that refer to something that has already been stated or is already known:
  As I told you last week, I'm going away tomorrow.
  As you know, some friends are staying with me at the moment.

3 We use **as** after certain verbs for giving descriptions or talking about attitudes:
  She **described** her boss **as** short and hairy.
  I **regard** her **as** my best friend.

4 We use **as** in the phrases **such as**, **the same as** and **as usual**:
  Some sports, **such as** golf, don't interest me.
    (= for example)
  I really like buildings **such as** this.
    (= of the same type)
  His income is about **the same as** mine.
  As usual, she gave me some very good advice.

5 We use **like** + noun/pronoun for comparing, with the meaning 'similar to':
  He doesn't behave **like other people**.
  Like most boys of his age, he's keen on sports.
  I wish I could sing **like you**.

6 We use **like** + noun/pronoun with the meaning 'in a similar way to':
  If you cook it **like this**, it always tastes better.

7 We use **like** + noun/pronoun with the meaning 'such as':
  Some people, **like my brother**, really love their jobs.
  I really enjoy music **like this**.

8 We use **look**, **sound**, **taste**, **feel** + **like** + noun/pronoun to talk about the appearance of someone/something or the impression something gives us:
  She doesn't **look like her sister** at all.
  He **sounds like his father** when he speaks.
  This **tastes like coffee**.

(See also **Unit 33**.)

9 We use **as if**/**as though** + subject, verb, etc. with the meaning 'in a way that suggests …'.

We use **as if**/**as though** + subject to describe how something seems:
  He talks **as if** he's an expert on the subject.
    (= he isn't or may not really be an expert)
  She acted **as though** we had never met before.
    (= but we had met before)

A Complete these sentences taken from reviews of new music, using *as* or *like*.

♦ This song sounds exactly *like* _____ the band's previous one.
1 At the moment, there is no one quite _____ this singer on the music scene.
2 Many people regard her _____ one of the best singers in the country at the moment.
3 Although she looks _____ a small and delicate girl, she has a very big voice.
4 _____ everyone knows, this band shot to fame last year.
5 He describes this new album _____ an experiment in a new style of music.
6 Bands _____ this tend to be popular for only a short time.

Prepositions

B Complete the dialogues using *as* or *like*.

♦ A: What did you do before this job?
B: I spent seven years _as_ a teacher at a university.

1 A: Are you coming to the party tonight?
B: No, _____ I told you before, I'm going somewhere else.

2 A: Do you like this programme?
B: No, it's _____ all those reality TV shows, it's really boring.

3 A: I'm having trouble doing this job on the computer.
B: That's because you shouldn't try to do it _____ that. Look, I'll show you.

4 A: Let's stay at this hotel for the whole trip.
B: Yes, we can use it _____ a base for travelling around the region.

5 A: Did you enjoy the book I lent you?
B: Yes, I don't usually enjoy novels _____ that, but it was excellent.

6 A: Did you discuss the problem with William?
B: Yes, and _____ I thought, it was an easy one to solve.

7 A: What's your opinion of Anna?
B: I get on well with her most of the time, but sometimes she acts _____ a child.

8 A: That was a horrible thing to say.
B: Don't get upset. I only said it _____ a joke.

C Complete these sentences describing people using *as*, *like* or *as if/as though*.

♦ Felicity behaves _as if/as though_ she's more important than everyone else.
1 Sarah doesn't think _____ other people, she has her own ideas.
2 _____ most people know, Matt has not had an easy life.
3 Helen dresses _____ the girls she sees in magazines.
4 Toby talks _____ money is the only thing in life that matters.
5 _____ all his friends, James is extremely interested in football.
6 When he talks, Simon sounds _____ someone who is not from this area.
7 _____ a student, Ruth works very hard and is very serious.

D Complete these sentences using *as*, *like* or *as if/as though*.

♦ He's a very good guitarist and he sounds _like_ a professional when he plays.
1 People _____ him really make me angry.
2 This doesn't taste _____ anything I've eaten before.
3 The thief was described _____ tall and thin.
4 _____ usual, she arrived late for work.
5 Older people such _____ my parents have different attitudes from mine.
6 Most people were shocked but she acted _____ nothing important had happened.
7 You sound _____ you've got a bad throat.
8 What you're telling me now is not the same _____ what you told me yesterday.

81 In; with; preposition + -ing

1 We can use **in** to describe what somebody is wearing:

Jasmine is the woman **in** the red dress.
I went to the interview **in** my new suit.
It was a sunny day, and everyone was **in** summer clothes.
Are you allowed to go to work **in** jeans?
We saw some soldiers **in** uniform.

2 We can use **with** to describe a part of somebody's body:

A small boy **with** red hair came into the shop.
Our teacher is a tall man **with** a beard.
Lisa is a pretty girl **with** blue eyes.
Jack was talking to a man **with** a big nose.

We can also use **with** to describe animals:

A rabbit is an animal **with** big ears and a small tail.

3 We can use **with** to talk about a part of something:

They live in a white house **with** a flat roof.
I bought a shirt **with** red stripes.
I used the pot **with** the wooden handle.
They have a garden **with** three apple trees.

4 We can use **with** before something, for example a tool, that we use in order to do something:

You clean your teeth **with** a toothbrush.
You open a tin **with** a tin opener.
I cleaned the table **with** a cloth.
Please eat **with** your knife and fork.

5 We use **by** + **-ing** (e.g. **by doing**) to describe how we do or did something:

She learnt French **by listening** to it.
You start a car **by turning** the key.
She became successful in business **by working** very hard.
The prisoners escaped **by climbing** over a wall.

We use **without** + **-ing** (e.g. **without doing**) to say that a particular action is not done or was not done:

She passed the exam **without doing** a lot of work.
They left **without waiting** for me.
He did the work **without making** any mistakes.

A Complete the sentences using *in* or *with*.

♦ A young man _with_ a moustache was driving the car.
1 He showed me a photograph of a woman _____ blue eyes.
2 It's the only house _____ the street.
3 A lot of businessmen _____ suits were on the train.
4 There was a plant _____ big green leaves in the corner of the room.
5 John was walking down the street with a woman _____ a black coat.
6 Look at that bull _____ those enormous horns!
7 One of the children was a girl _____ long, dark hair.
8 A man _____ a hat came into the cafe.
9 Soldiers _____ uniform were standing at the entrance to the building.
10 She wanted to buy a computer _____ a screen, a keyboard and a mouse.
11 We booked a hotel room _____ a bathroom.
12 It was cold, so I went out _____ a coat and scarf.
13 We've bought a television _____ a big screen.
14 He arrived for the meeting _____ a grey jacket.

Prepositions

B Match the first and second halves of the sentences. Then link the two halves with a preposition (*in*, *with*, etc.).

- ♦ You must speak to the woman
- 1 A giraffe is an animal
- 2 I want a shirt
- 3 She cleans her teeth
- 4 They live in a house
- 5 I like my coffee
- 6 He's digging the garden
- 7 She painted the kitchen
- 8 You should always cut meat
- 9 They got into the house
- 10 The soldiers do all their exercises
- 11 She has a car
- 12 He dried his hair
- 13 You can't make an omelette
- 14 Some women prefer men

- a a sharp knife.
- b sitting in the sun.
- c a spade.
- d lots of sugar.
- e beards.
- f a brush.
- g the green skirt.
- h breaking a window.
- i four chimneys.
- j uniform.
- k toothpaste.
- l a very long neck.
- m a round collar.
- n breaking eggs.
- o four-wheel drive.

- ♦ in (g)
- 1 ....
- 2 ....
- 3 ....
- 4 ....
- 5 ....
- 6 ....
- 7 ....
- 8 ....
- 9 ....
- 10 ....
- 11 ....
- 12 ....
- 13 ....
- 14 ....

C Rewrite the sentences using *by* or *without*.

- ♦ She sat in the corner. She didn't say anything.
  She sat in the corner without saying anything.
- ♦ He opened the door. He turned the key.
  He opened the door by turning the key.
- 1 He repaired the car. He changed some of the parts.

- 2 She answered the question but she didn't read it carefully.

- 3 He left. He didn't say thank you.

- 4 She got the money because she sold her car.

- 5 I threw the letter away. I didn't open it.

- 6 We worked all day and we didn't eat anything.

- 7 He lost weight. He went on a strict diet.

- 8 I went out, but I didn't lock the door.

82 Other uses of prepositions

There are many common phrases that have prepositions in them.

1 We use **at** in these phrases:

> at the beginning/end of, at first, at last, at the moment, at the weekend, at once (= 'immediately' or 'at the same time')

She'll be back **at the beginning of** next week.
At first, I didn't believe what he was saying.
I waited for weeks and **at last** the letter arrived.
Are you busy **at the moment**?
You don't have to do everything **at once**.

We also use **at** for speeds:

He was driving **at** over 150 km an hour.

2 We use **by** with means of transport:

> **by** car/bike/bus/plane/boat/ship/train, etc.

Do you go to work **by train** or **by car**?

But we say **on foot** (= walking):

I came here **on foot** because I wanted to get some exercise.

We use **the car/in my, our**, etc. to talk about someone's car:

It was only a short journey but we went **in my/our/the car**.

We use **on my, our**, etc. with **bike**:

He came **on his bike**.

We use **on the** before other means of transport:

I met her by chance **on the train**.

We use **by** in phrases describing processes (e.g. sending something, ordering something, paying for something, making something):

I'll send the information **by post/email**.
Can you book tickets **by phone**?
You can pay **by card** or **by bank transfer**.
All these products were made **by hand**.

But we say **in cash**:

I paid for the holiday **in cash**.

We also use **by** in these phrases:

> **by** chance, **by** accident, **by** mistake

3 We use **for** in these phrases:

> for example, for sale, for ever (OR forever)

Their house is **for sale**.
I'd like to live here **for ever**.

4 We use **in** in these phrases:

> in advance, in danger, in future, in a hurry, in charge (of), in control, in fashion, in general, in love, in my opinion, in the past

You are advised to book a table **in advance**.
I can't talk to you now, I'm **in a hurry**.
In general, she has a good life.

Notice also: **in writing/pen/pencil/capitals**

Please write your name **in capitals** in this box.
Put your complaint **in writing**.
 (= write a letter or email)

5 We use **on** in these phrases:

> on business/on holiday/on a trip, on (the) TV/televison, on the radio, on the internet, on (a/the) computer, on the phone (= speaking, using it), on strike, on fire, on the floor

I'm going away **on holiday/on business** next week.
All this work is done **on computers** these days.
There are no trains because the drivers are **on strike**.
I found a lot of useful information **on the Internet**.
She was **on the phone** when I went into the room.

6 Notice also the common prepositions **except (for)** and **instead of**:

Everyone was happy **except (for)** Elaine.
 (= Elaine was the only person who wasn't happy.)
I'd prefer a cold drink **instead of** a coffee at the moment.

We use an **-ing** form after **instead of**:

I walked to work **instead of going** by car.

Prepositions

A Match the first and second halves of the sentences.

- ♦ I waited for ages until the parcel arrived at
1. You should buy your tickets well in
2. As part of her job she has to travel a lot on
3. I didn't plan to meet him, it happened by
4. I won't make the same mistake in
5. This kind of music is currently in
6. Their plane was late because some pilots were on

a fashion.
b strike.
c advance.
d last.
e business.
f chance.
g future.

♦ d   1 ____   2 ____   3 ____   4 ____   5 ____   6 ____

B Complete these official instructions by putting in the correct prepositions.

- ♦ We can be contacted *by* phone at the number below.
1. Complaints must be put _____ writing and sent to the address below.
2. Please complete your personal details _____ capitals.
3. Applications sent _____ post will be dealt with as soon as possible.
4. Payment can be made _____ credit card or _____ bank transfer but not _____ cash.
5. Feel free to contact me _____ email at any time.

C Complete Nick's email to a friend using the words from the box and the correct preposition.

| first   holiday   once   ~~hurry~~   charge   ever   example   mistake |

Hi Pete,

I've been living in this city for a couple of months now. It's a very crowded and busy place and everyone seems to be ♦ *in a hurry* all the time. Nobody is willing to wait for anything, they want to have it ¹ _____. I see this all the time. ² _____, I was in a restaurant the other day and the man at the next table demanded to speak to the person ³ _____ because he'd been waiting five minutes for his meal! When the waiter then brought the wrong meal ⁴ _____, he went completely mad! ⁵ _____ I thought I'd like living here, but now I've decided it's a good place to stay if you're ⁶ _____. I wouldn't want to live here ⁷ _____.
Nick

D Complete these sentences with the correct prepositions.

- ♦ Did you have a good time *at* the weekend?
1. _____ my opinion, you're wasting your time.
2. A few minutes later, the whole building was _____ fire.
3. They've been _____ love ever since they first met.
4. They've won every game _____ one, which they lost badly.
5. She does most of her work _____ her laptop.

179

83 Verb + preposition

1 After some verbs we use a particular preposition* (e.g. **for**, **to**, **on**):

VERB + PREPOSITION	
wait for:	I was **waiting for** a bus.
listen to:	She **listens to** the radio a lot.
belong to:	Does that book **belong to** you?
ask for:	Have you **asked for** the bill?
apply for:	He has **applied for** another job.
depend on:	The salary **depends on** your age.
agree with:	I don't **agree with** you.

2 Now look at these examples:

▶ **arrive at/in**:

We **arrived at the airport**. (You **arrive at** a place, for example a building.)

We **arrived in Portugal**. (You **arrive in** a town or country.)

▶ **look at/for**:

Look at that strange **man** over there! (You **look at** something you can see.)

I'm **looking for** my **diary**. (You **look for** something that you are trying to find.)

▶ **talk to/about**:

She was **talking to** some friends. (You **talk to** somebody.)

They were **talking about** politics. (You **talk about** something.)

3 In questions that begin with a question word like **What**, **Who** or **How many**, we usually put the preposition at the end:

Who are you waiting **for**?

What does their decision depend **on**?

4 We do not usually use a preposition after these verbs:

phone/ring/call: He **phoned/rang/called** me last night. (NOT *He phoned/rang to me* …)

discuss: We often **discuss** sport. (NOT … *discuss about sport*.)

answer: She didn't **answer** me. (NOT … *answer to me*.)

reach (= arrive): I **reached** the office at nine o'clock. (NOT … *reached to the office* …)

5 Note that we **pay someone**, but we **pay for something**:

She paid **him** yesterday. (You pay a person.)

I paid **for the books**. (You **pay for** something that you receive.)

But note that we **pay** a bill: I'll **pay the bill**.

*Another term for verb + preposition is prepositional verb.

A Complete these sentences with the correct prepositions (*to*, *for*, etc.). In some sentences no preposition (–) is required.

- ♦ I'm waiting *for* a phone call.
- ♦ We reached *–* the airport after 11 o'clock.
- 1 I'll ask _____ some information.
- 2 Let's listen _____ some music.
- 3 Where do I pay _____ this shirt?
- 4 Let's discuss _____ the arrangements for tomorrow.
- 5 Who's going to pay _____ the taxi driver?
- 6 We paid _____ the bill and left the restaurant.
- 7 I'll phone _____ the theatre and book two tickets.
- 8 The price of the holiday depends _____ when you want to travel.

Prepositions

9 He walked out of the room without answering _____ me.
10 A lot of people don't agree _____ you.
11 I've applied _____ a visa.
12 Who does this pen belong _____ ?

B Complete the story with prepositions. For some gaps no preposition is required.

When Jack arrived ♦ at the theatre, Alice was waiting ¹ _____ him. 'Where have you been?' she asked ² _____ him. 'We can talk ³ _____ that later,' said Jack. 'I tried to phone ⁴ _____ you to say that I was going to be late, but you didn't answer. Let's go into the concert.' 'OK,' said Alice, 'but as you were late, you have to pay ⁵ _____ the tickets!' 'What?' said Jack. 'I don't want to argue ⁶ _____ it, but I don't agree ⁷ _____ you. It's not fair!'

C Complete the questions using the words in brackets ( ). Add the correct preposition.

Tim: What are you doing here, Grace?
Grace: I'm just waiting.
Tim: (who/you/wait) ♦ Who are you waiting for?
Grace: Sara. She's talking to the boss.
Tim: (what/they/talk) ¹ _____
Grace: She wants more money.
Tim: (how much/she/ask) ² _____
Grace: I don't know, but she's started looking for a new job.
Tim: (how many jobs/have/she/apply) ³ _____
Grace: Five or six, I think. By the way, is that a new phone that you've got?
Tim: Yes, I got it the other day.
Grace: And (what/you/listen) ⁴ _____
Tim: My favourite Beatles album. It's great!

D Complete the postcard by putting in the prepositions that are necessary. Sometimes, no preposition is required.

Dear Sam,

We arrived ♦ in Greece at about 11 o'clock. We got a taxi from the airport to the port, and found the boat going to our island. I enjoyed looking ¹ _____ the scenery on the way. When we reached ² _____ the island, we looked ³ _____ our villa but we couldn't find it. I talked ⁴ _____ a local man, and I asked ⁵ _____ directions. He offered to take me there. When we arrived ⁶ _____ the villa, I offered to pay ⁷ _____ him, but he didn't want any money. The weather's lovely. I'll call ⁸ _____ you when we get back from our holiday.

Love,

Tina

84 Adjective + preposition

1 Some adjectives can be followed by a preposition + noun:

ADJECTIVE	+ PREPOSITION	+ NOUN
I'm afraid	of	dogs.
She's good	at	maths.

Here are some more examples:
Some people are **afraid of** thunder.
John is very **angry with** me.
I was **annoyed with** my sister.
Jenny is **brilliant at** maths.
Tom was **busy with** his work.
William is **careless with** his money.
Anna's mother was **cruel to** her.
France is **famous for** its cheese.
Peter is very **fond of** children.
Our cat is **frightened of** your dog.
The rooms were **full of** old furniture.
Are you **good at** sport?
They were **grateful for** our help.
She's **interested in** old coins.
He's very **keen on** chess.
Your sister was very **kind to** us.
I'm often **lucky at** games.

Ian was **pleased with** the result.
They're **proud of** their children.
Are you **sure about** her name?
I was **surprised by** her anger.

2 Some adjectives are followed by a preposition + *-ing* form:

ADJECTIVE + PREPOSITION + -ing FORM
He was **sick of washing** dishes.

I'm not very **good at running**.
Robert is very **fond of talking**.
Anna is **used to working** at night.
(= She often works at night, and she doesn't mind it.)

3 A few adjectives can have an *-ing* form without a preposition:

busy   no good   not worth

ADJECTIVE + -ing FORM

They were **busy getting** things ready.
It's **no good worrying** about the weather.
It's **not worth taking** the car, we can walk.

A Complete these sentences using prepositions (e.g. *with*, *of*).

♦ Mary was pleased _with_ her exam results. She had got good marks in most subjects.
1 Thank you very much. I am very grateful _____ your help.
2 I'm not sure _____ the price, but I think they cost about £5.
3 It was the day of the concert, and everyone was busy _____ the preparations.
4 I didn't expect to win the match. I was quite surprised _____ the result.
5 Amber was very brave. We are very proud _____ her.
6 I like geography and I'm very interested _____ history as well.
7 We've got plenty of food. The fridge is full _____ things to eat.
8 Mary didn't like the director. She was annoyed _____ him.
9 John is very clever. He's brilliant _____ physics and chemistry.
10 Jasmine doesn't like small animals, but she's very fond _____ horses.
11 Julian should look after his glasses. He's very careless _____ them.
12 Lucy and Jasmine like sports. They are particularly keen _____ hockey.
13 Matt must be good _____ French. He got top marks in the exams.
14 Mike has never learnt to swim because he's afraid _____ water.

Prepositions

B Write these dialogues in the Present Simple or Continuous. Use the words in brackets ( ) and any prepositions (e.g. *with, of, at*) that you need.

- A: (Jasmine, why/be/you/angry/Peter?)   B: (Because he/be/very careless/his money)
  A: Jasmine, why are you angry with Peter?
  B: Because he is very careless with his money.

1. A: (be/their daughter/good/school work?)   B: (Yes, in fact she/be/brilliant/everything)
   A:
   B:

2. A: (Why/be/Mr Bell's dog/hide?)   B: (Because it/be/afraid/fireworks)
   A:
   B:

3. A: (be/Jenny/fond/classical music?)   B: (Yes, she/be/very keen/Bach, for example)
   A:
   B:

4. A: (be/you/pleased/Peter's exam results?)   B: (Yes, we/be/very proud/him)
   A:
   B:

C Complete the dialogue using the words from the box and a preposition if it is necessary.

| busy | famous | full | good | interested | ~~kind~~ | no good | sick | used | worried | worth |

Isaac: How did your job interview go?
Chloe: All right, I think. The company director was quite ♦ *kind to* me.
Isaac: What does the company make?
Chloe: Clothes. It's [1] _____ its sports clothes, in fact. I had to wait for a while because the director was [2] _____ talking to some clients. The corridor where I waited was [3] _____ boxes with clothes in them.
Isaac: And what did he ask you?
Chloe: She. The director's a woman. She asked me if I was [4] _____ maths. I said yes. She asked me if I was [5] _____ working under pressure, and I told her that I prefer to be busy at work so that it was no problem. Then she asked me why I was [6] _____ changing jobs, and I told her that I was [7] _____ working hard for so little pay. I'm a bit [8] _____ that answer now; perhaps it wasn't the best thing to say.
Isaac: It's [9] _____ thinking about it now. What do you think your chances are?
Chloe: I'm not sure. I'm not really sure that I want to change jobs just now, but I think it's [10] _____ going to an interview from time to time because it gives you practice and makes you more confident.

Test H: Prepositions

A This is a weather forecast on a local radio station. Complete the missing words.

'Good morning. This is the weather ◆at _____ six o'clock in the morning ¹o_____ Thursday 7 February. It's cold ²o_____, and there's ice ³o_____ the roads, so don't drive too close to the car ⁴i_____ f_____ of you! There should be 40 metres ⁵b_____ you and that car! If you're driving ⁶i_____ the city ⁷t_____ morning, pay attention to schoolchildren walking ⁸a_____ the road. Remember, you might be ⁹n_____ t_____ a school! Traffic is moving very slowly ¹⁰t_____ the city centre at the moment. There was an accident ¹¹l_____ night, so if you're driving ¹²p_____ Central Library, the police may stop you and ask you a few questions. That's all for now. More weather news ¹³e_____ hour, ¹⁴f_____ six ¹⁵i_____ the morning ¹⁶t_____ six at night, this is the KC News Network making sure you're up to date with the news on the road!'

B Anthony is talking to Michelle. Complete their conversation by writing in the missing words from the box.

at   by (x2)   in   good   of   with (x3)   without   ~~without~~   worth.

Anthony:	Jack says he can learn a new language ◆without working.
Michelle:	Who's Jack?
Anthony:	He's that new boy ___ the bright blue jumper. The one ___ long hair. He's bought an audiobook, and he says he learns ___ listening to it while he's asleep.
Michelle:	I think that's silly.
Anthony:	But you're good ___ learning new words, aren't you? I might try Jack's audiobook. I'm sick ___ making mistakes all the time.
Michelle:	It's no use worrying about mistakes. We learn ___ making mistakes.
Anthony:	It's easy for you. You can pass French exams ___ doing much work. How do you do it?
Michelle:	I just sit down ___ a dictionary and a French newspaper. It's not ___ buying an expensive audiobook, in my view.

C Melanie is sending an email to Emilia. Cross out the wrong words.

Hi Emilia,

I want to be ◆on/~~in~~ holiday! It's too hot to work. The office is ¹as/like an oven ²on/at the moment. It looks ³as/like if my boss will be in Germany ⁴on/in business next week so I'll be ⁵at/in charge. Are you enjoying yourself in Cancun? Is Mexico good ⁶like/as a holiday destination? ⁷Like/As usual, I haven't booked my holiday yet, but I think I'll go to Spain ⁸by/in car and visit my old friend Pilar in Madrid. You really sounded ⁹as/like though you were ¹⁰on/in love when I spoke to you ¹¹by/on the phone last week. ¹²As/Like you know, I think your new boyfriend is a really nice guy. I'm sure you'll be happy together.

Love,

Melanie

Prepositions

D A tour guide is showing tourists a Roman camp near Hadrian's Wall in the north of England. Complete the tour using words from the box.

> reach   busy   interested   waiting   talk   sure   proud
> ~~Listen~~   depended   grateful   surprised   brilliant

'◆ Listen to me now, please. Can you hear me? I'm going to ¹ _____ to you today about daily life for Romans living in the camp. I think you will be ² _____ by some of the things that you see. This part of the camp was the kitchen. Imagine 15 cooks ³ _____ with the meals for the soldiers and their families! The cooks ⁴ _____ on local farms for the food, and they were ⁵ _____ at keeping food for a long time, using salt for example. If you're ⁶ _____ in cooking, please ask for more information at the tourist centre. Shall we continue? Who are we ⁷ _____ for? We're not ⁸ _____ about this part of the camp, but we think it was a bathing area, and we know that the Romans were ⁹ _____ of their bathrooms. I expect that the people living here were ¹⁰ _____ for hot water in winter. Let's move on. In a moment we'll ¹¹ _____ the family part of the camp, and I'll let you look around by yourselves.'

E Olivia and Dan are talking on the phone. In gaps 1–7, circle the correct preposition. In gaps 8–20, write the correct preposition.

Olivia: Hi! Is that you, Dan? I'm glad you haven't left yet. When you come to the conference tonight, could you bring the green file? It's ◆ onto/(on) my desk, ¹behind/between the phone. Can you see it? That's right. It's ²across/under the dictionary. Great! Now, do you know how to get to the hotel?

Dan: I think so. After I've driven out ³from/of London, I go north ⁴in/up the A54, through Watford, ⁵as/like though I was going to Milton Keynes. But in fact I take the B254 ⁶on/to Halton before I reach Milton Keynes. I think I should get there about nine o'clock, shouldn't I?

Olivia: That's right, unless you get lost ⁷as/like me!

Dan: Isn't there a big house ⁸ _____ sale, just before the Halton road?

Olivia: Yes. It's ⁹ _____ the left. I didn't see it, so I had to ask ¹⁰ _____ directions.

Dan: Is the boss there already? I plan to arrive at the hotel ¹¹ _____ jeans instead ¹² _____ my suit and tie. I hope that's OK. By the way, did you apply ¹³ _____ Phil's job?

Olivia: I wasn't sure about it, but yes, I did apply. I was a bit annoyed ¹⁴ _____ the advertisement on the website, though. There was a sentence ¹⁵ _____ the end of it, saying 'You must be good ¹⁶ _____ talking to people.'

Dan: What's wrong with that?

Olivia: Well, Phil was very good at talking to people, but he wasn't fond ¹⁷ _____ doing any work, was he?

Dan: You sound ¹⁸ _____ you didn't really like Phil.

Olivia: Well, I thought he was a bit cruel ¹⁹ _____ his co-workers.

Dan: Yes, I think they were frightened ²⁰ _____ him, weren't they? Look, I'd better go. See you later!

185

85 Have and have got

1 Look at this example with **have**:
   They always **have** breakfast at seven o'clock.

POSITIVE		
I/you/we/they	have	
He/she/it	has	
NEGATIVE	**FULL FORM**	**SHORT FORM**
I/you/we/they	do not have	don't have
He/she/it	does not have	doesn't have
QUESTIONS		
Do	I/you/we/they	have …?
Does	he/she/it	

2 Look at this example with **have got**:
   I**'ve got** three brothers.

POSITIVE	FULL FORM	SHORT FORM
I/you/we/they	have got	've got
He/she/it	has got	's got
NEGATIVE		
I/you/we/they	have not got	haven't got
He/she/it	has not got	hasn't got
QUESTIONS		
Have	I/you/we/they	got …?
Has	he/she/it	

3 We can use **have** or **have got**:

▶ to talk about the things we possess:
   We **have** a house in Spain.
   We**'ve got** a house in Spain.
   Paul **doesn't have** a car.
   Paul **hasn't got** a car.
   Do you **have** any money?
   Have you **got** any money?

▶ to talk about our families:
   Jasmine **has** a brother and a sister.
   Jasmine**'s got** a brother and a sister.

▶ to describe people:
   She **has** blue eyes.
   She**'s got** blue eyes.
   Does your brother **have** long hair or short hair?
   Has your brother **got** long hair or short hair?

▶ to say that we are not feeling well:
   I **have** a headache.
   I**'ve got** a headache.

4 We use **have** (NOT ~~have got~~) to talk about meals and holidays, and with a bath, a shower, or a wash:
   Do you normally **have** a big **breakfast**?
   Have a good **holiday**!
   She's **having a shower** at the moment.
   I always **have a wash** before I go out.

A Write positive or negative sentences or questions, using *have got* and the words in brackets ( ).

♦ (she/not/brown eyes.) *She hasn't got brown eyes.*
1 (he/a flat/in the town centre.) ....
2 (you/a car?) ....
3 (I/not/a brother.) ....
4 (she/a headache.) ....
5 (Steve/brown hair?) ....

Verbs

Now write sentences or questions using *have* in the Present Simple (*have, has, don't have,* etc.).

- ♦ (we/always/eggs/for breakfast) We always have eggs for breakfast.
- 6 (John/always/a holiday in August)
- 7 (she/a bath/every Friday)
- 8 (you/a shower/in the morning?)
- 9 (I/always/lunch/in the park.)
- 10 (They /not/a swimming pool.)

B Put the words in brackets ( ) in the correct order to complete the dialogues.

- ♦ (got – I've – two brothers)
  A: Have you got any brothers or sisters?
  B: Yes, I've got two brothers.
- 1 (in Edinburgh – a flat – she's got)
  A: Does your sister live in Scotland?
  B: Yes,
- 2 (you – got – have – a headache?)
  A: What's the matter?
  B: No, but I feel tired.
- 3 (blonde hair – she – got – hasn't)
  A: Jasmine's tall and blonde.
  B: No, you're wrong.
- 4 (have – you – do – a holiday every year?)
  A:
  B: No, I don't.
- 5 (he's – a shower – having)
  A: Where's Michael? Is he ready?
  B: No,
- 6 (a car – I – got – haven't)
  A: Are you going to drive to Scotland?
  B: No,
- 7 (you – dinner at seven o'clock? – have – do)
  A:
  B: No, we always eat at seven-thirty.

C Some of the sentences are wrong. Rewrite the wrong sentences and tick (✓) the correct sentences.

- ♦ We've got a holiday in Mexico every year. We have a holiday in Mexico every year.
- ♦ Paul's got a sister in Scotland. ✓
- 1 She is tired, but she doesn't have a cold.
- 2 I haven't got lunch every day.
- 3 Have you got a shower every day?
- 4 Have you got an English dictionary?
- 5 Do you have a headache?
- 6 We've got a large garden.
- 7 I've got a bath at ten o'clock and I go to bed at eleven o'clock.
- 8 They're having got dinner at the moment.
- 9 They've got two dogs.
- 10 Have got a good weekend!
- 11 Have you got a motorbike?

86 Make, do, have, get

1 There are many phrases in which a particular verb is used together with a particular noun, for example:

   make a cup of **coffee**
   do some **work**
   have breakfast

2 We often use **make** in sentences about producing or creating something:

   They **made** a **fire** in the woods.
   Shall I **make** some **coffee**?
   He **made** some **sandwiches** for lunch.

3 We also use **make** in these phrases:

   Excuse me. I have to **make** a **phone call**.
   He **makes** a lot of **mistakes** in his work.
   I couldn't sleep because the neighbours were **making** a lot of **noise**.

4 We often use **do** in sentences about working, or about doing particular jobs:

   Have you **done** your **homework**?
   He offered to **do** the **washing-up**.
   We're going to **do** some **shopping**.
   I haven't **done** much **work** today.

5 We use **have** + noun to describe activities:

   I'm going to **have** a **shower** in the morning.
   We usually **have lunch** at about one o'clock.
   I'm **having fish** for dinner tonight.
   I **had** a **swim** in the sea this morning.

6 We use **get** with adjectives that describe feelings, to say that we begin to have the feeling:

   I'm **getting tired** now. I need a rest.
   They're late and I'm **getting worried**.
   I **got angry** and shouted at them.

7 We use **get** in some phrases that describe a change of situation:

   We **got lost** in Paris. (= We became lost …)
   It's **getting cold**. (= It's becoming cold.)
   Jasmine was very ill, but she's **getting better**.
   They **got married** three years ago.
   It rained heavily and I **got very wet**.

8 We use **make** + **someone** + adjective to talk about the cause of a feeling:

   He **made us** very **angry**.
   The news **made him happy**.

A Complete the sentences, using the correct forms of *make*, *do*, *have* or *get*. Be careful that you use the correct tense.

   ♦ He was _making_ a cup of coffee in the kitchen.
   ♦ We _has_ lunch in a very pleasant little restaurant yesterday.
   1 She always _____ excited before her birthday.
   2 A: Helen's ill.
     B: Oh dear. I hope she'll _____ better soon.
   3 We have to _____ some homework every evening.
   4 I think I've _____ a terrible mistake.
   5 They _____ the shopping and then they went home.
   6 I was late because I _____ lost on my way there.
   7 It always _____ very hot here during the summer.
   8 Could I _____ a quick phone call, please?
   9 Please don't _____ so much noise.
   10 It was a lovely surprise and it _____ me very happy.
   11 Her parents are _____ old. They are 60 or 70.
   12 How old were you when you _____ married?

Verbs

B Look at the notes in the table about what Laura did yesterday. Complete the text using the correct forms of *make*, *do*, *have* or *get*. Sometimes more than one answer is possible.

7.30	Got up. Shower.
8.00	Breakfast (fruit juice and toast).
8.30–9.00	Walk to work. Rain.
9.00–1.00	Work. Very busy.
1.00–2.00	Lunch in office. Sandwiches.
2.00–5.00	Work. Finished everything.
5.30	Shopping. Home.
7.00	Pizza for dinner. Washed up.
8.00–11.00	TV. Tired. Bed.

It was a normal day for Laura yesterday. She got up at 7.30 and she ♦ _had_ a shower. Then she ¹_____ breakfast. For breakfast she ²_____ fruit juice and toast. While she was walking to work, it rained and she ³_____ wet. She ⁴_____ angry about this. In the morning she ⁵_____ a lot of work. She ⁶_____ lunch at about one o'clock. She ⁷_____ sandwiches for lunch. When she had ⁸_____ all her work in the afternoon, she went home. On the way home she ⁹_____ some shopping. She ¹⁰_____ a pizza for dinner. She ¹¹_____ the washing-up and then she watched TV for three hours. By 11 o'clock she felt quite tired, and so she went to bed.

C Complete the dialogues using the correct form of *make*, *do*, *have* or *get*.

♦ **A:** Was the film good?
B: No, I _got_ bored in the middle of it.

1 **A:** Could you _____ some shopping for me?
B: Yes, what do you want me to buy?

2 **A:** Were you pleased by the news?
B: No, it _____ me very unhappy.

3 **A:** Was it a warm day?
B: Yes, but it _____ rather cold in the evening.

4 **A:** Are you hungry at the moment?
B: No, I _____ a big meal a couple of hours ago.

5 **A:** Did he pass the test?
B: No, he _____ a lot of mistakes.

6 **A:** Are you ready to go out?
B: No, I'm not. I want to _____ a wash first.

7 **A:** Could you repair this for me?
B: Yes, but I can't _____ the job until tomorrow.

87 Phrasal verbs (1): meanings and types

1 We can use many verbs together with another word to form 'phrasal verbs', e.g. **put on**, **get up**.

The same verb can go with several different words to form phrasal verbs with different meanings, e.g. **put away**, **put on**, **put up**.

The meaning of a phrasal verb is not always clear from the two parts. You should check the meaning of phrasal verbs in a dictionary.

2 Grammatically, there are three types of phrasal verb.

▶ One type consists of verb + adverb and there is an object, e.g.:
  She **put on** the hat.
  She **put** the hat **on**.

Some common verbs of this type are:

bring up, calm down, cross out, fill in, find out, give in, give out, look up, pick up, point out, pull off, put away, put up, take off, try on, turn off, work out

When the object is a pronoun, it goes between the two parts of the verb, e.g.:
  She **put** it **on**. (NOT ~~She put on it.~~)

▶ The second type of phrasal verb consists of verb + adverb but there is no object, e.g.:
  I usually **get up** at seven o'clock.

Some common verbs of this type are:

break down, check in, get off, get up, go on, go out, hang about, look out, set off, show up, stay up, take off, turn out, turn up

▶ The third type consists of verb + adverb + preposition and there is an object, e.g.:
  We're **looking forward to** your news.

Some common verbs of this type are:

do away with, face up to, run out of, look up to

(See also **Unit 88**.)

A Complete these dialogues with a phrasal verb and a pronoun.

♦ A: Has Mary put her hat on?
  B: Yes, she's _put it on_.

1 A: Who brought up the children?
  B: Their uncle _____.

2 A: Did you cross out the wrong words?
  B: No, the teacher _____.

3 A: When do we have to give in the homework?
  B: We have to _____ tomorrow.

4 A: Can you pick Ellie up after school?
  B: OK, I'll _____ on my way home.

5 A: Children, can you put your toys away now please.
  B: Can't we _____ later?

B Rewrite each sentence replacing the underlined expressions with the correct form of the phrasal verbs from the box.

break down   give out   go on   keep off   ~~look out~~   look up to   put up

♦ Be careful! Don't step into the hole!
  Look out! Don't step into the hole!

1 The young boys really admire the first team players.
  The young boys really _____ the first team players.

2 The teacher <u>distributed</u> the exam papers.
   The teacher _____ the exam papers.

3 You don't have to go home now. We can <u>give you a bed</u> for the night.
   You don't have to go home now. We can _____ you _____ for the night.

4 What's <u>happening</u> here? What are you doing?
   What's _____ here? What are you doing?

5 James's old car <u>stopped working</u> completely last weekend.
   James's old car _____ completely last weekend.

C Ellie and Jasmine are staying in Barcelona and are planning to do some shopping. Complete the dialogue with the correct form of the verbs from the box. Use a dictionary to check the meanings.

| find out | get off | look up | put on | run out of | set off | take off | try on | ~~work out~~ |

Ellie: Have you ♦<u>worked out</u> _____<u>worked out</u>_____ where the best shopping centre is?
Jasmine: Yes, I ¹_____ it _____ in the guidebook. We can take the metro right across the street and we ²_____ at the fourth station.
Ellie: By the way, I've ³_____ euros so we'll have to call at a bank.
Jasmine: We can go to the hotel reception and ⁴_____ if there's a cash machine near here. What are you going to wear?
Ellie: If we're going to ⁵_____ clothes, I think I'll wear a skirt. It's more difficult to ⁶_____ jeans and ⁷_____ them _____ all the time.
Jasmine: OK, as soon as you've changed we can ⁸_____.

D Choose the correct words in the story to complete the phrasal verbs. Use a dictionary to check the meanings

We were looking forward ♦<u>to</u>/~~on~~ our holiday, but the night before we were going to leave we stayed ¹down/<u>up</u> talking until about three o'clock. We didn't hear the alarm so we got ²<u>up</u>/in late and we were late getting to the airport. When we went to check ³<u>in</u>/up, we were lucky because some passengers hadn't shown ⁴<u>up</u>/out so there were still some seats left. When we got on the plane, Tim was a bit nervous because he hadn't flown before but I gave him a herbal pill and that calmed him ⁵<u>down</u>/out. The cabin crew told us to turn ⁶in/<u>off</u> our mobiles. Then the lights went ⁷up/<u>off</u> and Tim thought something was wrong but I pointed ⁸<u>out</u>/up that they always do that before the plane takes ⁹out/<u>off</u>. When we got to Rome, we went to pick ¹⁰<u>up</u>/off our cases. Mine was one of the first to come out, but Tim's didn't appear. We hung ¹¹<u>about</u>/up for a long time but it didn't turn ¹²<u>up</u>/out. We went to an office to report it and Tim had to fill ¹³<u>in</u>/on all his details on a form. After several phone calls, it turned ¹⁴<u>out</u>/up that Tim's case was in Athens. Luckily we got it back that same evening. As soon as it arrived, Tim pulled ¹⁵out/<u>off</u> his sweaty clothes, had a cold shower and put ¹⁶<u>on</u>/in a clean shirt and trousers. We were just in time to go and have dinner.

88 Phrasal verbs (2): separability

1 Grammatically, phrasal verbs fall into three* groups. Some phrasal verbs can belong to different groups (see **Unit 87**), sometimes with different meanings. For example, **clear up**:

   Who's going to **clear up** the mess?
      (= remove)
   The weather soon **cleared up**.
      (= improved)

2 Verbs in the first group consist of verb + adverb and they have an object. When the object is a noun, there are two possible positions:

   Tim **cleared up** the mess.
   Tim **cleared** the mess **up**.

However, when the object is a pronoun, it goes between the two parts of the verb:

   Tim **cleared** it **up**. (NOT ~~Tim cleared up it.~~)

Some common verbs in this group are:

break off, carry on, draw out, get off, give up, knock down, lay off, let out, make up, pay in, put on, rub out, set up, shut down, sort out

3 Verbs in the second group consist of verb + adverb but there is no object, e.g.:

   Where did you **grow up**?

Some common verbs in this group are:

call in, come about, cut down, drop in, go on, hang on, look out, stay in

4 Verbs in the third group consist of verb + adverb + preposition and they have an object:

   I can't **put up with** all this noise.

Some common verbs in this group are:

do away with, face up to, get away with, put up with

* Some people also classify prepositional verbs (**Unit 83**) as phrasal verbs.

A Complete these dialogues with the phrasal verb and a pronoun.

♦ A: Has somebody put the lights on?
   B: I think Joe's _put them on_ .

1 A: When did they knock down the cinema?
   B: They _____ several months ago.

2 A: Look at this skirt! How can I get the ink off?
   B: I think the only way to _____ is to take it to the cleaner's.

3 A: Somebody's rubbed out my name.
   B: Well, I haven't _____ .

4 A: Ellie and Pete have broken off their engagement.
   B: Oh no! When did they _____ ?

B Replace the underlined expressions in the sentences with the correct form of the phrasal verbs from the box.

| drop in   get away with   hang on   ~~knock down~~   put up with   sort out |

♦ They're going to <u>demolish</u> those old houses.
   They're going to _knock down_ those old houses.

1 The gang <u>escaped taking</u> £5 million.
   The gang _____ £5 million.

2 I'm going out. I can't <u>stand</u> the smoke in here.
   I'm going out. I can't _____ the smoke in here.

3   Maddie says she's going to visit us on Thursday.
    Maddie says she's going to _____ on Thursday.
4   Wait! I've just got to get my jacket.
    _____! I've just got to get my jacket.
5   We still haven't arranged who does the different jobs.
    We still haven't _____ who does the different jobs.

C Complete this interview using the correct form of the phrasal verbs from the box.

carry on   come about   cut down   do away with   draw out   drop in   face up to   give up
go on   ~~grow up~~   lay off   let out   make up   pay in   set up   shut down   stay in

Interviewer: I understand that your early life was not easy. Can you tell us a little about it? Where were you born?
Ruth: In Barnsley, in the north of England, and that's where I ♦ *grew up* _____.
Interviewer: Were you lonely as a child?
Ruth: I had three sisters and two brothers so it was never quiet. There was always something ¹_____. The house was never empty because neighbours ²_____ all the time.
Interviewer: Do you remember any particularly happy moments?
Ruth: Yes, when we went to bed my mother always told us stories. She didn't have a book – she just ³_____ them _____ herself.
Interviewer: And then things went wrong. How did that ⁴_____?
Ruth: Well, in the first place my father smoked a lot. He always said that he was going to ⁵_____, but he smoked more rather than less. He got very ill and he was in hospital for several weeks. Even when the hospital ⁶_____ him _____, he wasn't well. He had to ⁷_____ and keep warm so that his bronchitis wouldn't start again. But at least he had the sense to finally ⁸_____ smoking.
Interviewer: But things got worse.
Ruth: Yes, while he was recovering we heard that the factory where he worked had ⁹_____ a lot of workers. At first he wasn't affected but then we heard that they were going to ¹⁰_____ the factory _____.
Interviewer: And then things got better.
Ruth: Yes, my parents had to ¹¹_____ their new situation. They said that businesses could ¹²_____ factory workers but they would always need office staff. Luckily they had a savings account and every week they had ¹³_____ something _____. Now they decided to ¹⁴_____ their savings and ¹⁵_____ a little business selling office equipment. It did quite well and when they retired I decided to ¹⁶_____ it _____.
Interviewer: Well, that is a story with a happy end. Thank you for speaking to me.

89 Passive sentences (1)

1 We form the Present Simple passive like this:

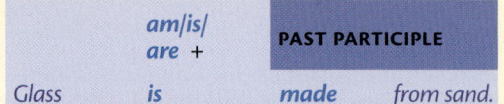

POSITIVE AND NEGATIVE

This programme **is shown** on TV every Thursday.

These computers **aren't produced** any more.

QUESTIONS

When **is** breakfast **served** in this hotel?

(For information on the forms of regular past participles see **Appendix 2** on page 243, and for irregular past participles see **Appendix 3** on page 244.)

2 We form the Past Simple passive like this:

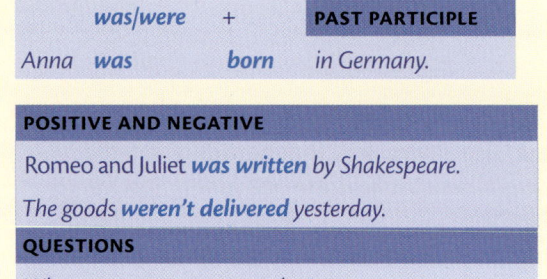

3 Look at these sentences:

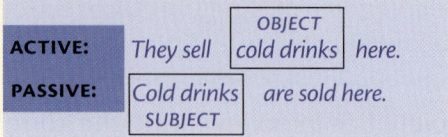

Notice that the object in the active sentence (**cold drinks**) is the same as the subject in the passive sentence. We use the passive when it is not important who does the action, or when we don't know who does it:

These cars are made in Japan. (We don't need to say …~~by Japanese workers~~.)

This castle was built in the 12th century. (We don't know who built it.)

4 Now look at these examples:

(i) **Alfred Hitchcock** was a great film-maker. **He** directed this film in 1956.

(ii) This is a wonderful **film**. **It** was directed by Alfred Hitchcock.

In (ii) we use the passive because we have been talking about something (**the film**), and not the person who did it (**Hitchcock**). We use **by** to say who does, or did, the action:

*This film was directed **by** Hitchcock.*

POSITIVE AND NEGATIVE

Romeo and Juliet **was written** by Shakespeare.

The goods **weren't delivered** yesterday.

QUESTIONS

When **was** your camera **stolen**?

A Complete these sentences using the correct form of the verbs from the box. Use the passive form of the Present Simple or Past Simple.

| build | check | found | hold | ~~make~~ | produce | ~~repair~~ | sell | speak | write |

- Scotch whisky _is made_ in Scotland.
- The car _was repaired_ last week.
1. The Olympic Games .... every four years.
2. English .... in many countries.
3. 'Yesterday' .... by John Lennon and Paul McCartney.
4. Car speeds .... by radar.
5. The Channel Tunnel .... to connect Britain with Europe.
6. Souvenirs .... at all popular tourist places.
7. The first Volkswagen Beetles .... in 1937.
8. *The Times* newspaper .... in 1785.

Verbs

B Now write questions for the sentences in exercise A, using the passive form.

- Where is Scotch whisky made?
- When was the car repaired?
1. How often
2. Where
3. Who
4. How
5. Why
6. Where
7. When
8. When

C Change the active sentences into passive sentences. Use the words in brackets ( ).

- We sell tickets for all shows at the box office. (Tickets for all shows/sell/at the box office)
  Tickets for all shows are sold at the box office.
1. Thomas Edison invented the electric light bulb. (The electric light bulb/invent/by Thomas Edison)

2. Someone painted the office last week. (The office/paint/last week)

3. Several people saw the accident. (The accident/see/by several people)

4. Where do they make these cars? (Where/these cars/make)

5. Six countries signed the agreement. (The agreement/sign/by six countries)

6. A stranger helped me. (I/help/by a stranger)

7. They don't deliver the post on Sundays. (The post/not/deliver/on Sundays)

D Complete the text using the correct active or passive form in brackets ( ).

Fiat ♦ was started (started/was started) by a group of Italian businessmen in 1899. In 1903, Fiat ¹_____ (produced/was produced) 132 cars. Some of these cars ²_____ (exported/were exported) to the United States and Britain. In 1920, Fiat ³_____ (started/was started) making cars at a new factory at Lingotto, near Turin. There was a track on the factory roof where the cars ⁴_____ (tested/were tested) by technicians. In 1936, Fiat launched the Fiat 500. This car ⁵_____ (called/was called) the Topolino - the Italian name for Mickey Mouse. The company grew, and in 1963 Fiat ⁶_____ (exported/was exported) more than 300,000 vehicles. Today, Fiat is based in Turin, and its cars ⁷_____ (sold/are sold) all over the world.

90 Passive sentences (2)

1 Here is a summary of passive tenses. Note that a passive verb always includes a past participle (e.g. **repaired**, **taken**). For more information on past participles, see **Appendices 2** and **3** on pages 243–4.

▶ Present Simple:

	VERB (PRESENT)	+ PARTICIPLE
ACTIVE:	Someone **repairs** the machine.	
PASSIVE:	The machine **is repaired**.	

▶ Past Simple:

	VERB (PAST)	+ PARTICIPLE
ACTIVE:	Someone **took** my phone.	
PASSIVE:	My phone **was taken**.	

▶ Present Perfect:

	have/has	+ PARTICIPLE
ACTIVE:	She **has packed** the books.	
PASSIVE:	The books **have been packed**.	

▶ Past Perfect:

	had	+ PARTICIPLE
ACTIVE:	Rob **had paid** the bill.	
PASSIVE:	The bill **had been paid**.	

▶ Present Continuous:

	am/is/are + -ing	+ PARTICIPLE
ACTIVE:	They **are mending** the car.	
PASSIVE:	The car is **being mended**.	

▶ Past Continuous:

	was/were + -ing	+ PARTICIPLE
ACTIVE:	They **were building** the bridge.	
PASSIVE:	The bridge **was being built**.	

▶ **will**, **can**, **must**, etc.

	+ INFINITIVE + PARTICIPLE
ACTIVE:	We **will finish** the job.
PASSIVE:	The job **will be finished**.
ACTIVE:	We **must do** the work.
PASSIVE:	The work **must be** done.

2 In all passive sentences, the first verb (= auxiliary verb) is singular if the subject is singular, and plural if the subject is plural:

	AUXILIARY VERB	
The house	**is**	being built.
The houses	**are**	being built.

We also use the auxiliary verb to make questions and negatives:

Have the books been packed?
The bill **hadn't** been paid.

A Make questions from the passive sentences in brackets ( ).

♦ (That car was made in Germany.) Where _was that car made?_
1 (Mary was examined by the doctor this morning.) When _____
2 (The food will be prepared on Friday.) When _____
3 (This window has been broken three times.) How many times _____

B Write the negative forms of the sentences in brackets ( ) from exercise A.

♦ That car _was not made in Germany._
1 Mary _____
2 The food _____
3 This window _____

Verbs

C Complete these passive sentences using the correct form of the words in brackets ( ).

- Nowadays, most bread _is made_ (be/make) from white flour.
- Two workers died while these houses _were being built_ (be/be/build)
1. Good chips .... (be/make) from good potatoes.
2. You mustn't smoke while your car .... (be/be/fill) with petrol.
3. This work .... (must/be/finish) by this afternoon.
4. These bones .... (be/find) last year in a cave.
5. Some money .... (have/be/steal) from Tom's jacket.

D Make these active sentences passive. Use a phrase with *by*.

- Your manager must write the report.
  The report _must be written by your manager._
- The children are organizing the Christmas party.
  The Christmas party _is being organized by the children._
1. The French team has won the silver medal.
   The silver medal ....
2. A Danish specialist was training the guard dogs.
   The guard dogs ....
3. People of all ages can play this game.
   This game ....
4. A large crowd was watching the match.
   The match ....
5. My daughter designed the decorations.
   The decorations ....
6. Two different teachers have marked the exams.
   The exams ....
7. A police car is following that green van.
   That green van ....

E Complete the sentences with the correct passive form of the verb in brackets ( ).

- The castle _was built_ (build) in 1546.
- These mountains can _be seen_ (see) from a great distance.
1. These houses .... (build) in 1946.
2. The repairs must .... (finish) by tomorrow.
3. The room has .... (paint) in several different colours.
4. The decision has already .... (take).
5. The newsletter will .... (send) tomorrow morning.
6. White wine can .... (make) from red grapes.
7. The accident happened while the cars .... (load) onto the lorries.
8. The new models will .... (deliver) next week.

91 Have (something) done

1 Look at this sentence:
   *Mary and Tim **painted** their flat.*

This tells us that Mary and Tim were the painters; they painted their flat.

Now look at this sentence with **have something done**:
   *Jenny and John **had** their flat **painted**.*

This tells us that Jenny and John wanted their flat painted, and that someone painted it for them.

2 Here are some more examples:

HAVE +	SOMETHING +	DONE
I **have mended**	my bike.	
I **have had**	my bike	**mended**.

*Michelle **is going to cut** her hair.*
*Michelle **is going to have** her hair **cut**.*
   (= Someone is going to cut it for her.)
*She **washes** her car every Sunday.*
*She **has** her car **washed** every Sunday.*
   (= Someone washes her car for her.)
*I **must clean** my suit this week.*
*I **must have** my suit **cleaned** this week.*
   (= I must pay someone to clean it for me.)

*I'll **mend** that broken window.*
*I'll **have** that broken window **mended**.*
   (= Someone will mend that window for me.)

3 We sometimes use **get** instead of **have**:
   *I must **get** my suit **cleaned**.*

4 Now look at this example:

*Lucy is very cross. She **had** her bike **stolen**.*

Here, we use **have something done** to talk about something that happens to someone, usually something unpleasant. Here is another example:
   *The group **had** two concerts **cancelled** because of bad weather.*

A Make sentences with a form of *have something done* for these situations. Use the correct tense.

♦ **SITUATION:** Tom's windows were dirty, but he didn't have time to clean them himself.
   Last Saturday, Tom *had his windows cleaned*.

1 **SITUATION:** The shop delivers Mary's food.
   Mary _____

2 **SITUATION:** At the butcher's Jacob said, 'Please cut the meat into small pieces'.
   Jacob _____ into small pieces.

3 **SITUATION:** The hairdresser cuts Rachel's hair about twice a year.
   Rachel _____ about twice a year.

4 **SITUATION:** Last week, the optician checked Mr Stone's eyes.
   Last week, Mr Stone _____

5 **SITUATION:** Mrs Frost's doctor says to her: 'When you come to see me next week, I'll check your blood pressure.'
   When Mrs Frost goes to see the doctor next week, she _____

6 **SITUATION:** Last week, the garage serviced Jasmine's car.
   Last week, Jasmine _____

7 **SITUATION:** A builder is going to mend the roof on our house.
   We _____ on our house.

Verbs

B Look at these signs from some shops and a garage. Write what people think when they see the signs using the words in brackets ( ) and *have* or *had*.

- WE REPAIR ALL KINDS OF BOOTS AND SHOES

    (That reminds me. I/must/my brown boots/repair)
    That reminds me. I must have my brown boots repaired.

1. LET US CLEAN YOUR CARPETS AND CURTAINS

    (My parents use that company. They/their carpets/clean/there)
    My parents use that company.

2. CAN WE CHECK YOUR OIL AND TYRES?

    (That reminds me. I/must/the tyres/check)
    That reminds me.

3. WE MAKE KEYS OF ALL TYPES

    (I'd almost forgotten. I/ought to/a new key/make/for the front door)
    I'd almost forgotten.

4. OUR SPECIALITY: PAINTING HOUSES AND FLATS

    (I don't think I can afford to/our flat/paint)
    I don't think I can afford to

5. WE MEND WATCHES AND CLOCKS

    (That shop isn't expensive. I/my watch/mend/there last week)
    That shop isn't expensive.

6. WE TEST YOUR EYES FOR FREE

    (Ah, yes! My husband/his eyes/test/there last winter)
    Ah, yes!

7. WE REMOVE ALL KINDS OF STAINS FROM ALL KINDS OF CLOTHES

    (Wonderful! I'll take my suit there and/that coffee stain/remove)
    Wonderful! I'll take my suit there and I'll

C Some unpleasant things happened to these people last week. Use the sentences in brackets ( ) to write sentences with *had (something) done*.

- (Mary's bag was pulled off her shoulder.)

    Mary had her bag pulled off her shoulder.

1. (Peter's driving licence was taken away by the police.)

    Peter

2. (Olivia's bike was stolen from the garage.)

    Olivia

3. (Fiona's glasses were broken.)

4. (John's clothes were torn in a fight.)

5. (Jasmine's flat was burgled at the weekend.)

6. (Our electricity was cut off because we had forgotten to pay the bill.)

92 Infinitive with/without to

1 Look at this example:

> to + INFINITIVE
>
> I want **to buy** some stamps.

We use **to do**, **to buy**, **to start**, etc. (**to + infinitive**) after some verbs, e.g.:

want	decide	
agree	promise	
forget	offer	+ TO + INFINITIVE
hope	plan	
arrange	try	

She **agreed to lend** him some money.
He **forgot to book** the tickets.
I'm **hoping to get** a new bike soon.
I've **arranged to play** tennis tonight.
They've **decided to start** a new company.
You **promised to help** me.
She **offered to do** the washing-up.
We're **planning to go** away this weekend.
He's **trying to learn** French.

2 We can also say **want** + **someone** + **to**:
His parents **want him to go** to university.
Do you **want me to help** you?

3 Now look at this example:

> INFINITIVE
>
> He can **speak** Spanish.

Can is a modal verb. We use **do**, **speak**, **see**, etc. (infinitives) after a modal verb. Some of the most common modal verbs are:

| will ('ll) | should | may | |
| might | can | could | must | + INFINITIVE |

I'**ll see** you soon.
She **won't agree**.
Where **should I sit**?
We **may go** by train.
It **may not cost** much.
Can I park here?
I **couldn't hear** her.
We **must pay** now.

4 We can use **make** + **someone** + infinitive, to mean 'cause' or 'force':
The film **made me cry.** (= It caused me to cry.)
They **made us leave**. (= They forced us to leave.)

5 We can use **let** + **someone** + infinitive, to mean 'allow':
She **let me stay**. (= She allowed me to stay.)

A Complete these sentences using the verbs in brackets ( ). Use an infinitive (*call*) or *to + infinitive* (*to call*).

♦ You can't _smoke_ (smoke) here. Smoking is not allowed in this building.
1 I'm sorry I forgot _____ (call) you yesterday. I was very busy.
2 Don't worry. The exam may not _____ (be) very difficult.
3 Her mother makes her _____ (clean) her room.
4 It's not a very good film. You won't _____ (enjoy) it.
5 She didn't want _____ (wait) any longer, so she left.
6 How many people are you planning _____ (invite) to the wedding?
7 She couldn't _____ (reply) because she didn't know what to say.
8 This kind of music makes me _____ (feel) good.
9 My friend let me _____ (drive) her car.
10 I'm afraid I've forgotten _____ (bring) the map.
11 They might not _____ (receive) the information until next week.

Verbs

B Complete each sentence so that it has the same meaning as the sentence in brackets ( ).

♦ (I don't think it's a good idea to argue with him.)
I don't think you should _argue with him._

1 (I won't be able to come to the meeting on Friday.)
I can't

2 (I'm meeting some friends tonight.)
I've arranged

3 (Listen to what I'm telling you.)
I want you

4 (It's important that you lock the door when you go out.)
Don't forget

5 (Perhaps we'll go out for a meal this evening.)
We may

6 (Allow me to pay for the meal.)
Let

7 (I'd like to do a course in Art History.)
I want

8 (He said, 'I'll pay the bill.')
He offered

9 (Should I sit in this chair?)
Do you want me

10 (His stories were very funny, and I laughed a lot.)
His funny stories made

11 (Perhaps he'll phone you tomorrow.)
He might

12 (It's possible that Tom won't be angry with you.)
Tom might not

13 (Jasmine allowed me to drive her new car.)
Jasmine let

C Complete the conversation using the verbs in brackets ( ) with or without *to*.

Charlie: I want ♦ _to do_ (do) something interesting this weekend. Can we
¹ _____ (do) something together?

Laura: Well, I've arranged ² _____ (go) on a trip to the coast with some friends.
Do you want ³ _____ (come) with us?

Charlie: Yes, that sounds good. When are you planning ⁴ _____ (leave)?

Laura: Well, we've decided ⁵ _____ (start) about nine o'clock tomorrow morning,
and I've promised ⁶ _____ (take) the others in my car. We're hoping
⁷ _____ (reach) the coast by about 11 o'clock. So, you must ⁸ _____
(meet) me here just before nine.

Charlie: OK, good. I won't ⁹ _____ (be) late.

93 Verb + -ing; like and would like

1 Look at this example:

-ing FORM
I **like** **listening** to music.

(For details on **-ing** forms, see **Appendix 2** on page 243.)

We can use certain verbs with an **-ing** form:

| like   enjoy   love   keep | |
| finish   stop   mind   hate | + **-ing** FORM |

   She doesn't **like cooking**.
   Do you **enjoy driving**?
   They **love living** in a village.
   He **keeps saying** the same things.
       (= He says the same things many times.)
   Have you **finished eating**?
   Suddenly she **stopped talking**.
   I don't **mind waiting**.
   She **hates using** a drill.

2 Compare this pair of sentences:
   I **like working** here. (= I enjoy my job here.)
   I'd like (= I would like) to get a better job.
       (= I want to get a better job.)

We use **like** + **-ing** (e.g. **like listening**, **like working**) to talk about things that we enjoy doing. We use **would like to** to say that we want to do something.:
   She **likes painting** pictures. (= She enjoys painting pictures.)

She **would like to be** an artist.
   (= She wants to be an artist.)
I **like going** to the theatre.
   (= I enjoy going to the theatre.)
I**'d like to go** to the theatre tonight.
   (= I want to go to the theatre tonight.)
Do you **like playing** cards?
   (= Do you enjoy playing cards?)
Would you **like to play** cards now?
   (= Do you want to play now?)

In offers and requests it is more polite to say **would like** than **want**:
   Would you **like to come** for dinner? (OFFER)
   I**'d like to leave** work early, please. (REQUEST)

3 We use **go** + **-ing** for sports and hobbies that we go out to do, and with **shopping**:
   We often **go skiing** in the winter.
   Let's **go swimming** this afternoon.
   She **goes dancing** at weekends.
   I'm **going shopping** this afternoon.

4 We can use the **-ing** form of a verb as the subject of a sentence to talk about activities:
   Swimming is a healthy activity.

In sentences like this, we can use a noun, adverb or prepositional phrase after the **-ing** form:
   Riding motorbikes can be dangerous.
   Exercising regularly is good for you.
   Dancing to this kind of music can be difficult.

A Complete the sentences using a Present Simple form of the first verb in brackets ( ). Study the example first.

♦ She _likes playing_ (like/play) tennis, but she _doesn't like watching_ (not/like/watch) it.
1 The buses .... (stop/run) at midnight.
2 I .... (not/mind/listen) to his problems.
3 He's not very good at chess, so he .... (keep/lose).
4 She .... (enjoy/go) to other countries and she .... (like/meet) new people.
5 I .... (keep/make) the same stupid mistakes!
6 They usually .... (finish/eat) at about eight-thirty in the evening.
7 She .... (not/enjoy/drive), but she .... (love/cycle).

B Complete the sentences using *like/not like* + *-ing* or *would like* + *to* with the words in brackets ( ).

- She _doesn't like working_ (work) here. She hates this job and is going to look for a better one.
- _Would you like to watch_ (you/watch) a different programme, or do you want to watch this one?
1. I _____ (live) here. I have lived here for many years and I think it's a nice town.
2. Sarah _____ (be) a journalist when she leaves university. She wants to work for a newspaper or a magazine.
3. I _____ (get up) so early every morning, but I have to do it.
4. I _____ (go out) for dinner in an Italian restaurant tonight.
5. Clare _____ (find) a job in the United States. She wants to work in Boston or in New York.
6. I _____ (watch) television all the time; I think it's a waste of time.
7. Mary _____ (lie) on the beach when she's on holiday. She doesn't like swimming or going on trips.

C Look at the pictures. They show what John did last week on holiday. Complete the sentences using the correct form of *go* and a verb from the box.

dance ~~shop~~ sail swim ski cycle

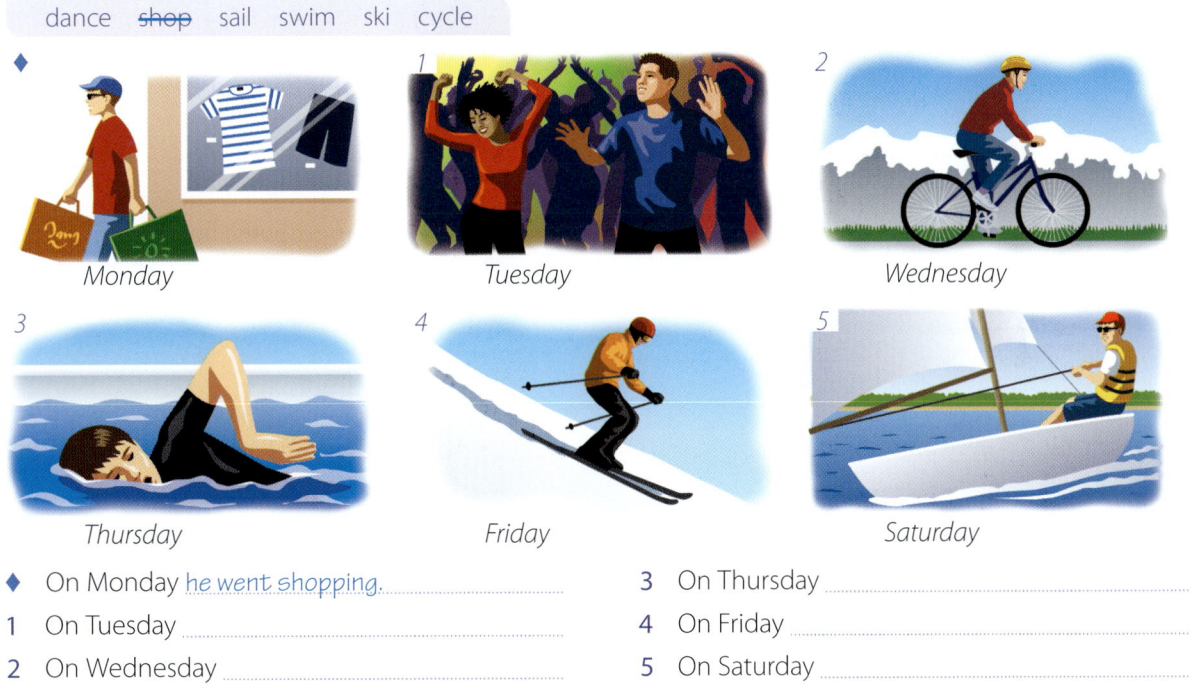

- On Monday _he went shopping._
1. On Tuesday _____
2. On Wednesday _____
3. On Thursday _____
4. On Friday _____
5. On Saturday _____

D Complete these sentences using the *-ing* form of the verbs in brackets.

eat play ~~walk~~ drive

- _Walking_ in the countryside is very pleasant at this time of year.
1. _____ the guitar is his favourite hobby.
2. _____ on motorways can be very tiring.
3. _____ fatty foods all the time is sure to be bad for you.

94 Verb + to or verb + -ing

1 Look at these sentences:
*My sister **promised to help** me.*
*John doesn't **want to wait**.*

We use **to** + infinitive after some verbs, e.g.:

afford	dare	decide	
deserve	want	hope	
learn	mean	offer	+ TO +
pretend	promise	refuse	INFINITIVE
seem	plan	agree	
arrange	have (='must')		

2 Look at these sentences:
*Have they **finished painting** the garage?*
*We **enjoy sitting** in the garden.*

We use an **-ing** form after other verbs, e.g.:

avoid	dislike	enjoy	
finish	give up	imagine	+ -ing
keep	practise	stop	

3 Look at these sentences:
*Jenny **likes to stay** at home.*
*Jenny **likes staying** at home.*

These verbs can usually take an **-ing** form or **to** + infinitive with no difference in meaning:

begin	continue	hate	intend
like	love	prefer	start

But after **would hate**, **would like**, **would love** or **would prefer**, we use **to** + infinitive:
***Would** you like to go for a walk?*
*I'**d love to visit** Australia.*

4 We can use an **-ing** form or **to** + infinitive after these verbs, but the meaning is different:

try   remember   forget

▶ I **tried to lift that** heavy stone. (= make an attempt: I made an attempt to lift the stone.)
*If you can't read where you are, **try sitting** nearer the window.* (= Test something out: sit nearer the window and see if you can read there.)

▶ **Remember to go** to the bank. (= Remember that you must go to the bank.)
*She **remembers going to** the bank.* (= She remembers that she went to the bank.)

▶ *Don't **forget to phone** Mrs Grey.* (= Remember that you must phone Mrs Grey.)
*I'll never **forget seeing** that castle.* (= I saw that castle, and I'll always remember it.)

A Complete the sentences using the correct form of the verb in brackets ( ).

♦ Paul dared *to argue* (argue) with the police.
♦ I can't imagine *living* (live) in the country.
1 We've decided _____ (go) to the beach.
2 I stopped _____ (play) tennis when I got married.
3 I meant _____ (buy) some butter, but I forgot.
4 Did you promise _____ (take) the children to the zoo?
5 Have the men finished _____ (repair) the roof yet?
6 I'd love _____ (visit) China.
7 You shouldn't avoid _____ (talk) about your problems.
8 Peter refused _____ (help) us.
9 Would you prefer _____ (pay) now or later?
10 I couldn't afford _____ (live) in London.
11 Why does Peter keep _____ (talk) about his mother?

Verbs

B Complete this conversation between Jessica and Sian using the correct form of the verbs in brackets ( ).

Jessica: What do your children ♦ *want to do* (want/do) when they leave school?

Sian: Well, Anna ♦ *enjoys writing* (enjoy/write), so she's ♦ *hoping to work* (hope/work) for a newspaper. But I don't know about Paul. He [1] _____ (give up/study) months ago. He seems to [2] _____ (enjoy/do) nothing now. He doesn't [3] _____ (deserve/pass) his exams. And he [4] _____ (refuse/listen) to us when we tell him to [5] _____ (keep/study).

Jessica: With our children in the past, if we [6] _____ (offer/help) them, they always [7] _____ (promise/study) hard. Nowadays if they [8] _____ (want/talk) to us, that's fine, but I've learnt to [9] _____ (stop/ask) them questions. I suppose they [10] _____ (dislike/listen) to my suggestions. They [11] _____ (seem/think) that they don't [12] _____ (need/study) hard, but one day they'll [13] _____ (have/find) a job.

C Complete the sentences using an *-ing* form, or *to* + infinitive, of the word in brackets ( ).

♦ You say that I've met Jessica, but I can't remember her.
  I can't remember *meeting* (meet) Jessica.

1. Please remember that you must buy some fruit.
   Please remember _____ (buy) some fruit.

2. We wanted to open the door, but we couldn't.
   We tried _____ (open) the door.

3. John met Madonna once. He'll never forget it.
   John will never forget _____ (meet) Madonna.

4. Michelle intended to call Peter, but she forgot.
   Michelle forgot _____ (call) Peter.

5. Jenny had a headache. She took an aspirin, but it didn't help.
   Jenny tried _____ (take) an aspirin for her headache.

6. I have a special soap that will probably get your hands clean.
   Try _____ (wash) your hands with this special soap.

7. It will not be easy to do all the work today.
   We'll try _____ (finish) the work before tonight.

8. I stayed in Jasmine's flat while she was on holiday. I remembered that I had to feed her cats every day.
   I remembered _____ (feed) Jasmine's cats every day while she was on holiday.

9. Remember that you must invite Mary to the party next week.
   Don't forget _____ (invite) Mary to the party next week.

95 Purpose: for ...ing

1 Look at this dialogue:
   A: **What's** this machine **for**?
   B: It's **for cutting** cloth.

The question **What is it for?** asks about the purpose of something (what we use something for). When we describe the purpose of a thing, we use **for** + **-ing**. Here are some more examples:
   This is an instrument **for measuring** wind speed.
   This tool is used **for making** holes.

2 Now look at this dialogue:
   A: **What** does he need my camera **for**?
      (= Why does he need my camera?)
   B: He needs it **for his work**. (= His work is the reason why he needs the camera.)

The question **What ... for?** asks about purpose. To talk about someone's purpose, we can use **for** + noun. Here are some more examples:
   A: **What** did he go to the shops **for**?
   B: He went to the shops **for some fruit**.
      (= He wanted to buy some fruit.)
   I buy the newspaper **for the sports news**.
      (= ... in order to read the sports news.)

3 Now look at this dialogue:
   A: **What** does he need my camera **for**?
   B: He needs it **to take** some photos.
      (= ... in order to take some photos.)

To talk about someone's purpose, we can also use **to** + infinitive (e.g. **to take**). Here are some more examples:
   He went to the shops **to buy** some fruit.
      (= ... in order to buy some fruit.)

*John phoned the police **to tell** them about the burglar.*

A Write definitions for the things in box A using one of the phrases from box B.

A
telescope — instrument
~~hammer — tool~~
fridge — appliance
kettle — appliance
thermometer — instrument
vacuum cleaner — appliance
drill — tool
speedometer — instrument
freezer — appliance

B
boil water
measure temperature
~~knock in nails~~
clean carpets
see things at a distance
keep food cold
measure speed
keep food frozen
make holes

♦ A hammer _is a tool for knocking in nails._
1 A kettle
2 A thermometer
3 A vacuum cleaner
4 A fridge
5 A telescope
6 A speedometer
7 A freezer
8 A drill

B Write the dialogues using the words in brackets ( ). Use *What … for?* to make questions and *for* to make replies.

♦ A: (/did/Tom/go/to the park/?) What did Tom go to the park for?
 B: (He/go/to the park/some fresh air.) He went to the park for some fresh air.

1 A: (/does/Mary/want/the money/?)
 B: (She/want/the money/a train ticket.)

2 A: (/does/Raphael/want/the flour/?)
 B: (He/want/the flour/a cake.)

3 A: (/did/William/go/to the butcher's/?)
 B: (He/go/to the butcher's/some sausages.)

4 A: (/does/Helen/want/the polish/?)
 B: (She/want/it/her shoes.)

5 A: (/did/Alice/go/to the library/?)
 B: (She/go/to the library/a book on India.)

6 A: (/did/Jasmine/phone/Anna/?)
 B: (She/phone/Anna/some advice.)

C Rewrite the replies from exercise B using the verbs from the box.

borrow   buy (x2)   clean   get (x2)   make

♦ Tom: He went to the park to get some fresh air.
1 Mary:
2 Raphael:
3 William:
4 Helen:
5 Alice:
6 Jasmine:

D Find the errors and rewrite the sentences correctly.

♦ This machine is for make pasta. This machine is for making pasta.
1 For what did he come?
2 A bus is for carry passengers.
3 She went to the baker's for to buy some bread.
4 The mayor came for give the prizes.
5 The woman jumped into the river to saving the child.
6 I'm training hard for to get fit.
7 This is a computer program for make three-dimensional drawings.
8 Can I use your pen for signing this form?

96 Verb + object (+ to) + infinitive

1 Look at these examples:

Laura said to Rob:
'Make some coffee please.'
We can say:
Laura **asked Rob to make** some coffee.

Anna said to Rose:
'Can you come to my party, Rose?'
We can say:
Anna **invited Rose to come** to her party.

Tom thinks Chris should see a doctor. He can say:
I'll **persuade Chris to go** to the doctor's.

The structure is:

VERB +	OBJECT +	TO +	INFINITIVE
She asked	Charlotte	to	wait.
She asked	her	to	wait.

We use these verbs in this structure:

tell	force	teach	
help	allow	would like	
ask	invite	encourage	+ OBJECT + TO
want	forbid	persuade	
advise	remind		

2 Note that the first verb can change its tense, but the second verb is always **to** + infinitive (**to make**):

She **is asking** Rob
She **will ask** Rob } to make some coffee.
She **has asked** Rob

Note that if we use a pronoun, we use **me**, **him**, **her**, **it**, **us**, **you**, **them** (object pronouns) after the verb:

Laura asked **him** to make some coffee.

3 Now look at these two sentences:

The teacher **let Jasmine leave** school early.
I **made him tell** me the truth.

Let here means 'allow', and **make** means 'force' or 'order'. **Make** and **let** are followed by an infinitive (without **to**):

	VERB +	OBJECT +	INFINITIVE
She	let	Jasmine	leave.

Feel, **hear**, **see** and **watch** can also be followed by an infinitive (without **to**):

I **heard** your sister **shout** 'Fire!'
   (NOT … to shout …)
Tom **saw** a car **come** round the corner.

A Write sentences using the words in brackets ( ). Be careful to use the correct tense.

♦ (Tomorrow/I/encourage/Jessica/enter/the competition.)
   Tomorrow I will encourage Jessica to enter the competition.

♦ (I was already tired, but I/force/myself/go on working.)
   I was already tired, but I forced myself to go on working.

1 (Anna/teach/Mary/drive/last year.)

2 (Don't worry! Tomorrow I/persuade/my father/see/a doctor.)

3 (The boss has/forbid/his staff/wear/jeans in the office.)

4 (Last Sunday, John/invite/Michelle/come/for lunch.)

5 (Next year, the teachers/allow/the students/use/calculators in exams.)

Verbs

B Complete the sentences using the words in brackets ( ).

♦ (Police officer: 'Can everyone please stay indoors?')
The police officer asked everyone _to stay indoors._

1 (Jasmine: 'Remember to come home early, Tim.')
Jasmine reminded Tim

2 (Manager: 'You must work more quickly.')
The manager wants us

3 (Captain: 'Let's do our best in the game.')
The captain encouraged us

4 (Jo: 'Can you come to my party on Saturday?')
Jo invited me

C Answer the questions, changing the nouns (e.g. *Michael*) to pronouns (e.g. *him*). Be careful to use the correct tense.

♦ A: Did Nicola tell Michael to be careful?
B: Yes, _she told him to be careful._

1 A: Would Kate like Peter to stay?
B: Yes,

2 A: Did Mrs Slater help her son to finish?
B: Yes,

3 A: Did the doctor advise Michael to stay in bed?
B: Yes,

4 A: Does Lucy allow her children to go to late-night parties?
B: Yes,

5 A: Did Mary remind Mark to call the office?
B: Yes,

D Write sentences with a similar meaning using the verb in brackets ( ).

♦ The police told everyone to leave the building. (make) _The police made everyone leave the building._

1 The driver allowed the old man to travel on the bus without a ticket.
(let)

2 Jack told his younger brother to wash the dishes.
(make)

3 I don't allow people to smoke in my house or in my car!
(let)

E Combine the two sentences into one.

♦ Your sister shouted 'Fire!'. I heard her. _I heard your sister shout 'Fire!'._

1 Tom prepared the sandwiches. Diane watched him.
Diane

2 The ground shook. We felt it.
We

3 Noah left early. Did you see him?
Did you

Test 1 — Verbs, passives, infinitives, -ing forms

A Chris and Toby are walking in the mountains. If the words in brackets ( ) are incorrect, cross them out and rewrite them. If they're correct, put a tick (✓).

Toby: (We're getting) ✦ ✓ lost. What shall we do?
Chris: (We did) ✦ We made a mistake an hour ago. We took the wrong road.
Toby: (I've got) ¹ _____ a headache, and (I'm making) ² _____ more and more tired.
Chris: Try not to worry. (I got) ³ _____ some aspirin in my bag.
Toby: It's cold! (Do you have) ⁴ _____ an extra jumper?
Chris: I think we'll have to stop for the night. (It's getting) ⁵ _____ dark.
Toby: What do you mean? (We haven't done) ⁶ _____ a tent!
Chris: Try to stay calm. (We'll make) ⁷ _____ a fire and (we'll have got) ⁸ _____ a meal.
Toby: I suppose you're going (to make) ⁹ _____ the shopping!
Chris: We're OK. (I've got) ¹⁰ _____ some tea and some pasta in my bag.
Toby: What if it rains?
Chris: Stop worrying! I've got a job for you (to make) ¹¹ _____. Go and find some wood.
Toby: I want (to have got) ¹² _____ a rest first!
Chris: Now (you're making) ¹³ _____ me angry. Let's get on with it!

B Christine is talking to her doctor. Insert the missing words from the box.

| it (x3) | ~~gets~~ | put | ran | out | in | down |

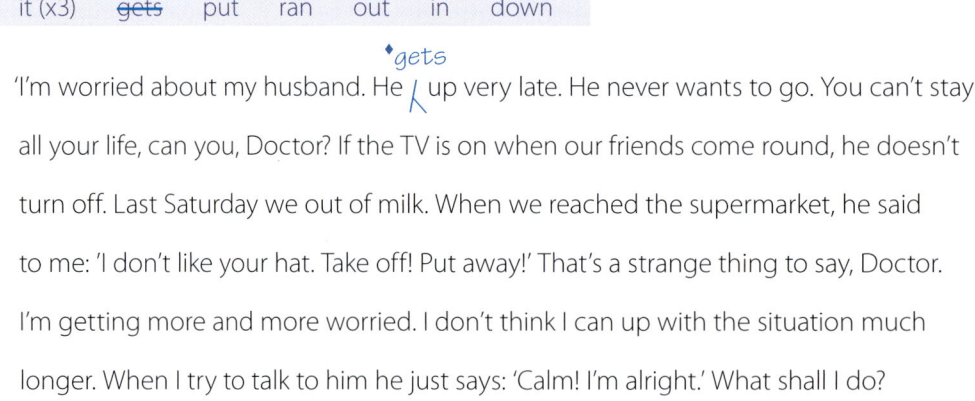

'I'm worried about my husband. He ✦gets⌄ up very late. He never wants to go. You can't stay

all your life, can you, Doctor? If the TV is on when our friends come round, he doesn't

turn off. Last Saturday we out of milk. When we reached the supermarket, he said

to me: 'I don't like your hat. Take off! Put away!' That's a strange thing to say, Doctor.

I'm getting more and more worried. I don't think I can up with the situation much

longer. When I try to talk to him he just says: 'Calm! I'm alright.' What shall I do?

C Look at this conversation. Make it more natural by rewriting some of it. Use the passive form and *someone*.

Anna: Well, we watched this TV programme about moving to Spain, and we decided to go. ✦<u>Someone has packed our bags</u>. We're ready to leave!
Celia: We wouldn't leave England, would we, John? ¹<u>Someone decorated our house last month</u>. It looks beautiful. ²<u>And someone is designing a summer house for the garden</u>.
John: ³<u>But someone also stole our car last week</u>. Perhaps Spain is a good idea, after all.

210

Verbs

Celia: Anyway, I hope you two know what you're doing! Our neighbours went to France, and when they got there ⁴someone hadn't built their new house! So they bought an old farmhouse instead. It was only after ⁵someone repaired the windows ⁶and someone mended the roof that they were happy. It took a long time.

Mike: ⁷Well, someone has made our decision. ⁸Someone booked our flight yesterday. ⁹Someone is selling our house next month. We're on our way!

♦ Our bags _have been packed._
1 Our house
2 And a summer house
3 But our car
4 their new house
5 their windows
6 and the roof
7 Well, our decision
8 Our flight
9 Our house

D Maddie is replying to a message from a new friend. Complete her reply using the words in brackets ( ). Use the infinitive without changing it, or add *to* or change it to the *-ing* form.

It was nice to hear from you. You asked me to tell you as much as I could about myself, so I will! To begin with, I don't like ♦ _cooking_ (cook). And I hate ¹ _____ (wash) up. I can't ² _____ (drive), but I'm planning ³ _____ (learn) one day! I gave up ⁴ _____ (smoke) ten years ago. You don't ⁵ _____ (smoke), do you? What else can I ⁶ _____ (tell) you? Onions and old films make me ⁷ _____ (cry). I go ⁸ _____ (dance) on Sunday afternoons. And I don't mind ⁹ _____ (walk) in the rain. I think that's almost everything about me. Oh yes. Some time ago I decided ¹⁰ _____ (get) fit. ¹¹ _____ (Jog) regularly makes me ¹² _____ (feel) better, but I don't like ¹³ _____ (cycle), and I love ¹⁴ _____ (eat) chocolate! If you want me ¹⁵ _____ (continue), you'll have to write back! (But I'd rather hear about you.)

E Will is talking to his boss. Rewrite the words in brackets ( ), adding *to* if necessary, or changing the infinitive to the *-ing* form.

Will: You promised (give/me) a new job after two years here. ♦ _to give me_
Boss: Yes, but you must (finish/do) the job you've got. ¹
Will: But I would (prefer/start) something new now. ²
Boss: Try (be/patient)! What did you join the company for? ³
Will: I wanted (do/something) interesting, I suppose. ⁴
Boss: And I allowed (you/do) lots of different things, didn't I? ⁵
Will: And now you are asking (me/do) the same thing every day! ⁶
Boss: I've seen (you/improve) so much! Just keep going a little longer. ⁷
Will: You can't make (me/stay) in this job. ⁸
Boss: No, I can't. But I can encourage (you/think) about the future. ⁹

97 Zero Conditional and First Conditional

1 Look at this:

IF	+ PRESENT SIMPLE	+ PRESENT SIMPLE
If	I **eat** too much,	I **feel** bad.

(= Every time I eat too much, I feel bad.)

We use this structure (**if** + Present Simple + Present Simple) for facts that are generally true. This structure is called the Zero Conditional:

If I **don't get** enough sleep, I **feel** tired.
(= Every time I don't get enough sleep, I feel tired.)
If you **want** to become a doctor, you **have** to study hard. (= Anyone who wants to become a doctor has to study hard.)

2 We can say the same thing by reversing the two parts of the sentence:

PRESENT SIMPLE	+ IF	+ PRESENT SIMPLE
I **feel** bad	if	I **eat** too much.

Note that we do not use a comma (,) before **if**.

3 Now look at this:

IF +	PRESENT SIMPLE +	+ WILL/WON'T
If	I'm late,	she'll be angry.

(= Perhaps I will be late; then she'll be angry.)

We use this structure (**if** + Present Simple + **will**/**won't**) to talk about things that may happen in the future. The verb after **if** is Present Simple, but we use it for a possible future action or situation; we use **will**/**won't** + verb for the result. This structure is called the First Conditional:

	FUTURE POSSIBILITY	+ RESULT
If	we **don't hurry**,	we **won't finish**.

4 We can reverse the order:
She'll be angry **if** I'm late.
We won't finish **if** we don't hurry.

5 We do not use **will**/**won't** after **if**:
NOT *If I will be late, she'll be angry.*

A Rewrite these sentences about various types of people using *if* + Present Simple + Present Simple. Make *you* the subject of both parts of the sentence.

♦ Doctors treat people who are ill.
 If you're a doctor, you treat people who are ill.

1 Vegetarians don't eat meat.
 If you're a vegetarian, ...

2 People who live in a hot country don't like cold weather.
 If you live ....

3 Teachers have to work very hard.
 If you're a teacher, ...

4 People who do a lot of exercise stay fit and healthy.
 If you ....

5 Mechanics understand engines.
 If you're a ....

6 People who read the news know what's happening in the world.
 If you ....

Conditionals and reported speech

B Complete these sentences with *if* + Present Simple + *will/won't*, using the words in brackets ( ). Sometimes you do not need to change the words in brackets.

♦ If _it rains_ (it/rain), _we won't go_ (we/not/go) out.
1. If _____ (the weather/be) nice tomorrow, _____ (we/drive) to the coast.
2. If _____ (she/post) the parcel now, _____ (they/receive) it tomorrow.
3. _____ (Fiona/be) angry if _____ (John/arrive) late again.
4. _____ (I/go) to their party if _____ (I/have) enough time.
5. If _____ (she/not/pass) this exam, _____ (she/not/get) the job that she wants.
6. _____ (you/learn) a lot if _____ (you/take) this course.
7. If _____ (I/get) a ticket, _____ (I/go) to the concert.
8. _____ (I/buy) that phone if _____ (it/not/cost) too much.
9. If _____ (you/run) very fast, _____ (you/catch) the bus.
10. _____ (I/go) to the doctor's if _____ (I/not/feel) better tomorrow.
11. If _____ (they/win) this game, _____ (they/be) the champions.

C Complete the dialogues with the Present Simple or *will/won't* forms of the words in brackets ( ). Sometimes you do not need to change the words in brackets.

♦ **A:** We must be at the airport at two o'clock.
   B: Well, if _we take_ (we/take) a taxi at one o'clock, _we won't be_ (we/not/be) late.
1. **A:** I'd like a newspaper.
   B: Well, _____ (I/buy) one for you if _____ (I/go) to the shop later.
2. **A:** Has John called yet?
   B: No, and if _____ (he/not/call) this afternoon, _____ (I/call) him this evening.
3. **A:** Is Fiona there, please?
   B: No, but if _____ (you/want) to leave a message, _____ (I/give) it to her.
4. **A:** Is Tim going to pass his exam?
   B: Well, _____ (he/fail) if _____ (he/not/work) harder.
5. **A:** Could I have some information about this year's concerts, please?
   B: Yes, if _____ (you/give me) your email, _____ (I/send) it to you.

98 Second Conditional

1 Look at this sentence:

*If Amy Winehouse **was** alive today, she **would be** over 30 years old.*

Winehouse isn't alive today. The sentence imagines something that is not true. The verb after **if** is Past Simple, but it refers to the present. This structure is called the Second Conditional:

IF +	PAST SIMPLE	+ WOULD (OR 'D)
If	he **worked** harder,	he **would do** better.

Another example is someone who doesn't have enough money to buy a new car and says:

*I'**d buy** a new car if I **had** enough money.*

Note that we do not use a comma (,) before **if**.

2 We can use the same type of sentence to talk about the future:

IF +	PAST SIMPLE	+ WOULD (OR 'D)
If	I **won** a lot of money,	I'**d buy** a big house.

This sentence describes an unlikely future situation: it is unlikely that I will win a lot of money.

3 We can use **wish** to say that we want something to be different from how it is now. Note that the verb after **wish** is past (e.g. **could**, **was**, **had**):

I **wish** you **could** talk.

*She **wishes** (that) her dog **could** talk.*
*Mary **wishes** she **had** enough money for a new dress.*
*I **wish** I **was** very rich.*

4 After **if** and after **wish**, we sometimes use **I/he/she/it** with **were**:

*If she **were** (OR was) alive today, …*
*I **wish** Amy Winehouse **were** (OR was) still alive.*

Notice also the expression **if I were you,** when you give someone advice:

*If I **were** you, I'd go to the police.*
(NOT ~~If I was you, …~~)

A Complete these sentences using the words in brackets.

♦ If Ellie lived in Brighton, she _would be_ (she/be) near her parents.
♦ Jacob would read more if _he didn't work_ (he/not/work) so hard.
1 If Elizabeth didn't have to work in the evenings, _____ (she/go) to concerts.
2 Lucy wouldn't go to work by car if _____ (she/live) near a train station.
3 Oliver wouldn't be overweight if _____ (he/not/eat) so much.
4 If Peter didn't live in a flat, _____ (he/have) a dog.
5 Grace would definitely learn French if _____ (she/get) a job in France.
6 If Mark wanted to be healthy, _____ (he/not/smoke).

Conditionals and reported speech

B Look at the predictions for the next few years and complete the sentences.

> It is unlikely that astronauts will visit Mars.
> ~~It is unlikely that they will stop making weapons.~~
> It is unlikely that doctors will find a cure for cancer.
> It is unlikely that they will discover oil in Ireland.
> It is unlikely that everyone will stop using plastic.

♦ If they stopped making weapons, the world would be safer.
1 If _____, the Irish would be very happy.
2 If _____, this terrible disease would disappear.
3 If _____, our rivers would be much cleaner.
4 If _____, we would learn a lot about the planet.

C A manager tells people why they can't have a job. Write the people's thoughts with *I wish*.

♦ You don't have a driving licence, so you can't have the job.
  I wish I had a driving licence.
♦ You can't have the job because you can't type.
  I wish I could type.
1 You can't have the job because you don't have good eyesight.
  I wish _____
2 You can't speak German, so you can't have the job.
  I wish _____
3 You don't have a degree, so you can't have the job.
  I wish _____
4 You can't have the job because you are not 18 years old.
  I wish _____

D Imagine how life nowadays could be better. Complete the sentences using the words in brackets ( ) and any other words you need.

♦ People don't do enough exercise, so there is a lot of heart disease.
  (more, less) If people did more exercise, there would be less heart disease.
1 There are too many cars. The city is very polluted.
  (fewer) I wish there _____, then the city would be less polluted.
2 People drive too fast, so there are a lot of accidents.
  (more slowly) I wish people _____, then there would be fewer accidents.
3 People watch too much TV, so they don't have much time for reading.
  (more) If people watched less TV, they _____.
4 Children have bad teeth because they eat too many sweets.
  (fewer) Children would have better teeth if they _____.
5 Not enough people travel by bus, so the roads are crowded.
  (more) I wish _____, then the roads would be less crowded.
6 People haven't got enough time to cook, so they eat a lot of fast food.
  (more, less) If people _____, they _____.

99 Third Conditional

1 Look at this sentence:

*If Amy Winehouse **had died** in 2013, she **would have been** 30 years old.*

Winehouse did not in fact die in 2013. She died before she was 30 years old. The sentence imagines something that did not happen in the past. This structure is called the Third Conditional:

> **IF + PAST PERFECT + WOULD HAVE (OR 'D HAVE) + PAST PARTICIPLE**
>
> *If he **had tried** harder, he **would have** won.*

Here is another example:

*If Jasmine **had come** on her usual train, I **would have seen** her.* (= She didn't come on her usual train, so I didn't see her.)

Notice how we can also use the negative forms **wouldn't have** and **hadn't**:

*John F. Kennedy **wouldn't have died** in 1963 if he **hadn't gone** to Dallas.* (= Kennedy died in 1963 because he went to Dallas, but this sentence imagines the opposite.)

*I would have phoned you if I **hadn't lost** your phone number.* (= I didn't phone you because I lost your phone number.)

*I **wouldn't have gone** to the museum if I had known it was shut.* (= I went to the museum because I didn't know it was shut.)

2 We can use **wish** + **had done** to talk about the past when we are sorry that something didn't happen, and we imagine that it did:

*He **wishes** he **hadn't driven** so fast.* (= He drove fast and now he's sorry about it.)

*I woke up very late this morning. I **wish** I **had gone** to bed earlier last night.*

We can use a negative form (**wish ... hadn't done**) to say that we are sorry that something did happen:

*Many people **wish** that John F. Kennedy **hadn't gone** to Dallas.* (= Many people are sorry that John F. Kennedy went to Dallas.)

A Read this story about Ellen and write sentences using the words in brackets ( ).

In May 2014 Ellen lost her job in London. She didn't have much money in the bank, so she was very worried. She looked in the newspapers and she saw an advertisement for a job as a translator from German into English. She didn't speak German very well, so she didn't apply for it. In June, she heard about some teaching jobs abroad because a friend phoned to tell her about them. She phoned the company, and they asked her to go for an interview with the director. Ellen thought the interview went badly, but in fact the director was happy with the interview and offered Ellen a job in Spain. However, Ellen couldn't start at once because she didn't know any Spanish. She took a course to learn the language. She was good at languages and she made rapid progress. So, by September she had a new job, and she still had a little money left in the bank.

♦ (If Ellen/have/a lot of money in the bank, she/not/be/so worried.)
  If Ellen had had a lot of money in the bank, she wouldn't have been so worried.

♦ (If she/not/search/online, she/not/see/the advertisement.)
  If she hadn't searched online, she wouldn't have seen the advertisement.

Conditionals and reported speech

1 (If she/speak/German very well, she/apply/for the job.)

2 (If her friend/not/call, she/not/hear about the teaching jobs.)

3 (If she/not/contact/the company, they/not/ask/her to go for an interview.)

4 (If the interview/go/badly, the director/not/offer/Ellen a job.)

5 (If Ellen/know/some Spanish, she/start/at once.)

6 (If she/not/be/good at languages, she/not/make/rapid progress.)

B Complete the sentences using the information in brackets ( ).

♦ (Sam didn't get the job as a translator because he failed the exam.)
Sam _would have got_ the job as a translator if he _had_ not _failed_ the exam.

1 (Oliver lost our phone number, so he didn't call us.)
If Oliver _____ not _____ phone number, he _____ us.

2 (Ellie broke her leg, so she didn't go on holiday.)
If Ellie _____ not _____ her leg, she _____ on holiday.

3 (We didn't make a cake because we forgot to buy any eggs.)
We _____ a cake if we _____ not _____ to buy some eggs.

C Write sentences about these people who are sorry about things they did in the past. Use *wish* or *wishes*.

♦ Owen wasted his time at school; now he's sorry.
Owen wishes he hadn't wasted his time at school.

1 I didn't tell the truth; now I'm sorry.
I wish _____

2 John borrowed some money from his mother; now he's sorry.
John _____

3 Mary didn't get up early; now she's sorry.
Mary _____

4 Peter didn't go to the party; now he's sorry.
Peter _____

5 I didn't send Charlotte a birthday card; now I'm sorry.
I _____

6 Fiona didn't help her sister; now she's sorry.

7 He shouted at the children; now he's sorry.

100 Reported speech (1)

1 When we report something that somebody said earlier, we usually change the tense of the verb like this:

ACTUAL WORDS	REPORTED SPEECH
Present Simple →	Past Simple
'I **live** in a small flat,' she said.	She said (that) she **lived** in a small flat.
Present Continuous →	Past Continuous
'**I'm leaving** on Tuesday,' I said.	I said (that) I **was leaving** on Tuesday.
Past Simple / Present Perfect →	Past Perfect
'I **learnt** a lot,' he said.	He said (that) he **had learnt** a lot.
'Mr Jackson has **left**,' she said.	She said (that) Mr Jackson **had left**.
will →	would
'**I'll help** you,' she said.	She said (that) she **would help** me.
am/is/are going to →	was/were going to
'**We're going to be** late,' I said.	I said (that) we **were going to be** late.
can →	could
'I **can't find** my money,' he said.	He said (that) he **couldn't find** his money.

2 Note that it is not necessary to use **that** in reported speech:

She said (**that**) she knew the answer.

3 Compare **say** and **tell** in these sentences:

She **said** (that) she lived in a small flat.
She **told me** (that) she lived in a small flat.

Note that with **say** we do not mention the person.

She said (that) she was going to be late.
(NOT ~~She said me she was~~ …)
I said that I disagreed with him.
(NOT ~~I said him that I~~ …)

Note that with **tell** we must mention the person.

He told **me** (that) he was happy.
(NOT ~~He told he was happy.~~)
He told **me** that he would pay me immediately.
(NOT ~~He told that he would pay me immediately.~~)
She told **Jacob** (that) she was going to meet someone.
(NOT ~~She told that she was going to meet someone.~~)

A Look at these pictures of people coming through passport control at an airport. Change the things they said into reported speech.

◆ I am visiting friends.
1 I am going to a conference.
2 I have lost my passport.
3 We have been on holiday.
4 I don't understand.

◆ He said *that he was visiting friends.*
1 She said
2 He said
3 They said
4 She said

> Conditionals and reported speech

B Read this conversation and then report what Claudia and Nicole said.

Nicole: How long have you been in France?
Claudia: Six weeks.
Nicole: Are you enjoying your stay?
Claudia: Yes, I'm enjoying it a lot.
Nicole: Have you been here before?
Claudia: Yes. I've been to France many times.
Nicole: What are you doing here?
Claudia: I'm on holiday.
Nicole: Are you staying in a hotel?
Claudia: No, I'm staying with some friends.
Nicole: Where do they live?
Claudia: They have a flat in the city centre.
Nicole: How long are you staying?
Claudia: I'm leaving in March.
Nicole: Can you speak French very well?
Claudia: No, I can't. I'm going to have some lessons.
Nicole: I'll teach you.

- ♦ Claudia said _(that) she had been_ in France for six weeks.
- 1 Claudia said _____ her stay a lot.
- 2 Claudia said _____ to France many times.
- 3 Claudia said _____ on holiday.
- 4 She said _____ with some friends.
- 5 She said _____ a flat in the city centre.
- 6 She said _____ in March.
- 7 She said _____ French very well.
- 8 She said _____ some lessons.
- 9 Nicole said _____ Claudia.

C Complete the sentences with *said* or *told*.

- ♦ She _said_ she wasn't feeling very well.
- 1 Alex _____ me that he would buy the tickets.
- 2 They _____ that the train was going to be late.
- 3 She _____ him that she was very angry with him.
- 4 She _____ him that she couldn't help him.
- 5 Who _____ you that I was leaving? It's not true!
- 6 They _____ us that they were leaving in the morning.
- 7 He _____ that he didn't know what was wrong with the car.
- 8 She _____ she had four sisters.
- 9 She _____ me that Tom worked in a factory.
- 10 He _____ me that he was a doctor, but he _____ Anna that he was a dentist.

101 Reported speech (2)

1 Requests

There are different ways to make a request, e.g.:
- Sarah: Please wait a minute, Tom.
- Sarah: Will you wait a minute, please?
- Sarah: Tom, could you wait a minute, please?

We can report all of these requests in the same way, using **asked**:
- Sarah **asked** Tom to wait a minute.

We do not usually use **please** in a reported question.

2 Orders

There are different ways to give an order:
- 'Stand up, John.'
- 'You must work harder.'

We can report orders like this, using told:
- He **told** John to stand up.
- He **told** me to work harder.

3 Advice

We can give advice like this:
- 'You ought to stay in bed, Peter.'
- 'You should stop smoking, John.'

We can report advice like this, using advised:
- He **advised** Peter to stay in bed.
- She **advised** John to stop smoking.

4 In reported speech, we use **ask**, **tell** and **advise** like this:

VERB	+	OBJECT	+	TO	+	INFINITIVE
Sarah		asked		Tom		to wait.
She		told		him		to stand.
He		advised		Jasmine		to stop smoking.

Here is a list of common verbs that we use in this structure:

advise	ask	tell	order
persuade	remind	forbid	warn

Examples:
- I'll remind them to come early.
- I advised them to go to the police.

We cannot use **say** in this structure:
- She said (that) he should wait.
- (NOT She said him to wait.)

5 To report a negative request, order, etc. (e.g. 'Don't laugh'), we use **not** + **to** + infinitive:

VERB	+	OBJECT	+	NOT + TO + INFINITIVE
Sara		told	Tom	**not to** laugh.
They		warned	Owen	**not to borrow** money.
I		reminded	John	**not to be** late.

A Rewrite the sentences using an object + *to* + infinitive.

♦ 'Make some coffee please, Rob.'
Laura asked *Rob to make some coffee.*

1 'You must do the homework soon, Jasmine.'
She told ....

2 'Remember to buy a map, Anna.'
He reminded ....

3 'You should see a doctor, Mrs Clark.'
He advised ....

4 'Keep all the windows closed, William.'
They warned ....

5 'Go home, Paul.'
Francis told ....

Conditionals and reported speech

B Report what these people said using the words in brackets ( ) and the Past Simple.

♦ Jacob said, 'Anna, would you lend me £5, please?'
(ask) Jacob asked Anna to lend him £5.

1 I said to John, 'Remember to call Ellie.'
(remind) ....

2 'You must wash your hands, children,' the teacher said.
(tell) ....

3 'Mary, please lend me your bicycle pump,' said Paul.
(ask) ....

4 She said, 'Children, stay away from the water.'
(warn) ....

5 'You should see a lawyer,' the police officer said to Mark.
(advise) ....

C Complete the conversations using the words in brackets ( ). You will also need a pronoun (e.g. *me, him, them*) and the word *not*. Use the Past Simple.

♦ A: Did you tell the children to clean the car?   B: (Yes, but I/tell/to use too much water.)
   B: Yes, but I told them not to use too much water.

1 A: Did you ask William to come to the meeting?   B: (Yes, and I/tell/to be late.)
   B: ....

2 A: Did the doctor tell Lucy to keep warm?   B: (Yes, and she/warn/to go outside the house.)
   B: ....

3 A: Did you ask Michael to go to the butcher's?   B: (Yes, and I/tell/to forget the bacon.)
   B: ....

4 A: Did the police officer advise everyone to stay indoors?   B: (Yes, and he/tell/to go near the windows.)
   B: ....

5 A: Did the dentist advise you to eat carefully?   B: (Yes, and she particularly/warn/to eat nuts.)
   B: ....

D Complete the sentences using the words in the box.

advise   ask   order   remind   tell   warn

♦ The official said to George, 'Go to Room 23.' The official *told him to go* to Room 23.

1 'Girls, you mustn't touch these wires. It can be dangerous,' said the guide.
The guide .... the wires.

2 'The bus is all right, Anna, but it's better for you to take the train,' we said.
We .... the train.

3 'Bring the money, Simon. Don't forget,' Mrs Walters said.
Mrs Walters .... the money.

4 'This is the police,' the voice said. 'Spectators must leave at once.'
The police .... at once.

5 I said, 'Please come in, Mr Tufnell.'
I .... in.

102 Reported questions

1 'Yes/no' questions have a form of **be** (e.g. **is**, **are**) or an auxiliary verb (e.g. **can**, **do**, **have**) that goes before the subject:

	SUBJECT	
'Are	they	English?'
'Can	John	type?'

We report these questions with **ask if/ whether**:

		SUBJECT		
She asked	**if**	they	**were**	English.
She asked	**if**	John	**could**	type.

OR:
  She asked **whether** they **were** English.
  She asked **whether** John **could** type.

Note that in a reported question we do not put **be** or an auxiliary before the subject (NOT *She asked were they English.*)

2 Many questions begin with a question word (**Who**, **What**, **Where**, etc.):

	SUBJECT	
'Where does	Anna	live?'
'Why has	Jasmine	gone?'

We report these questions with **ask**:

	SUBJECT		
They asked **where**	Anna	lived.	
She asked **why**	Jasmine	had gone?'	

3 We can also **ask someone something**:
  The manager asked **me** if I could type.
  They asked **him** where Sarah lived.

4 Note that when we report a question that somebody asked earlier, we usually change the tense of the verb:
  'Can John swim?'
  He asked if John **could** swim.

The most common tense changes are:

▶ Present → Past:
  am/is → **was**   **are** → **were**
  is living → **was living**   **live** → **lived**

▶ Present Perfect → Past Perfect:
  has gone → **had gone**

▶ Past Simple → Past Perfect:
  arrived → **had arrived**

▶ Modals:
  will → **would**   **can** → **could**

We often also change other words, for example:
  'Have **you** finished, Mike?'
  She asked Mike if **he** had finished.

5 We can use wanted to know and wondered instead of asked:
  She **wanted to know** if they were English.
    (OR She wanted to know **whether** they were English.)
  She **wondered** why Jasmine had gone.

A Change each sentence into reported speech or a direct question by filling in the gaps. End each sentence with a full stop (.) or a question mark (?).

♦ (Did they come?) She asked _if_ they had come.
♦ (I asked him where he worked.) _Where_ do you work?
1 (Do you speak English?) They asked me _____ I spoke English _____
2 (I wanted to know why he had taken my key.) _____ did you take my key _____
3 (How many people came to the party?) I asked _____ people had come to the party _____
4 (Does Anna work on Saturdays?) I asked _____ Anna worked on Saturdays _____
5 (Can we meet tomorrow?) I asked _____ we could meet tomorrow _____
6 (I asked what he had done.) _____ has he done _____

222

Conditionals and reported speech

7   (When are your parents leaving?) I asked her _____ her parents were leaving _____

8   (Why has Jasmine gone home?) I asked _____ Jasmine had gone home _____

9   (Where do you go for your holidays?) I wanted to know _____ they went for their holidays _____

10 (Is William coming to the party, Jasmine?) I asked Jasmine _____ William was coming to the party _____

B Use the words in brackets ( ) to write questions. Then complete the reported questions.

♦   (Where/have/Maria/go/?) Question: *Where has Maria gone?*
    Reported question: I asked *where Maria had gone.*

1   (Do/James/often/play/football/?) Question: _____
    Reported question: I wondered if _____

2   (What/have/the children/eat/?) Question: _____
    Reported question: She wanted to know _____

3   (Where/be/Mark/going/?) Question: _____
    Reported question: I asked _____

4   (When/will/the next bus/leave/?) Question: _____
    Reported question: We wanted to know _____

5   (Have/Anna/see/the film/?) Question: _____
    Reported question: Tom asked _____

C Steve Ellis robbed a bank and the police believe that Alan Reeves helped him. Complete what Reeves told the police officer using the questions from the box.

> ♦ ~~How long have you been out of prison?~~
> 1 Have you worked since then?   4 Do you know Steve Ellis?
> 2 Does your sister give you money?   5 How long have you known Steve?
> 3 Who else gives you money?   6 Have you seen Steve recently?

♦   I asked him *how long he had been out of prison*, and he replied that he had left prison six months ago.

1   Then I asked him _____. He told me that he hadn't found a job.

2   I asked him _____, and he said she did give him some money, but not very much.

3   Then I asked him _____. He replied that nobody else did.

4   I asked him _____, and he said that he and Steve were friends.

5   So I asked him _____ and he said that he had known him for six years.

6   Then I asked him _____, and he said that he couldn't remember.

Test J — Conditionals and reported speech

A Antonio and Ellie are having a break at work. Complete their conversation with the verbs in brackets ( ) in the right tenses. Use contracted forms, if they sound more natural.

Antonio: I feel old and useless.
Ellie: You're OK. Don't worry so much.
Antonio: If I ◆ _was_ (be) in a different job, I might be happier.
Ellie: You always talk like this if you ¹ _____ (be) tired.
Antonio: Yes, but if I had applied for other jobs, I ² _____ (get) something more interesting by now. I wouldn't be so tired.
Ellie: If I ³ _____ (be) you, I'd take a holiday.
Antonio: I wish I ⁴ _____ (have) enough money.
Ellie: If you saved up, you ⁵ _____ (be) able to have holidays. We've had this conversation before, haven't we?
Antonio: Yes, I know. But if I ⁶ _____ (not talk) to you, I won't find an answer.
Ellie: I wish I ⁷ _____ (can) help you more.
Antonio: But I would have stopped work completely if I ⁸ _____ (not met) you, Ellie!
Ellie: If people ⁹ _____ (not speak) to each other, they lose hope. That's my opinion. What makes you happy, anyway?
Antonio: I wish I ¹⁰ _____ (know). The only thing I know is that I ¹¹ _____ (sing) if I'm happy. Does that help?
Ellie: Perhaps. Where do you sing?
Antonio: In the shower mostly.
Ellie: Perhaps you ¹² _____ (be) happier if you got a job in music?
Antonio: Perhaps. But I have to get back to work. I'll talk to you later.

B Peter is making a political speech in the town centre. Improve his speech by using Second and Third Conditionals instead of the underlined text.

'Please listen to me. ◆<u>We don't work together, so we don't succeed.</u> ¹<u>You didn't vote for me at the last election, so your lives have not improved.</u> Don't go away. I know it's raining! ²<u>Churchill isn't alive today.</u> ³<u>Life isn't better, and he isn't our Prime Minister.</u> Come back, sir! I haven't finished. ⁴<u>Our teachers aren't happy because our schools are short of money.</u> ⁵<u>I won't become Prime Minister, so I won't give every child a new phone.</u> ⁶<u>I didn't bring my wife with me today.</u> ⁷<u>She isn't here because she's busy with her own work.</u>'

◆ If _we worked together, we would succeed._
1. If you _____
2. I wish Churchill _____
3. Life would _____
4. Our teachers would _____
5. If I _____
6. I wish I _____
7. If she wasn't _____

Conditionals and reported speech

C Luke's parents got divorced ten years ago. Luke has just met his father, William, for the first time in five years. In this conversation, he is telling his girlfriend what his father said. Report it.

What William said:
- ~~'Are you living on your own?'~~
1. 'Please get enough sleep.'
2. 'You should get some qualifications.'
3. 'Don't take any drugs.'
4. 'Why did Paul leave the flat?'
5. 'Where do you work?'
6. 'Please give me your new address there.'

Michelle: What did he say?
Luke: ♦ (ask) *He asked me if I was living on my own.*
Michelle: None of his business! What else?
Luke: ¹(advise) _____
Michelle: What does he think you've been doing for five years? What about college?
Luke: ²(tell) _____
Michelle: Did he get any himself? Anything else?
Luke: ³(warn) _____
Michelle: I suppose that's sensible. Did he say anything about your friend Paul?
Luke: ⁴(ask) _____
Michelle: Did you talk about work?
Luke: ⁵(ask) _____
Michelle: So you told him about the job in Sheffield?
Luke: Yes and ⁶(persuade) _____

D Now use William's report to his second wife to write what Luke actually said.

William's report:
- ~~He said I didn't look very well.~~
1. He said he would give me the name of his doctor.
2. He told me to eat more fruit.
3. He told me he was living in a flat on his own.
4. He said he had tried sharing with his friend, Paul, but Paul had left.
5. He said he was going to live in Sheffield.

Luke: ♦ *You don't look very well.*
William: I'm alright actually.
Luke: ¹ _____
William: But I'm never ill.
Luke: ² _____
William: Perhaps. Anyway, what are you doing these days?
Luke: ³ _____
William: Don't you get lonely?
Luke: ⁴ _____
William: Really? What are you going to do next, anyway?
Luke: ⁵ _____

103 And, but, so, both … and, either, etc.

1 We use **and** and **both … and** to link two similar ideas in one sentence:

　　She is tired.　　She is hungry.
　　↓
　　She is tired **and** hungry.
　　She is **both** tired **and** hungry.
　　We found **both** our tickets **and** our money.

2 We use **but** to contrast two different ideas:

　　He swims. He doesn't play tennis.
　　He swims, **but** he doesn't play tennis.
　　I live in Bristol, **but** I work in London.

3 We use **so** to talk about the result of something (see **Unit 104**); it links two actions (= and therefore …):

　　SITUATION:　　　　RESULT:
　　I'm tired.　　　　I'm going to bed.

　　I'm tired, **so** I'm going to bed.
　　They were late, **so** they missed the train.

4 We use **or** and **either … or** to talk about two possibilities:

　　POSSIBILITY A:　　POSSIBILITY B:
　　She's French.　　She's Swiss.
　　↓
　　She's French **or** Swiss.
　　She's **either** French **or** Swiss.
　　That man is **either** a footballer **or** an actor.
　　I never work all day. I work **either** in the morning **or** in the afternoon.

5 We use **neither … nor** to put two negative statements together:

　　Peter didn't come.　　Jess didn't come.
　　↓
　　Neither Peter **nor** Jess came.

The verb form (**came**) is positive, because **neither … nor** makes the sentence negative:
　　NOT ~~Neither Peter nor Jess didn't come.~~

6 When we talk about two things, we can also use **both**, **either** and **neither** like this:

	PLURAL VERB	
Both of these suitcases	are	heavy.

I haven't seen **either of the films**.

	SINGULAR OR PLURAL VERB	
Neither of his sisters	was/were	there.

We can also say:

both/either/neither + of + them/us

He has two cars, but **neither of them** works.

A Complete the second halves of the sentences with *but* or *so*.

◆ The film was very long,　　but　it was interesting.
　　　　　　　　　　　　　　so　　we got home late.

1 The restaurant is very expensive,　　　　the food is terrible.
　　　　　　　　　　　　　　　　　　　　only rich people go there.

2 I'm studying hard,　　　　I don't have much free time.
　　　　　　　　　　　　　I'm not making much progress.

3 I've got her email address,　　　　I can write to her.
　　　　　　　　　　　　　　　　　I haven't got her mobile number.

4 We wanted to swim,　　　　we went to the seaside.
　　　　　　　　　　　　　the sea was too cold.

5 They didn't have any money,　　　　they wanted to eat in a restaurant.
　　　　　　　　　　　　　　　　　　they couldn't go to a restaurant.

6 I lost my bag,　　　　I went to the police station.
　　　　　　　　　　　I found £10 in my pocket.

Building sentences

B Combine these sentences with *both ... and*.

- Jasmine owns a shop. She owns a restaurant. *Jasmine owns both a shop and a restaurant.*
1. This restaurant is cheap. It is good.
2. Jo bought a dress. She bought a jumper.
3. They play golf. They play tennis.
4. The film was funny. It was exciting.

C Now combine these sentences with *either ... or*.

- POSSIBILITY A: She's at the office. POSSIBILITY B: She's at the airport.
  She's either at the office or at the airport.
1. POSSIBILITY A: Paul's at home. POSSIBILITY B: Paul's at the gym.
2. POSSIBILITY A: The shop is in East Street. POSSIBILITY B: The shop is in Fox Street.
3. POSSIBILITY A: Her father is a doctor. POSSIBILITY B: Her father is a dentist.
4. POSSIBILITY A: The museum is in Oxford. POSSIBILITY B: The museum is in Bath.

D Now combine these sentences with *neither ... nor*.

- Chris didn't have time to take a holiday. Michelle didn't have time to take a holiday.
  Neither Chris nor Michelle had time to take a holiday.
1. The bus didn't arrive on time. The train didn't arrive on time.
2. David doesn't play tennis. Mike doesn't play tennis.
3. The restaurants aren't good. The hotels aren't good.
4. The English team didn't play well. The Scottish team didn't play well.

E Complete the sentences with *both/either/neither + of + us/them* (e.g. *neither of us*).

- I went to the concert with Mary, but *neither of us* enjoyed it very much because it was a bit boring.
1. There are two flights we can catch to New York. Both flights cost the same amount, so we can choose ....
2. I played two games against Harry, and I lost .... because he is a much better player than me.
3. I saw Jasmine and Alice walking down the street and I waved at them, but .... saw me because they were talking.
4. I looked at George, and George looked at me. Then .... started to laugh because it was such a funny situation.
5. A man spoke to us but .... could understand him, so we didn't answer.
6. Tim and I wanted to go to the game, but .... could get tickets, so we watched it on TV.

227

104 Because, in case, so, so that

1 We use **because** to give the reason for something:

	REASON
Jack is in bed	**because** he's got the flu.

We couldn't go out **because** the weather was terrible.
I took a taxi **because** I was in a hurry.

We use **because of** with a noun (e.g. **flu**, **weather**, **noise**):

	REASON
Jack is in bed	**because of** his flu.

We couldn't go out **because of** the storm.
I couldn't sleep **because of** the noise.

2 We use **in case** when the reason is something that might happen:

	REASON
I'm taking an umbrella	**in case** it rains.

(= I'm taking an umbrella because it might rain.)
I'll phone John, **in case** he wants to come with us. (= ... because he might want to come with us.)

3 We use **so** to talk about the result of something:

	RESULT	
I was in a hurry	**so**	I took a taxi.

Jack's got the flu **so** he's in bed.
The weather was terrible **so** we couldn't go out.
My neighbours were having a party and making a lot of noise **so** I couldn't sleep.

4 We use **so that** to talk about the purpose of an action:

	PURPOSE	
I took a taxi	**so that**	I would arrive on time.

I listen to the news in the morning **so that** I know what's happening in the world.
Tom goes jogging every day **so that** he'll stay fit.
I took a taxi **so that** my friends would not have to wait for me.

(We can also use **to** + infinitive to talk about purpose; see **Unit 95**.)

A Write each sentence in a different way using the words given.

♦ Tom didn't want to go out because he had a cold.
  Tom didn't want to go out because of *his cold*.

♦ Take some money because you might need to take a taxi.
  Take some money in case *you need to take a taxi*.

♦ John and I asked for a drink because we were thirsty.
  John and I were thirsty so *we asked for a drink*.

1 Mary went to bed because she was tired.
  .... so ....

2 I couldn't sleep because it was so hot.
  .... the heat.

3 Charlotte doesn't like apples so she doesn't eat them.
  .... because ....

4 The streets were crowded because of the football match.
  .... there was a football match.

5 I'll give Jasmine a key to the house because she might get home before me.
  .... in case ....

Building sentences

B Complete the sentences with *because*, *in case* or *so*, and a phrase from the box. Use each phrase once.

> I'll take a book to read
> I want to lose weight
> she's at home
> ~~they had to wait for the next one~~
> he lost his passport
> his wife was ill
> more people come to the party

- They missed one bus *so they had to wait for the next one.*
1. I don't know where my sister is, but I'll try phoning her
2. I'm eating less these days
3. Peter had trouble at the airport
4. It's a long journey
5. We've bought more food
6. Mr Smith didn't go to the meeting

C Write out complete sentences using the words in brackets ( ), making any necessary changes and including *so that*.

- (Mark/go/swimming every day/he can stay healthy.)
  Mark goes swimming every day so that he can stay healthy.
1. (Last week, my brother/lend/me £60/I could buy some new trainers.)
2. (Last month, the Government/pass/new traffic laws/there will be fewer accidents.)
3. (Our school has/open/a new library/we can have more books.)
4. (Anna always/write/everything in her diary/she doesn't forget her appointments.)
5. (Last Friday, we/leave/home early/we could avoid the morning traffic.)

D If the sentence is correct, put a tick (✓). If it is incorrect cross out any incorrect words and, if necessary, write in the correct word.

- A: Why are they tired? ✓
  B: Because ~~that~~ their long journey. *of*
1. I can't come tomorrow, so that I came today.
2. Take a sandwich with you in case you get hungry.
3. Julie had to go to the shops so she needed something for lunch.
4. A: Good morning. I've come because of my back hurts.
   B: You mean you've come so a check-up? O.K. But we're very busy today so you'll have to wait about an hour.

105 Since, as, for

1 We can use **because**, **since** and **as** to express a reason for something. Normally we use **because** when the reason has not been mentioned previously; the reason usually comes in second place:

*We stayed at home **because** Tom was ill.*

If the conversation has already mentioned that Tom was ill, we normally express the reason with **since** or **as**; the reason usually comes in first place:

*Tom wasn't feeling well. **Since/As** Tom was ill, we stayed at home.*

2 We can use **for** to express purpose or reason with different structures. We can use it with a noun to express a purpose:

*I went to the shops **for** some cheese.*
*We stopped **for** a drink.*

When the action and the purpose involve different people, we express this with **for** and a noun or pronoun followed by the infinitive with **to**:

*We stopped **for** the children to have a drink.*
*I waited **for** him to finish his homework.*

We can use **for** with a noun or an **-ing** form to give the reason for a reaction:

*The teacher sent Charlotte home **for** cheating.*
*My cousin was arrested **for** robbery.*
*Johnson is in prison **for** dangerous driving.*
*Sam won a medal **for** saving a young boy.*

Here the reason happens before the reaction.

3 You will sometimes see **for** used in a way similar to **because**:

*Diane was pleased to receive the books, **for** she was fond of reading.*

However, this is not common and you can always use **because** in these cases.

4 We can also use prepositions **due to** and **owing to** with a noun to express a reason:

*Many people arrived late **due to/owing to** the heavy rain.*
***Due to/Owing to** the road repairs, we had to take a different route.*

If we use these prepositions with a clause, we have to include **the fact that**:

*The concert was cancelled **due to/owing to** **the fact that** the pianist had appendicitis.*

Note that we can use noun + **be** + **due to** + noun:

*The delay **was due to** fog.*

We cannot use **owing to** in this way:

NOT ~~The delay was owing to fog.~~

Here the reason happens before the action or fact.

A Complete the sentences with an expression from the box.

due to a problem with the brakes	for the children
for the best drawing	for some bottled water
since Carolyn's a vegetarian	owing to the underground strike
~~for a cup of coffee~~	

♦ The workers had a break *for a cup of coffee*.
1 She kept a box of toys .... to play with.
2 Amber won a prize ....
3 .... , we can't take her to our usual restaurant.
4 Jasmine's accident was ....
5 Jack has gone to the shops ....
6 Many people were late for work ....

Building sentences

B For each pair of sentences, complete the second so that it means the same as the first. In some cases there is more than one possibility.

- Lucy went to the kitchen to get some ice cubes.
  Lucy went to the kitchen for *some ice cubes*.

1. Jonny's mother sent him to his room because he misbehaved.
   Jonny's mother sent him to his room for ....
2. The ferry was late due to the heavy winds.
   The ferry was late due to .... it was very windy.
3. Nathan hit his sister and his father punished him.
   Nathan's father punished him for ....
4. We had the meeting in the annex because they were repairing the main building.
   We had the meeting in the annex owing to .... the main building.
5. The boss gave Isaac a bonus because he worked at the weekend.
   The boss gave Isaac a bonus for .... at the weekend.
6. I can't get into the bathroom because Emily's there.
   Since .... , I can't get in there.
7. The road is blocked because some trees have fallen.
   The blocked road is due to ....
8. They waited while the sheep crossed the road.
   They waited for .... cross the road.

C Here is a story about a day out for the Long family. Choose the correct options to complete it.

Mr Long is a careless driver. In fact he has a reputation as a dangerous driver ◆ because/~~owing to~~ the police have fined him three times [1] because/for speeding. [2] Due to/Since he drives carelessly, his wife usually drives the family car, especially when the children are with them. The children often feel sick in the car [3] due to the fact that/owing to they are not good travellers, and when this happens Mrs Long has to stop the car [4] for/as them to have a break. Some people take pills for travel sickness, of course, but Mrs Long doesn't like the idea [5] because/due to she doesn't think they work. One hot summer's day the family were on their way to visit Mrs Long's mother [6] owing to the fact that/owing to it was her birthday. [7] Since/For it was a special day the children were wearing their best clothes, so it was obviously a bad day [8] for/because them to get dirty. Very soon the children were feeling sick, probably due [9] to/for the heat, so Mrs Long stopped the car several times [10] for/since them to get out for some fresh air. When they finally arrived, grandmother said, 'You're a bit late but I suppose that's [11] due to/owing to the traffic.' 'Not really,' said Mrs Green. 'The journey took longer than usual [12] because/owing to the heat and we had to stop several times [13] to/for a break.' At their grandmother's the children soon felt better and they had a great afternoon. After lunch they went for long walk with Grandma's dog, Queenie. On the way home they were tired and fell asleep straightaway in the car.

106 Although, while, however, despite, etc.

1 We can contrast two ideas or situations within a sentence with **although**:

Although the weather was very cold, we decided to go for a walk.
The government passed the new law although many people opposed it.

Informally we can use **though** in the same way:

Though the weather was very cold, we decided to go for a walk.
The government passed the new law though many people opposed it.

While is not possible here.

2 We can use **while** to contrast two aspects of the same thing or two similar things within a sentence:

While I agree with the idea, I don't think it's very practical.
Some of my friends have found work while others are still unemployed.

(**Al**)**though** is also possible here.

3 When the contrast is expressed in a separate sentence, we use **however**:

The government passed the new law. However, many people were against it.
I agree with the idea. I don't think it's very practical, however.

We use a comma to separate **however** from the rest of the sentence.

Though can also go at the end of a separate sentence:

I agree with the idea. I don't think it's very practical, though.

Although is not possible here.

4 We can use prepositions **in spite of** and **despite** with a noun (but not usually a personal pronoun) to express concession or contrast:

In spite of/Despite the cold weather, we decided to go for a walk.
The government passed the new law in spite of/despite the opposition.

If we use these prepositions with a clause, we have to include **the fact that**, e.g.:

The government passed the new law in spite of/despite the fact that many people were against it.

A In each question, complete the second sentence (or pair of sentences) so that the meaning is the same as the first sentence (or pair of sentences).

♦ Jacob is older than Megan but she is taller than he is.
   Although Jacob is older than Megan, she is taller than he is .

1 In spite of the fact that it was dangerous, many people helped in the rescue.
   Many people helped in the rescue although _____ .

2 Some people continue to smoke cigarettes although there is a serious warning on every packet.
   _____ the warning on every packet, some people continue to smoke cigarettes.

3 There were several stronger teams but it was Greece that won the cup.
   There were several stronger teams. It was Greece that won the cup, _____ .

4 Although London is more expensive than the rest of Britain, many people prefer to live there.
   Many people prefer to live in London despite _____ it is more expensive than the rest of Britain.

5 My work is interesting but it is not very well paid.
   While _____ , it is not very well paid.

6 Although Amy complained about the exams, she got very good marks.
   Amy complained about the exams. _____ , she got very good marks.

Building sentences

B Complete this speech about drugs by putting in *although*, *despite*, *however* or *while*. In some cases there is more than one possibility.

Ladies and gentlemen. Today I want to explain why I think drugs should be legalized. Many people think that all drugs are illegal. ♦ _However_, the legal situation is different in different countries. For example, ¹_____ coca leaves are legal in some parts of South America, they are banned in the USA and many other countries. But even in the USA and Europe, it is not true that all drugs are illegal. ²_____ tobacco and alcohol are seriously addictive, they are a regular aspect of most social gatherings in our countries. Not everybody who smokes tobacco or drinks alcohol is an addict, of course. Many regular smokers would like to cut down or stop, ³_____, and in fact many have tried several times. ⁴_____ their many attempts, they continue smoking, precisely because nicotine is so addictive. Anyway, what are the disadvantages of the illegal drugs remaining illegal? In the first place, illegality means that there is no quality control to protect the consumer. People think they are buying cocaine, for example, ⁵_____ the substance is often mixed with dust or even poisonous powders. Also drugs on the street are fairly expensive so ⁶_____ consumers might not have a job, they need their drugs and this quickly leads to stealing and prostitution in order to pay for them. Second, the drug industry generates enormous quantities of money, enough to corrupt many police officers and politicians. We like to think that our authorities control crime. The reality, ⁷_____, is that in some countries crime controls the authorities. Ladies and gentleman, ⁸_____ you may not like drugs, as long as drugs are illegal, they are outside democratic control.

Anthony and Grace are discussing the talk about drugs. Complete their conversation using the expressions from the box.

~~although~~   although   despite   however   in spite of the fact that   though

Anthony: What did you think of the talk?

Grace: I don't agree with her, ♦ _although_ I have to accept that her talk was clever. It's true that the present situation isn't perfect. ¹_____, if they legalize drugs, things will be much worse.

Anthony: Oh, I don't know. Society seems to manage all right with tobacco and alcohol ²_____ they're perfectly legal.

Grace: You make it sound as if they're harmless. I think it's truer to say that society functions ³_____ they're legal because they cause problems for a lot of people.

Anthony: A few people misuse them. Most people use them sensibly, ⁴_____.

Grace: It doesn't make sense to say that you can smoke sensibly. That's why there are health warnings on the packets. People are stupid enough to smoke ⁵_____ all the warnings.

107 Relative clauses (1)

1 If we use a sentence like:
   The police have found the boy.
it may not be clear which boy.
We can make it clear like this:
   *The police have found the boy **who disappeared last week**.*

Who links the relative clause (**who disappeared last week**) to the main clause (**The police have found the boy**).

2 When we talk about people, we use **that** or **who**:
   *I talked to the girl **that** (OR **who**) won the race.*

When we talk about things or animals, we use **that** or **which**:
   *I like the car **that** (OR **which**) won the race.*

3 **That**, **who** or **which** can be the subject of the relative clause, like this:

	SUBJECT	
I talked to the girl	who	won.
	The girl	won.
That is the dog	that	attacked me.
	The dog	attacked me.

There is no other pronoun (e.g. **it**, **they**):
   NOT *That is the dog that it attacked me.*

4 **That**, **who** or **which** can be the object of the relative clause, like this:

	OBJECT	
The card	which	Jon sent was nice.
Jon sent		the card.
The man	that	I saw was very rude.
I saw		the man.

There is no other pronoun (e.g. **him**, **them**):
   NOT *The man I saw him was very rude.*

When **that**, **who** or **which** is the object of the relative clause (e.g. *The card **which** Jon sent*), we can leave it out:
   *The card **Jon sent** was nice.*
   *The man **I saw** was very rude.*

5 Now look at this sentence with **whose**:
   *Lucy is the woman **whose husband is an actor**.* (= Lucy's husband is an actor.)

We use **whose** in place of **his**, **her**, **their**, etc. We only use it with people, countries and organizations, not things. It has a possessive meaning. Here is another example:
   *The man **whose** dog bit me didn't apologize.*
   (= The man didn't apologize. **His** dog bit me.)

All these relative clauses that define a person or thing are called defining relative clauses.

A Complete the sentences using the information in brackets ( ) and *who* or *which*.

♦ (I went to see a doctor. She had helped my mother.)
  I went to see the doctor *who had helped* my mother.

1 (A dog bit me. It belonged to Mrs Jones.)
  The dog _____ belonged to Mrs Jones.

2 (A woman wrote to me. She wanted my advice.)
  The woman _____ wanted my advice.

3 (A bus crashed. It was 23 years old.)
  The bus _____ was 23 years old.

4 (Anna talked to a man. He had won a lot of money.)
  Anna talked to the man _____.

5 (Mary was wearing the red dress. She wears it for parties.)
  Mary was wearing the red dress _____.

6 (He's an architect. He designed the new city library.)
  He's the architect _____.

Building sentences

B Complete the sentences using the information in brackets ( ) and *that*.

♦ (Jack made a table. It's not very strong.)
The table *that Jack made* is not very strong.

1 (I read about a new computer. I had seen it on TV.)
I read about the new computer _____.

2 (Jasmine made a cake. Nobody liked it.)
Nobody liked the cake _____.

3 (Mary sent me a joke. It was very funny.)
The joke _____ was very funny.

4 (My sister wrote an article. The news is going to publish it.)
The news is going to publish the article _____.

5 (I met an old lady. She was 103 years old.)
The old lady _____ was 103 years old.

6 (I saw a house. My brother wants to buy it.)
I saw the house _____.

C Complete the sentences with one of the phrases in the box and *who* or *whose*.

interviewed me	has visited so many different countries
~~had saved their son~~	wives have just had babies
book won a prize last week	~~divorce was in all the papers~~
car had broken down	complain all the time

♦ The parents thanked the woman *who had saved their son*.
♦ The couple *whose divorce was in the newspapers* have got married again.

1 It is very interesting to meet somebody _____.
2 The person _____ asked me some very difficult questions.
3 In my office there are two men _____.
4 What's the name of that writer _____?
5 I don't like people _____.
6 We helped a woman _____.

D Complete the sentences with *who*, *that*, or nothing (–).

♦ The match – we saw was boring.
♦ Did I tell you about the people *who* live next door?
♦ The horse *that* won the race belongs to an Irish woman.

1 I love the ice cream _____ they sell in that shop.
2 The book _____ I'm reading is about jazz.
3 The woman _____ came to see us was selling magazines.
4 We'll go to a restaurant _____ has a children's menu.
5 The factory _____ closed last week had been there for 70 years.
6 Have you read about the schoolgirl _____ started her own business and is now a millionaire?
7 Ethel says that the house _____ Tom has just bought has a beautiful garden.

108 Relative clauses (2)

1 In informal English, in defining relative clauses, when **who**, **that** or **which** is the object of the verb, it can be omitted:

  The name of the woman I interviewed was Mrs Norris.
  The car they bought was quite expensive.

Notice that there is no pronoun in the relative clause:

  The name of the woman I interviewed ~~her~~ was Mrs Norris.
  The car they bought ~~it~~ was quite expensive.

2 When the verb has a preposition, in formal English the preposition goes with **whom** or **which**:

  That is the young man **to whom** I spoke.
  The job **for which** she's applied is in Paris.

Informally, we can omit the relative word and then the preposition goes at the end of the relative clause:

  That is the young man I spoke **to**.
  The job she's applied **for** is in Paris.

3 Informally, we often omit the relative word **when** after **day**, **year**, etc.:

  That was the **year** I finished university.

We often omit the relative word **where** after **place**, **somewhere**, etc.:

  Do you know **a place**/**somewhere** we can get a good sandwich?

We often omit the relative word **why** after **reason**:

  The real **reason** she came was to speak to me.

We often omit a relative expression after **way**:

  That's the **way** they make beer in Germany.

A Cross out the words in the sentences that are not possible or not necessary. If there are no such words, mark the sentence with a tick (✓).

  ♦ The first book ~~which~~ she wrote ~~it~~ was *Lost Steps*.
  ♦ This is the boy who broke the window. ✓
  1 Do you know the woman that my father's talking to?
  2 They're going to close the factories that they make too much smoke.
  3 People who live in flats shouldn't have dogs.
  4 An animal that comes out at night must have good eyes.
  5 The boat that my cousins sailed in it was hit by a bomb.
  6 An amphibian is an animal which can live on land or in water.
  7 People who are from Manchester are called Mancunians.

B In the following, if a sentence is incomplete, indicate where a word is necessary and write the word at the end. If the sentence is correct, mark it with a tick (✓).

  ♦ Is there a shop near here ⋀ sells stamps? *that*
  ♦ Mrs Thomas is the teacher my sister likes best. ✓
  1 The referee is the person takes the decisions.
  2 The bus they were waiting for never came.
  3 The old lady we saw was wearing a pink dress.
  4 Is this the train goes to Nottingham?
  5 There's a place near here you can get a good hamburger.
  6 It took a long time to find the doctor we wanted to see.
  7 Do you know anybody plays the piano really well?

Building sentences

C Combine the two sentences into one. Put in *who*, *that*, *which* or *where* only if it is necessary.

♦ I lent you a book. Have you read it?
   Have you read *the book I lent you*?

♦ My mother works in a factory. It makes parts for cars.
   The factory *where my mother works* makes parts for cars.

1 Sian's got a new mobile. It takes brilliant photos.
   Sian's got a new mobile that takes brilliant photos.

2 They lived in a block of flats. It was struck by lightning.
   The block of flats they lived in was struck by lightning.

3 The hotel had a magician. He was very clever.
   The hotel had a magician who was very clever.

4 The porters are paid a salary. They can't live on it.
   The porters can't live on the salary they are paid.

5 Nobody else wanted the food. My father ate it.
   My father ate the food nobody else wanted.

6 We ran out of petrol in a little village. It didn't have a petrol station.
   The village where we ran out of petrol didn't have a petrol station.

D Freda and Jacob are packing to go on holiday. Complete their conversation with the expressions from the box and include *that* if it is necessary.

you can take onto the plane	go with my green dress	~~has a lock~~
have just been mended	covers all the Mediterranean islands	a bit heavy
I can walk all day in	we bought in that second-hand bookshop	I knitted myself

Jacob: We'd better take two cases. The one ♦ *that has a lock* and that smaller one is a bit heavy.

Freda: Which camera do you want to take? The handy one or the big one you can take onto the plane?

Jacob: Let's take the smaller one. How about the travel guide? There's that big one we bought in that second-hand bookshop and that pocket-sized one – the one just about Corsica.

Freda: Perhaps the small one will be enough.

Jacob: I think I'll take my shoes that have just been mended. How many pairs of shoes are you taking?

Freda: Well, we'll need some comfortable ones I can walk all day in and perhaps for the evenings I'll take the new green ones, the ones that go with my green dress.

Jacob: It might be cool in the evenings. I suppose you're taking a sweater.

Freda: Yes, the white one. You know, the one I knitted myself. Anyway, let's have a break. I feel like a drink.

109 Relative clauses (3)

1 Look at these two sentences:

London has nearly 9 million inhabitants.
*London, **which is the capital of Britain**, has nearly 9 million inhabitants.*

The clause **which is the capital of Britain** gives us more information about London, but we do not need this information to define **London**. We can understand the first sentence without this extra information. **Which is the capital of Britain** is a non-defining relative clause. It has commas (**,**) to separate it from the rest of the sentence.

2 For things or animals, we use **which** (NOT ~~that~~) in non-defining relative clauses:

*Jacob sold his computer, **which he no longer needed**, to his cousin.* (NOT ... ~~that he no longer needed~~ ...)
*In the summer we stay in my uncle's house, **which is near the sea**.*

3 For people, we use **who** (BUT NOT ~~that~~) in non-defining relative clauses. We use **who** when it is the subject of the relative clause:

SUBJECT
*Elvis Presley, **who died in 1977**, earned millions of dollars.* (**Presley** died in 1977.)

We use **who** (or sometimes **whom**) when it is the object of the relative clause:

OBJECT
*My boss, **who** (OR **whom**) **I last saw before Christmas**, is very ill.* (I last saw **my boss** before Christmas.)

4 We use **whose** to mean **his**, **her**, or **their**:

*Marilyn Monroe, **whose real name was Norma Jean**, was born in Los Angeles.*
(**Her** real name was Norma Jean.)

5 We can also use **which** (BUT NOT ~~that~~) to refer to a whole fact:

*Anna did not want to marry Tom, **which** surprised everybody.*

Here, **which** refers to the fact that Anna did not want to marry Tom.

A Make one sentence from the two that are given. Use *who* or *which*.

♦ Mont Blanc is between France and Italy. It is the highest mountain in the Alps.
  Mont Blanc, which is between France and Italy, is the highest mountain in the Alps.

♦ Alfred Hitchcock was born in Britain. He worked for many years in Hollywood.
  Alfred Hitchcock, who was born in Britain, worked for many years in Hollywood.

1 The sun is really a star. It is 93 million miles from the earth.

2 John F. Kennedy died in 1963. He was a very famous American President.

3 Charlie Chaplin was from a poor family. He became a very rich man.

4 The 2016 Olympics were held in Rio de Janeiro. It was the capital of Brazil until 1960.

5 We went to see the Crown Jewels. They are kept in the Tower of London.

Building sentences

B From the notes, make one sentence. Use *who*, *whose* or *which* with the words in brackets ( ).

♦ Greta Garbo. (She was born in Sweden.) She moved to America in 1925.
Greta Garbo, who was born in Sweden, moved to America in 1925.

♦ Darwin. (His ideas changed our view of the world.) He travelled a lot when he was young.
Greta Garbo, who was born in Sweden, moved to America in 1925.

1 Football. (It first started in Britain.) It is now popular worldwide.
Football, ...

2 Margaret Thatcher. (She was the Prime Minister of Britain for 11 years.) She studied science at university.

3 Michelangelo. (He lived until he was 90.) He is one of Italy's greatest artists.

4 Barack Obama. (His wife is a brilliant lawyer and role model.) He became President of the USA in 2009.

5 The Nile. (It runs through several countries.) It is the longest river in Africa.

6 Madonna. (Her parents were born in Italy.) She is a famous American singer.

7 Gandhi. (He was born in 1869). He was assassinated in 1948.

8 Elephants. (They are found in Africa and India). They are the largest land animals.

9 The Beatles. (Their music is still popular.) They were probably the most famous pop group in the world.

10 Brands Hatch. (It is not far from London.) It is famous for its motor races.

C Complete this text about Lewis Carroll with *who*, *which* or *whose*.

Alice in Wonderland, ♦ *which* is one of the most popular children's books in the world, was written by Lewis Carroll, ¹................ real name was Charles Dodgson. Carroll, ²................ had a natural talent as a story-teller, loved to entertain children, including Alice Liddell, ³................ father was a colleague of Carroll's at Oxford University. One day Carroll took Alice and her sisters for a trip on the River Thames, ⁴................ flows through Oxford. After the trip, Carroll wrote in his diary that he had told the children a wonderful story, ⁵................ he had promised to write down for them. He wrote the story, illustrated it with his own drawings, and gave it to the children. By chance, it was seen by Henry Kingsley, ⁶................ was a famous novelist, and he persuaded Dodgson to publish it.

Test K — Building sentences

A Carlo is working on the busy reception desk of a large hotel in Bristol. Complete the dialogue with the words from the box.

| either | in case | nor | both | so (x2) | and | ~~Neither~~ | because | or |

Carlo: Can I help you, sir?

First man: I hope so. ♦Neither the shower ¹_____ the bath works in my room.

Carlo: I'm sorry, sir. We'll have them repaired this afternoon.

***

First woman: I've got an early flight, ²_____ I need an alarm call at five o'clock in the morning.

Carlo: No problem, Madam. I'll arrange that for you.

***

Second man: Can I borrow an umbrella ³_____ it rains? I don't want to get my suit wet.

Carlo: Of course you can, sir. Here you are.

***

Second woman: I'm unhappy ⁴_____ my room doesn't have a view. I'd like to see ⁵_____ the park ⁶_____ the river.

Carlo: I'll see what I can do, Madam.

***

Third man: Can you book me a taxi ⁷_____ that I can get to the airport by ten o'clock tonight?

Carlo: Certainly sir. I'll book it for half past nine.

***

Third woman: ⁸_____ the bed ⁹_____ the bath are too small for my husband and me.

Carlo: I'm sorry, Madam, but that's all we have at the moment.

B This is the first of two articles from a holiday magazine. Cross out the wrong words.

Beach, City or Lake?

♦Although/Since most British holidaymakers traditionally go to the seaside for their holidays, lakes and mountains are also popular places ¹as/for people to relax and enjoy themselves. ²While/However, a lake holiday usually costs more than a beach holiday because the local hotels and restaurants are more expensive.

³Since/Although most people think very carefully about prices, the beach is still the top location ⁴for/as a one-week or two-week holiday. ⁵While/However you may not think of a city as a place for relaxing, many people enjoy a short break or a long weekend in a nearby town.

⁶Although/In spite of the noise and the traffic, tourists love going to big cities and seeing the art galleries, museums, shops and nightlife. ⁷However/Although they are expensive, big cities all over the world welcome millions of visitors every year.

> Building sentences

C Joe and Beth have been invited to a neighbour's wedding. Cross out the underlined words if they are not necessary.

Joe: What would you like to drink?
Beth: Something ♦ that I haven't tried before, I think. Joe, can you see the man ♦ who is drinking orange juice?
Joe: Is he the man ¹ who repaired our roof in the summer?
Beth: I think so. The day ² when he came to our house was your birthday, wasn't it?
Joe: That's right. But the work ³ that he did wasn't very good, was it?
Beth: No, it wasn't. Do you know the woman ⁴ who is eating a piece of cake by the window?
Joe: Yes. I'm sure she's the woman ⁵ whose dog bit my leg a month ago.
Beth: Oh dear. Is there anyone here ⁶ that you want to talk to?
Joe: I'd like to find the man ⁷ that plays music in his garden at six in the morning!
Beth: Joe! Try to be friendly. The new neighbour ⁸ that I met in the street yesterday was really nice.
Joe: Yes, but did you think about the reason ⁹ why she was nice? She wanted to borrow two of our chairs.

D This is the second holiday article. Complete the article with the words from the box.

that has   that thousands   which means   you see   which has   that visit   ~~which has~~

Beautiful Ireland

Ireland, ♦ which has _____ a population of less than four million people, is a country with some of the world's most beautiful mountains and valleys. The first things ¹ _____ as you drive south from Dublin are the green grass and the hills of Wicklow. Further south, on the way to County Wexford, there are many small hotels, ² _____ you can find somewhere to stay without booking in advance. The place ³ _____ of tourists visit every year, however, is the west coast. This is the coast ⁴ _____ fantastic views of the Atlantic Ocean, and pretty seaside towns. Galway, for example, ⁵ _____ a wonderful bay, is well worth a visit. Or two visits! It is a fact that tourists ⁶ _____ Ireland always come back soon for a second or third holiday!

E Complete the announcement on a train from London to Lyon with words from the box.

case   but   ~~Although~~   nor   who   which   however   neither   due

'♦ Although we will arrive late in Paris, we still expect to reach Lyon by 19.00 this evening. Passengers ¹ _____ would like tea, coffee or cold drinks should visit the café in coach D. Please remember, ² _____ , that the café will close in 20 minutes ³ _____ to a problem with the refrigerator. Remember also to keep your ticket with you at all times in ⁴ _____ you pass the Ticket Inspector as he walks through the train. We are sorry to say that ⁵ _____ Coach F ⁶ _____ Coach K has air conditioning at the moment, ⁷ _____ if you are in one of these coaches we would like to offer you a free bottle of water. Finally, please remember that Coach B, ⁸ _____ is at the front of the train, is a quiet coach – the use of mobile phones is not allowed. Thank you. Enjoy your trip!'

Appendix 1 — Nouns

1 Plural nouns

1 We usually add **-s** to a noun to form the plural:
   - a book → some **books**
   - one kilo → ten **kilos**
   - shop → **shops**
   - tyre → **tyres**

2 After **-s**, **-ss**, **-sh**, **-ch** and **-x** we add **-es**:
   - bus → **buses**
   - dress → **dresses**
   - glass → **glasses**
   - dish → **dishes**
   - wish → **wishes**
   - beach → **beaches**
   - watch → **watches**
   - box → **boxes**

3 When a noun ends in a consonant* + **-y**, the **y** changes to **-ies**:
   - city → **cities**
   - family → **families**
   - lorry → **lorries**
   - story → **stories**

   We do not change **y** after a vowel*:
   - day → **days**
   - journey → **journeys**

4 Nouns ending in **-f** or **-fe** have the plural **-ves**:
   - leaf → **leaves**
   - shelf → **shelves**
   - life → **lives**
   - thief → **thieves**

5 A few nouns ending in **-o** have **-es**:
   - potato → **potatoes**
   - tomato → **tomatoes**
   - hero → **heroes**

   But most have **-s**:
   - kilo**s**   photo**s**   studio**s**   piano**s**   zoo**s**

6 Some nouns have irregular plurals:
   - child → **children**
   - fish → **fish**
   - foot → **feet**
   - man → **men**
   - mouse → **mice**
   - person → **people**
   - sheep → **sheep**
   - tooth → **teeth**
   - woman → **women**

2 Uncountable nouns

1 Here is a list of common uncountable nouns:

advice	ice	petrol
bread	information	rain
butter	luggage	snow
cheese	marmalade	sugar
coffee	meat	tea
cotton	milk	toast
glass	money	water
heat	news	work
homework	noise	

2 Uncountable nouns do not have a plural form:
   - petrol (NOT ~~petrols~~)   bread (NOT ~~breads~~)

3 We do not use **a/an** with uncountable nouns, but we can use **some/any**, **the**, **much** (NOT ~~many~~), **such** and **my/your/his**, etc.:
   - I always have **toast** and **marmalade** for breakfast.
   - I'd like **some tea**, please.
   - Look at **the snow** outside.
   - How **much luggage** have you got?
   - We've had **such** wonderful **news**.

4 Some nouns can be countable or uncountable:
   - I heard a **noise** from downstairs. (countable)
   - I can't sleep. The neighbours are making **so much noise**. (uncountable)

---

* **Consonants:** b c d f g h j k l m n p q r s t v w x y z
  Vowels: a e i o u
  Syllables: |hit| = 1 syllable |vi|sit| = 2 syllables |re|mem|ber| = 3 syllables

Appendix 2 — Regular verbs

1 Present Simple

1 Add an **-s** to make the **he/she/it** form of most Present Simple verbs:

I/you/we/they	he/she/it
leave	leaves
make	makes
say	says
work	works

2 After **-ss**, **-sh**, **-ch**, **-o** or **-x** (e.g. *finish*, *go*), we add **-es**:

I/you/we/they	he/she/it
catch	catches
finish	finishes
pass	passes
teach	teaches
do	does
go	goes
mix	mixes

3 When a verb ends in a consonant* + **-y**, the **y** changes to **-ies**:

I/you/we/they	he/she/it
fly	flies
try	tries
carry	carries
study	studies

2 The -ing form

1 For most verbs we add **-ing**:
 ask → asking   go → going

2 For verbs ending with a consonant + **-e**, we normally leave out **e** when we add **-ing**:
 hope → hoping   take → taking
 live → living

But we keep a double **e** before **-ing**:
 see → seeing   agree → agreeing

3 When a verb ends in **-ie**, it changes to **y** when we add **-ing**:
 die → dying   lie → lying

But **y** does not change:
 hurry → hurrying

4 When a word ends with one vowel* and one consonant (e.g. *run*, *swim*, *jog*), we double the final consonant:
 get → getting   run → running
 jog → jogging   swim → swimming

But note that we do not double the consonant:
▶ when it is **y**, **w** or **x** (e.g. *stay*)
 buy → buying   wax → waxing
 draw → drawing   stay → staying
▶ when the final syllable* is not stressed
 listen → listening   wonder → wondering
 visit → visiting

Note however that in British English **l** is usually doubled, even if the syllable is unstressed (e.g. *travel*):
 cancel → cancelling   travel → travelling

3 The past tense and past participles

1 Most verbs have **-ed** in the past tense; most past participles also end in **-ed**:

INFINITIVE	PAST TENSE	PAST/PASSIVE PARTICIPLE
happen	happened	happened
work	worked	worked

2 If the verb ends in **-e**, we add **-d**:
 live → lived   phone → phoned

3 When a verb ends in a consonant + **-y**, the **y** changes to **-ied**:
 study → studied   try → tried

4 When a word ends with one vowel and one consonant (e.g. *stop*), we double the final consonant:
 grab → grabbed   stop → stopped
 plan → planned

But note that we do not double the consonant:
▶ when it is **y**, **w** or **x** (e.g. *enjoy*)
 allow → allowed   enjoy → enjoyed
▶ when the final syllable is not stressed
 open → opened   discover → discovered
 listen → listened

Note however that in British English **l** is usually doubled, even if the syllable is unstressed (e.g. *travel*):
 cancel → cancelled   travel → travelled

Appendix 3: Irregular verbs

INFINITIVE	PAST TENSE	PAST/PASSIVE PARTICIPLE
be	was/were	been
beat	beat	beaten
become	became	become
begin	began	begun
blow	blew	blown
break	broke	broken
bring	brought	brought
build	built	built
burn	burnt	burnt
buy	bought	bought
catch	caught	caught
choose	chose	chosen
come	came	come
cost	cost	cost
cut	cut	cut
do	did	done
draw	drew	drawn
drink	drank	drunk
drive	drove	driven
eat	ate	eaten
fall	fell	fallen
feel	felt	felt
find	found	found
fly	flew	flown
forget	forgot	forgotten
get	got	got
give	gave	given
go	went	gone/been
grow	grew	grown
have	had	had
hear	heard	heard
hide	hid	hidden
hit	hit	hit
hold	held	held
hurt	hurt	hurt
keep	kept	kept
know	knew	known

INFINITIVE	PAST TENSE	PAST/PASSIVE PARTICIPLE
learn	learnt/learned	learnt/learned
leave	left	left
lend	lent	lent
let	let	let
lose	lost	lost
make	made	made
mean	meant	meant
meet	met	met
pay	paid	paid
put	put	put
read	read	read
ring	rang	rung
run	ran	run
say	said	said
see	saw	seen
sell	sold	sold
send	sent	sent
show	showed	shown
shut	shut	shut
sing	sang	sung
sit	sat	sat
sleep	slept	slept
speak	spoke	spoken
spend	spent	spent
stand	stood	stood
steal	stole	stolen
sweep	swept	swept
swim	swam	swum
take	took	taken
teach	taught	taught
tell	told	told
think	thought	thought
throw	threw	thrown
understand	understood	understood
wake	woke	woken
wear	wore	worn
win	won	won
write	wrote	written

Appendix 4: Adjectives and adverbs

1 Comparatives and superlatives

1. We form the comparative and superlative of short adjectives (adjectives with one syllable*) with **-er** and **-est**:
   - cheap → cheap**er**, the cheap**est**
   - long → long**er**, the long**est**
   - warm → warm**er**, the warm**est**

2. If the adjective ends in **-e**, we add **-r** and **-st**:
   - late → lat**er**, the lat**est**
   - nice → nic**er**, the nic**est**

3. When a one-syllable adjective ends with one vowel* and one consonant* (e.g. *big*), we double the final consonant:
   - big → big**ger**, the big**gest**
   - hot → hot**ter**, the hot**test**
   - wet → wet**ter**, the wet**test**

   Note that we do not double **w**:
   - few → few**er**, the few**est**

4. We put **more**/**the most** before adjectives of two or more syllables:
   - beautiful → **more** beautiful, **the most** beautiful
   - expensive → **more** expensive, **the most** expensive
   - polluted → **more** polluted, **the most** polluted

5. When an adjective ends in a consonant + **-y** (e.g. *happy*), the **y** changes to **-ier** or **-iest**:
   - dirty → dirt**ier**, the dirt**iest**
   - easy → eas**ier**, the eas**iest**
   - happy → happ**ier**, the happ**iest**
   - lucky → luck**ier**, the luck**iest**

6. Some adjectives have irregular comparative and superlative forms:
   - good → **better, the best**
   - bad → **worse, the worst**
   - far → **farther, the farthest**
     OR **further, the furthest**
   - little → **less, the least**

7. Be careful to use **fewer** with plural nouns (e.g. **shops**), and **less** with uncountable nouns (e.g. **money**):
   - There are **fewer shops** in the centre of town than there used to be.
   - John earns **less money** than Mary.

2 Adverbs

1. We form most adverbs by adding **-ly** to an adjective:
   - polite → polite**ly**
   - quick → quick**ly**
   - slow → slow**ly**

2. When an adjective ends in a consonant + **-y**, the **y** changes to **-ily**:
   - easy → eas**ily**
   - happy → happ**ily**
   - lucky → luck**ily**

3. When an adjective ends in a consonant + **-le**, the **e** changes to **-y**:
   - probable → proba**bly**
   - remarkable → remarka**bly**

4. Some adverbs are irregular:
   - good → **well**
   - fast → **fast**
   - hard → **hard**
   - late → **late**

---

* **Consonants:** b c d f g h j k l m n p q r s t v w x y z
  Vowels: a e i o u
  Syllables: |hit| = 1 syllable |vi|sit| = 2 syllables |re|mem|ber| = 3 syllables

Exit test

Choose the right answer (a, b, c, d) and write a, b, c, or d, as in the example.

♦ Russia is the __a__ country in the world.
 a) *largest*   b) *larger*   c) *most large*   d) *most largest*

Tenses: present

1 My sister and I ___ from Scotland.
 a) *we are*   b) *am*   c) *are*   d) *is*

2 How old ___?
 a) *are you*   b) *you are*   c) *you have*   d) *have you*

3 They ___ in London.
 a) *no live*   b) *don't live*   c) *live not*   d) *doesn't live*

4 Where ___ Mary live?
 a) *does*   b) *do*   c) *are*   d) *is*

5 Where are Sam and Anna? ___ in the garden.
 a) *They're siting*   b) *They sitting*   c) *There sitting*   d) *They're sitting*

6 What ___, Ellie?
 a) *you are*   b) *are you*   c) *do you*   d) *are you doing*

7 It's very cold today and ___ .
 a) *it's snowing*   b) *it snows*   c) *its snowing*   d) *it snowing*

8 ___ close the window please.
 a) *No*   b) *Not*   c) *Don't*   d) *You don't*

Tenses: past

9 Where ___ yesterday?
 a) *was you*   b) *you were*   c) *were you*   d) *did you be*

10 They ___ last week.
 a) *didn't come*   b) *came not*   c) *don't came*   d) *didn't came*

11 What ___ doing at nine o'clock yesterday evening?
 a) *Peter were*   b) *Peter was*   c) *did Peter*   d) *was Peter*

12 I didn't hear the phone because when it rang, I ___ a shower.
 a) *had*   b) *was having*   c) *have had*   d) *having*

13 My cousins ___ seen a kangaroo.
 a) *have never*   b) *never have*   c) *has never*   d) *haven't never*

14 Have you ___ to Canada?
 a) *ever been*   b) *ever gone*   c) *been ever*   d) *gone ever*

15 I'm sorry. Mrs Johnson hasn't ___ .
 a) *arrived just*   b) *already arrived*   c) *arrived already*   d) *arrived yet*

16 My husband and I ___ to Edinburgh in 2001.
 a) *have moved*   b) *moved*   c) *did moved*   d) *has moved*

17 I ___ to London five times already this week.
 a) *went*   b) *have gone*   c) *have been*   d) *was going*

18 Maddie has ___ here since February.
 a) *being worked*   b) *working*   c) *been working*   d) *been worked*

19 I'm a vegetarian. I ...... meat since I was a child.
    a) *haven't eaten*   b) *don't eat*   c) *haven't been eating*   d) *am not eating*

20 When we arrived, the train ...... the station.
    a) *already left*   b) *had already left*   c) *had left already*   d) *has left already*

21 When Laura was younger, she ...... in a jazz band.
    a) *use to sing*   b) *sang usually*   c) *was singing*   d) *used to sing*

Tenses: future

22 What ...... do tomorrow?
    a) *you are going to*   b) *are you going*   c) *you are going*   d) *are you going to*

23 Are you thirsty? ...... make you a drink?
    a) *Will I*   b) *Shall I*   c) *Do I*   d) *I'll*

24 My cousins ...... visit us next weekend.
    a) *will to*   b) *going to*   c) *are going to*   d) *are going*

25 I can't see you tomorrow. ...... lunch with Paul.
    a) *I'm having*   b) *I'll have*   c) *I'm going have*   d) *I will to have*

26 We can start as soon as they ....
    a) *arrive*   b) *are arriving*   c) *will arrive*   d) *are going to arrive*

27 Can somebody come and help me? ~ Yes, ... you.
    a) *I'll help*   b) *I'm helping*   c) *I will to help*   d) *I help*

Sentences and questions

28 They bought ....
    a) *in the country a big old house*   b) *a big old house in the country*   c) *an old big house in the country*
    d) *in the country an old big house*

29 Joe was thirsty so I made ....
    a) *a cup of tea to him*   b) *him a cup of tea*   c) *for him a cup of tea*   d) *to him a cup of tea*

30 Are you hungry? ~ ....
    a) *Yes, I am*   b) *Yes, I'm*   c) *No, I aren't*   d) *No, I no*

31 ...... did you get to Brighton? By train?
    a) *When*   b) *Where*   c) *Why*   d) *How*

32 Do you know that girl? ...... is her name?
    a) *How*   b) *Which*   c) *What*   d) *Who*

33 How ...... will the journey take? Two hours *a* more?
    a) *often*   b) *far*   c) *much*   d) *long*

34 Julie ...... her mother: very tall.
    a) *is like*   b) *is liking*   c) *likes*   d) *like*

35 How do you know? ...... you?
    a) *Who did tell*   b) *Who have told*   c) *Who has told*   d) *Who did told*

36 Whose is that bike? ~ ....
    a) *It's Tom's*   b) *It's Toms'*   c) *Its Tom's*   d) *Its Toms'*

37 Marc lives in Paris, ...
    a) *isn't it?*   b) *isn't he?*   c) *don't he?*   d) *doesn't he?*

38 Did they go to Canada? ~ Yes, they ....
    a) *went*   b) *did*   c) *did go*   d) *gone*

39 Jack doesn't speak French and ....
    a) *Charlotte doesn't neither*   b) *Charlotte neither*   c) *neither Charlotte*   d) *neither does Charlotte*

Modal verbs

40 When Raphael was at school, he ...... speak French quite well.
    a) *was able*   b) *could*   c) *able to*   d) *can*

41 Excuse me. ...... you help me?
    a) *Could*   b) *May*   c) *Shall*   d) *Do*

42 You ...... buy a ticket before boarding the bus.
    a) *might*   b) *must*   c) *might to*   d) *must to*

43 ...... go to the supermarket after work.
    a) *I've got to*   b) *I've get to*   c) *I was getting to*   d) *I have got*

44 It's a present so you ...... pay anything.
    a) *don't get to*   b) *haven't to*   c) *mustn't to*   d) *don't have to*

45 Who's the woman in that car? ~ ...... be Laura. She's in Germany.
    a) *It mustn't*   b) *She mustn't*   c) *It can't*   d) *She can't*

46 In my opinion, you ...... smoke so much.
    a) *shouldn't to*   b) *shouldn't*   c) *needn't*   d) *don't have to*

47 If you have stomach pains, you ...... to go to the doctor's.
    a) *had better*   b) *should*   c) *ought*   d) *must*

48 We've got enough blue paint. Your sister ...... to buy any more.
    a) *don't need*   b) *doesn't need*   c) *needn't*   d) *hasn't need*

49 ...... wear a uniform when you were at school?
    a) *Must you have worn*   b) *Must you wear*   c) *Had you to wear*   d) *Did you have to*

Articles, nouns, pronouns, etc:

50 What's her job? ~ She's ...... lecturer.
    a) *an university*   b) *a university*   c) *one university*   d) *university*

51 Are you a vegetarian? ~ Yes, I never eat ....
    a) *meat*   b) *the meat*   c) *some meat*   d) *a meat*

52 ...... is my favourite art.
    a) *A music*   b) *The music*   c) *Music*   d) *Some music*

53 ...... is your favourite – the White Horse *a* the Golden Hart?
    a) *Which one*   b) *What one*   c) *Which ones*   d) *What ones*

54 I'd like ...... , please.
    a) *four loaves of bread and two boxes of tomatoes*   b) *four loafs of bread and two boxs of tomatoes*
    c) *four loave of bread and two boxes of tomatos*   d) *four loaves of bread and two boxes of tomato*

55 Look at ...... cows in the field over there.
    a) *these*   b) *that*   c) *those*   d) *this*

56 Her eyes are blue and her ...... dark.
    a) *hair are*   b) *hair is*   c) *hairs are*   d) *hairs is*

57 We don't need to buy ...... milk.
    a) *a*   b) *some*   c) *any*   d) *no*

58 We saw Mary, but ....
    a) *him didn't see us*   b) *she didn't see we*   c) *her didn't see us*   d) *she didn't see us*

59 How many cinemas ...... near here?
    a) *are they*   b) *is there*   c) *are there*   d) *is it*

60 My bike is red but ...... blue.
    a) *she's*   b) *her is*   c) *hers is*   d) *her one is*

61 Your children are very good. They always help ...... a lot.
   a) *each other*   b) *themselves*   c) *them*   d) *each the other*

62 I want to check the meaning of these words. Can you ...... ?
   a) *get the dictionary for me*   b) *give to me the dictionary*   c) *get the dictionary to me*
   d) *give the dictionary for me*

63 Have you got ...... ?
   a) *many luggages*   b) *many luggage*   c) *much luggages*   d) *much luggage*

64 Have you got any money? ~ I've only got ....
   a) *little*   b) *a little*   c) *few*   d) *a few*

65 I don't know ...... near here to have lunch.
   a) *anything*   b) *something*   c) *anywhere*   d) *something*

66 They've got two cars. One is a Rover and ...... is a Mini.
   a) *the other*   b) *another*   c) *other*   d) *one other*

67 I didn't speak to all the people but I spoke to ....
   a) *most them*   b) *most of it*   c) *them most*   d) *most of them*

Adjectives and adverbs

68 Mrs Pearson had everything in a ...... bag.
   a) *plastic green large*   b) *large green plastic*   c) *green large plastic*   d) *green plastic large*

69 We thought the film was ....
   a) *very bored*   b) *much boring*   c) *very boring*   d) *much bored*

70 My birthday is the ...... of May.
   a) *twenty-eighth*   b) *twentyeth*   c) *twenty-nineth*   d) *twenty-forth*

71 Paris isn't ...... London.
   a) *big as*   b) *as big as*   c) *as big that*   d) *so big that*

72 Sara is only 15. She isn't ...... drive a car.
   a) *enough old to*   b) *enough old for*   c) *old enough for*   d) *old enough to*

73 It was ...... night that we didn't see the animals.
   a) *a so dark*   b) *so a dark*   c) *such a dark*   d) *a such dark*

74 In the photo Tom looks ...... his friends.
   a) *happier that*   b) *happier than*   c) *more happy than*   d) *more happy*

75 Which is the ...... the world?
   a) *longer river in*   b) *longer river of*   c) *longest river of*   d) *longest river in*

76 Jasmine drives carefully but her sister drives ....
   a) *fastly*   b) *very fast*   c) *more quick*   d) *very quick*

77 I take the bus but Tim ...... to work.
   a) *hardly ever walks*   b) *walks hardly ever*   c) *often walks*   d) *walks often*

78 Turn left at the garage then go ...... until you get to the school.
   a) *ahead*   b) *straight on*   c) *on ahead*   d) *on straight*

79 The way she said that made me ....
   a) *extreme angrily*   b) *angrily extreme*   c) *extremely angry*   d) *angry extremely*

80 He doesn't talk much and he doesn't listen much ....
   a) *too*   b) *neither*   c) *either*   d) *as well*

81 After 25 minutes take the meat ...... the oven.
   a) *out from*   b) *out of*   c) *from of*   d) *from out*

Prepositions

82 I think we can meet .... the bus stop.
    a) *on*   b) *at*   c) *in*   d) *behind*

83 The train has to go .... three tunnels.
    a) *across*   b) *along*   c) *through*   d) *under*

84 It happened .... Friday.
    a) *at lunch-time in*   b) *at lunch-time on*   c *in lunch-time on*   d) *on lunch-time at*

85 She described the thief .... a tall, bearded man.
    a) *like*   b) *such as*   c) *as*   d) *as though*

86 That student over there – the one ....
    a) *in the blonde hair*   b) *with the blonde hair*   c) *in blonde hair*   d) *blonde haired*

87 It was very late but .... last we reached the hotel.
    a) *in the*   b) *at the*   c) *in*   d) *at*

88 What time did they arrive .... the airport?
    a) *at*   b) *in*   c) *on*   d) *to*

89 She learnt French .... listening to tapes.
    a) *by*   b) *for*   c) *on*   d) *with*

90 The rooms were full .... old furniture.
    a) *of*   b) *with*   c) *from*   d) *off*

Verbs

91 Peter .... a car.
    a) *hasn't got*   b) *hasn't*   c) *haven't got*   d) *doesn't have got*

92 We're going to .... some shopping.
    a) *make*   b) *get*   c) *do*   d) *have*

93 The plane .... in bad weather.
    a) *pulled off*   b) *put up*   c) *got up*   d) *took off*

94 There was no truth to his story. He simply ....
    a) *made up it*   b) *made it up*   c) *drew it out*   d) *drew out it*

95 Fiat .... a group of Italian businessmen.
    a) *is started for*   b) *is started by*   c) *was started by*   d) *was started for*

96 Oh, no! My camera isn't here. It .... stolen!
    a) *has been*   b) *is*   c) *is being*   d) *has*

97 His hair is too long. He should .... cut.
    a) *let it be*   b) *get it be*   c) *make it*   d) *have it*

98 The film was very sad. It .... cry.
    a) *made us to*   b) *made us*   c) *let us*   d) *let us to*

99 The teacher .... go home early.
    a) *wanted that we*   b) *made us to*   c) *decided us to*   d) *let us*

100 When you've .... , I'll tell you what I think.
    a) *stopped talking*   b) *stopped to talk*   c) *been stopping talking*   d) *been stopped to talk*

101 Would you .... to the cinema?
    a) *to like go*   b) *like to go*   c) *like going*   d) *to like to going*

102 I'm going to India next year. .... Kerala, Goa and Mumbai.
    a) *I'm going to plan visiting*   b) *I plan visiting*   c) *I'm going to plan to visit*   d) *I plan to visit*

103 This is a machine .... boxes.
   a) *for make*   b) *for to make*   c) *for making*   d) *to making*
104 We invited .... come to the party.
   a) *them to*   b) *to them*   c) *that they*   d) *that they*

Conditionals and reported speech

105 Tomorrow we can go for a picnic if the weather .... fine.
   a) *is being*   b) *will be*   c) *would be*   d) *is*
106 If I .... you, I'd go to the police.
   a) *would be*   b) *should be*   c) *were*   d) *am*
107 I wish I .... to bed earlier last night.
   a) *went*   b) *had gone*   c) *was going*   d) *have gone*
108 Your cousin .... she lived in a small flat.
   a) *said me*   b) *said to me*   c) *told*   d) *told me*
109 Jasmine had a lot of work and so she asked .... help her.
   a) *me to*   b) *to me*   c) *that I*   d) *that I should*
110 Do you know where .... ?
   a) *lives Joe*   b) *do Joe lives*   c) *does Joe live*   d) *Joe lives*

Building sentences

111 Mr and Mrs Simpson neither came .... sent a message.
   a) *a*   b) *neither*   c) *nor*   d) *either*
112 Take your umbrella .... it rains.
   a) *because*   b) *because of*   c) *for*   d) *in case*
113 His mother told him off ....
   a) *for laughing*   b) *because laughing*   c) *for he laughed*   d) *because of laughing*
114 Most people go by train. The bus, ... , is cheaper and faster.
   a) *although*   b) *despite*   c) *while*   d) *however*
115 .... the fact that nobody thought he should do it, he did it.
   a) *However*   b) *While*   c) *In spite of*   d) *Because*
116 The team .... scored the most goals won the competition.
   a) *, which*   b) *, that*   c) *that*   d) *which it*
117 Do you know those boys .... are talking to Yvonne?
   a) *which*   b) *that they*   c) *who*   d) *who's*
118 We saw that woman .... was on TV.
   a) *the son of her*   b) *whose son*   c) *that the son*   d) *that the son*
119 I received your letter of 22 March, ... I'm very grateful.
   a) *which*   b) *that*   c) *for which*   d) *to which*
120 Raphael went to see the film *Robocop 4*, ... had already seen three times.
   a) *which*   b) *which he*   c) *that*   d) *that he*

Index

The numbers in this index are unit numbers unless they have the letter 'p' for 'page.'

a 49–50, 54, **Test F** pp140–1
  or **an** 49
  or no article 50
  or **the** 49, 50
a few 61
a little 61
a lot of 61
  such a lot of 70
ability: **can**, **can't**, **could**, **couldn't** 39
above 78
abroad 75
across 78
adjectives 27, **Test G** pp168–9, p245
  + adjective 76
  adverb + adjective 76
  and adverbs 73
  as ... as 68
  comparative 71, p245
  -ed or **-ing** 66
  order 65
  possessive 57
  + preposition 84
  'size' 76
  superlative 72, p245
adverbs 27, 73–7, **Test G** pp168–9, p245
  + adjective 76
  and adjectives 73
  as ... as 68
  comparative 73
  -ly ending 73, p245
  of certainty 77
  of completeness 77
  of direction 75
  of emphasis 77
  of frequency 74
  of manner 77
  of place 75, 77
  of sequence 75
  of time 77
  position in sentence 77
  superlative 73
advice 45, 101
advise 101
after
  after that 75
  for the future 25
afterwards 75
all 64
almost 77
along 78
already 15, 19

also 77
although 106
always 74
am 1, 2
an 49–50, **Test F** pp140–1
and 103
another 63
answers, short 37, 43, **Test D** p84
any 54, **Test F** pp140–1
any more 60
anybody 62
anyone 62
anything 62
anywhere 62
apostrophe (') 35, 57
are 1, 2
arrive at/in 83
articles 49–50, **Test F** pp140–1
as 80
  as ... as 68
  reason 105
  the same as 80
  such as 80
as if 80
as soon as: for the future 25
as though 80
as usual 80
ask 101
at
  place 78
  speed 82
  time 79, 82
auxiliary verbs 27
away 75

be
  Past Simple 9
  Present Simple 1–2
  questions 2
  there + **be** 2, 56
be going to 21, **Test C** pp58–9
  or **will** 23, 26
because 104
because of 104
been to and **gone to** 14
before: for the future 25
behind 78
beside 78
best 73
better 73
between 78
both ... and 103
but 103

by
  by car/bike/bus 82
  by chance/accident/mistake 82
  + **-ing** 81
  by post/email/phone 82

can **Test E** pp106–7
  ability 39
  permission 40
  questions 40
  requests 40
cannot 39
can't
  ability 39
  impossibility 44
cardinal numbers 67
case: **in case** 104
certainly 77
certainty
  adverbs 77
  must 44
comparative **Test G** pp168–9
  adjectives 71, p245
  adverbs 73
  (**not**) **as ... as** 68
conditionals 97–9, **Test J** p224
could **Test E** pp106–7
  ability 39
  possibility 44
  questions 40
couldn't: ability 39
countable nouns 53

dates 55, 67
definitely 77
despite 106
did: in questions 29
direct objects 59
do 86
  in negative forms 3
  in the Present Simple 3, 4
  in question tags 36
  in questions 4, 29, 30
  in short answers 43
does
  in negative forms 3
  in the Present Simple 3, 4
  in question tags 36
  in questions 4, 29, 30
  in short answers 43
don't have to 43
down 78
due to 105

each 63
each other 58
either 77, 103
   I'm not either 38
either ... or 103
else 62
enough 69
even 77
ever 13
   hardly ever 74
every 63, 74, 79
everybody 62
everyone 62
everything 62
everywhere 62
except (for) 82
extremely 76

fact: the fact that 105
fairly 76
fast 73
few 61
fewer p245
First Conditional 97
first(ly) 75
for
   for example/sale/ever 82
   purpose 95, 105
   reason 105
   and since 14, 17
forbid 101
forget 94
from
   place 78
   time 32, 79
front: in front of 78
future 26, **Test C** pp58–9
   be going to 21, 23, 26
   Present Continuous 24, 26
   when/before/after/until +
     Present Simple 25
   will 22, 23, 26
get 86
   get something done 91
go + -ing 93
going to see be going to
gone to and been to 14
got 85

had: in Past Perfect 19
had better 46, **Test E** pp106–7
had to do/go 42, 48
hard 73
hardly ever 74
have 85
   and have got 85
   + noun 86
   Present Continuous 6
   will have to 42

have got 85
have got to 42
have something done 91
have to 42, 43, **Test E** pp106–7
   don't have to 42
he 55, 58
her 55, 57, 58
here 75
hers 57
herself 58
him 55, 57, 58
himself 58
his 57
how 30, 33, **Test D** p85
How far? 32
How long? 17, 18, 32
How many? 18, 32, 60, **Test F** p141
How much? 18, 32, 60, **Test F** p141
How often? 32
How old? 32
however 106

I 55, 58
I am too 38
if: as if 80
I'm not either 38
imperative 8
impossibility 44
in 82
   clothing 81
   phrases 82
   place 78
   time 79
   transport 82
in case 104
in cash 82
in spite of 106
indirect objects 59
infinitive **Test I** p211
   to + infinitive 94
   with/without to 92
-ing forms **Test I** p 211, p243
   adjectives 66
   after a preposition 81
   after a verb 93, 94
   Past Continuous 11
   Present Continuous 5
   Present Perfect Continuous 17
   spelling 5, p243
instead of 82
into 78
is 1, 2
it 55, 56, 57, 58
its 57
itself 58

just
   = simply 77
   + past participle 15

last 79
least
   the least + adjective 72
   the least + adverb 73
left 75
less 73
let + someone + infinitive 92
like 80
   + -ing 93
   What ... like? 33
   would like 93, 94
little 61
look at/for 83
lots of 61 see also a lot of

make 86
   make + someone + infinitive 92
many 60
   as many ... as 68
   so many 70
may **Test E** pp106–7
   permission 40
   possibility 44
   questions 40
   requests 40
me 55, 57, 58
might 44
mine 57
modal verbs 39–48, **Test E**
   pp106–7
more
   comparative adjective 71, p245
   more + adverb 73
   quantity 60
most 64
   the most + adverb 73
   superlative adjective 72, p245
much 60
   as much ... as 68
   so much 70
must **Test E** pp106–7
   certainty 44
   for the future 41
   necessity 41, 43
   recommendation 41
mustn't 41, 43
my 57
myself 58

nearly 77
necessity 41, 43
need 47, **Test E** pp106–7
needn't 47
needn't have 47
negative forms 1, 3
neither 103
neither ... nor 103
Neither am I 38, **Test D** p85

never 13, 19, 74
next
  sequence 75
  time 79
next to 78
no 54
no one 62
nobody 62
none 64
normally 74
not ... any 54
nothing 62
nouns 27, **Test F** pp140–1
  countable 53
  + noun 76
  plural 51, **Test F** pp140–1, p242
  uncountable 32, 53, p242
nowhere 62
numbers 67

object pronouns 55, 57, 58, **Test F** p141
off 78
often 74
on
  on business/holiday/a trip 82
  place 78, 82
  time 79
  transport 82
  on TV/the radio/the internet 82
once a ... 74
one 51, **Test F** pp140–1
  one + singular noun/verb 63
  one of the/possessive + plural 63
  and **ones** 51
ones 51
only 77
onto 78
opinion 45
opposite 78
or 103
orders 101
ordinal numbers 67
other
  each other 58
  the/possessive + **other** + singular 63
  the/possessive/quantifier + **other** + plural noun 63
others 63
  the others 63
ought to 46, **Test E** pp106–7
our 57
ours 57
ourselves 58
out 75
out of 78
outside 78

owing to 105

passive sentences 89–90, **Test I** pp210–11
passive tenses 90
past 78
Past Continuous 11, **Test B** pp44–5
  or Past Simple 12
  passive 90
past participles 13, p243
  irregular verbs p244
  in passive 90
Past Perfect 19, **Test B** pp44–5
  passive 90
Past Simple 9–10, **Test B** pp44–5, p243
  be 9
  irregular verbs p244
  or Past Continuous 12
  or Present Perfect 16
  passive 89, 90
  and **used to** 20
pay 83
permission 40
persuade 101
phrasal verbs 87–8 see also prepositional verbs
place
  adverbs 75, 77
  prepositions 78, 82
  relative clauses 108
possessive forms **Test F** p141
  adjectives 57
  pronouns 57
  's, s' 35, 57
possibility 44, 103
prepositional verbs 83
prepositions 27, **Test H** pp184–5
  after adjectives 84
  after verbs 83
  + **-ing** 81
  of movement 78
  of place 78, 82
  of time 32, 79, 82
  phrases 82
Present Continuous 5–6, **Test A** p19
  for the future 24, 26, **Test C** pp58–9
  -ing form 5
  or Present Simple 7
  passive 90
  questions 6
Present Perfect 13–16, **Test B** pp44–5
  for the future 25
  or Past Simple 16
  or Present Perfect Continuous 18

  passive 90
Present Perfect Continuous 17, **Test B** pp44–5
  or Present Perfect Simple 18
Present Simple 1–4, **Test A** pp18–19
  be 1–2
  for the future 25, 26
  negative 3
  or Present Continuous 7
  passive 89, 90
  questions 2, 4
  regular verbs p243
present tense: **when, before, after, until,** etc. 25
probably 77
pronouns 27, **Test F** pp140–1
  object 55, 57, 58
  possessive 57
  reflexive 58
  subject 55, 58
purpose 95, 104, 105

question tags 36, **Test D** p85
questions 29–33, **Test D** pp84–5
  be 2
  Can? May? Could? 40
  How long/far/often ...? 32
  Present Continuous 6
  Present Simple 2, 4
  reported questions 102
  short answers 37, 43
  What ... like? 33
  where, when, why, how 30
  who, what, which 31
  'yes/no' questions 29
quite 76

rarely 74
rather 76
really 76
reason 104, 105
reason 108
reflexive pronouns 58, **Test F** p141
relative clauses 107–9
remember 94
remind 101
reported speech 19, 100–2, **Test J** p225
  advice 101
  orders 101
  questions 102
  requests 101
  say and **tell** 100, 101
requests 40, 101
result 103, 104
right 75

's, s' 35, 57
same: the same as 80

say 100
Second Conditional 98
shall 22, Test C pp58–9
she 55, 58
short answers, 37, 43, Test D pp84
short forms: be 1
should 45, 46, Test E pp106–7
   do you think I should …? 45
   I think we should 45
   should I? 45
should have done/gone 48
shouldn't 45
since
   and for 14, 17
   reason 105
so
   or such 70
   result 103, 104
so am I 38, Test D p85
so many 70
so much 70
so that 104
some 54, 64, Test F pp140–1
some more 60
somebody 62
someone 62
something 62
sometimes 74
somewhere 62, 108
soon: as soon as 25
straight on 75
subject pronouns 55, 58
such a lot of 70
such a/an 70
such as 80
such or so 70
superlative Test G pp168–9
   adjectives 72, p245
   adverbs 73

talk to/about 83
tell 100, 101
tests
   adjectives Test G pp168–9
   adverbs Test G pp168–9
   articles Test F pp140–1
   building sentences Test K pp240–1
   conditionals Test J p224
   infinitives Test I p211
   -ing forms Test I p211
   modal verbs Test E pp106–7
   nouns Test F pp140–1
   passive Test I pp210–11
   prepositions Test H pp184–5
   pronouns Test F pp140–1
   questions and answers Test D pp84–5
   reported speech Test J p225
   sentences Test D pp84–5

tenses – future Test C pp58–9
tenses – past Test B pp44–5
tenses – present Test A pp18–19
verbs Test I pp210–11
that 52
   relative pronoun 107, 108
   in reported speech 100
   so that 104
the Test F pp140–1
   or a/an 49
   or no article 50
their 57
theirs 57
them 55, 57, 58
themselves 58
then 75
there 75
there is/are 2, 56, Test F p141
these 52
they 55, 56, 58
think: Present Continuous 6
Third Conditional 99
this 52, 79
those 52
though 106
   as though 80
through 78
time
   adverbial phrases 77
   it 55, 56
   prepositions 32, 79, 82
to
   with infinitive 92, 94
   movement 78
too 69, 77
try 94
twice a … 74

uncountable nouns 32, 53, p242
under 78
until 25, 32
up 78
us 55, 57, 58
used to 20
usual: as usual 80
usually 74

verbs 27, Test I pp210–11
   + to 94
   auxiliary verbs 27
   + -ing 93, 94
   irregular verbs p244
   + object (+ to) + infinitive 96
   phrasal verbs 87–8
   + preposition 83
   regular verbs p243
very 76

warn 101
was 9

way 108
we 55, 58
weather 55, 56
well 73
were 9
what
   what 31
   what: subject and object 34
What … like? 33
when
   for the future 25
   in past tenses 11, 19
   relative adverb 108
   when 30
where
   relative adverb 108
   where 30
which
   relative pronoun 107, 108, 109
   which 31
Which one/ones? 51
while
   contrast 106
   in past tenses 11
who
   relative pronoun 107, 108, 109
   who 31
   who: subject and object 34
whom 108, 109
who's 35
whose 107, 109
Whose is this? 35
why
   after reason 108
   why 30
will 22, Test C pp58–9
   or be going to 23, 26
will be able to 39, Test E pp106–7
with 81
without + -ing 81
word order
   adjectives 65
   adverbs 77
   subject, verb, object 28
worst 73
would like 93, 94
Would you? 40

'yes/no' questions 29
yet 15
you 55, 57, 58
your 57
yours 57
yourself 58
yourselves 58

Zero Conditional 97